The Lincoln Forum

Abraham Lincoln, as he looked three days before his fifty-fifth birthday. The president sat for this photograph—as well as the poses later engraved for the copper penny and the $5 bill—on February 9, 1864, at the Washington galleries of Mathew B. Brady. The camera operator was Anthony Berger. "The whole physiognomy is as coarse a one as you would meet anywhere in the length and breadth of the United States," Nathaniel Hawthorne wrote after meeting Lincoln for the first time. "But withal, it is redeemed, illuminated softened, and brightened by a kindly though serious look out of his eyes, and an expression of homely sagacity, that seems weighted with rich results of village experience." (*Library of Congress*)

THE LINCOLN FORUM

Rediscovering Abraham Lincoln

JOHN Y. SIMON *and* HAROLD HOLZER,
Editors

DAWN RUARK, *Associate Editor*

Fordham University Press
New York
2002

The North's Civil War, No. 21
ISSN 1089-8719

Library of Congress Cataloging-in-Publication Data

The Lincoln forum: rediscovering Abraham Lincoln/John Y. Simon and Harold Holzer, editors; Dawn Ruark, associate editor.—1st ed.
    p. cm.
  Includes bibliographical references and index.
  ISBN 0-8232-2214-4 (hardcover)—ISBN 0-8232-2215-2 (pbk.)
  1. Lincoln, Abraham, 1809–1865. 2. Lincoln, Abraham, 1809–1865—Military leadership. 3. United States—History—Civil War, 1861–1865. I. Simon, John Y. II. Holzer, Harold. III. Ruark, Dawn
E457.8 .L738 2002
973.7'092—dc21   2002005505

Printed in the United States of America
02   03   04   05   06   5   4   3   2   1
First Edition

To Charles D. Platt

Co-founder, generous patron, and tireless executive
With the thanks of the entire Lincoln Forum

CONTENTS

FOREWORD AND ACKNOWLEDGMENTS

Frank J. Williams

ABRAHAM LINCOLN made but one major mistake when he delivered the Gettysburg Address on November 19, 1863. He modestly predicted that the world would "little note nor long remember" what he said that day at the dedication of the Soldier's National Cemetery on the site of the biggest, bloodiest battle of the American Civil War.

Instead, the world quickly and enthusiastically acknowledged that the president had created a masterpiece for the occasion, which not only commemorated the valor of the soldiers who died there, but consecrated the entire struggle to save the Union. That day, Abraham Lincoln declared a "new birth of freedom" for America and challenged his countrymen to complete the "unfinished work" yet required to fulfill the promise of the Declaration of Independence. Inspired by those words, they did precisely as Lincoln hoped.

Understandably, no presidential appearance, no presidential speech, before or after, ever stirred American audiences so powerfully. Generations of students have memorized it, books have been devoted to it, films have re-created it. And the spot where Lincoln delivered it has itself become a tourist mecca.

Appropriately, it has also served as a magnet for a national group created in 1995 to encourage scholarship, discussion, and debate about the man whose unforgettable words first stirred the country nearly a century and a half ago. That group is the Lincoln Forum. It has been dedicated for seven years now to the eternally, provocatively "unfinished work" of understanding and learning from our history.

At six consecutive annual symposia, the Forum has attracted hundreds of historians, students, and enthusiasts to Gettysburg to explore the deeper meanings of Lincoln's public and private lives, and his impact on his own time as well as ours. In formal papers, visual presentations, and lively panel discussions, scholars and audiences have speculated together on topics ranging from the Lincoln marriage to the Emancipation Proclamation, from Lincoln's prowess as a commander in chief to his skills as a public speaker.

So many of the earliest symposium contributions deserved wider circulation that in 1999 the Forum published its first volume of collected essays. That book, *The Lincoln Forum: Abraham Lincoln, Gettysburg, and the Civil War,* featured chapters by scholars like Richard Nelson Current and Edna Greene Medford, as well as important commentary by Associate Justice Sandra Day O'Connor of the United States Supreme Court. As I said in announcing the venture, the book represented "a tangible culmination of several years of intensive work to organize, build, and expand the Lincoln Forum" as well as an effort to "enlighten the many readers in this country" whose interest in the theme remains strong.

Since that time, an ever-widening roster of historians has appeared to address the annual Lincoln Forum symposium, and to offer still more important and original work. Old favorites have returned with new interpretations. Respected experts have asked and answered crucial historical questions. And younger scholars have also appeared, to share with our growing audiences their unique perspective on Civil War history. Their contributions are also worth preserving. The time was clearly right for a new volume of Lincoln Forum essays. And this is the result.

Some of the papers in the book have already aired on C-SPAN's Book TV network, but our goal for this project still seemed to us crucial: to share important historical research and commentary with those who have yet to hear it, and to provide a valuable permanent record for those who attended these Forums in person.

Like Lincoln himself—and the words he crafted to inspire his beleaguered country—these essays are not only well worth noting, but long remembering.

The Lincoln Forum is indebted to a number of individuals and groups who have made our annual symposium, and this book, possible, and all of them well deserve acknowledgments and thanks.

First, I must express gratitude to my colleagues in the leadership of the organization: Vice Chairman Harold Holzer, who successfully balances a daunting job at the Metropolitan Museum of Art, an exhausting schedule of writing and speaking, and much administrative work for the Forum, including the editing of our semiannual *Bulletin;* Treasurer Charles D. Platt, into whose retirement the Forum intruded to take full advantage of his skill as a business executive and his commitment as history devotee (both of which he has given cheerfully); Executive Committee member John Y. Simon, whose brilliance and wit have enlivened many symposia, and whose nationally recognized skill as an editor makes these volumes possible; and our Administrator, Annette Westerby, who has taken a part-time job and made it a full-time commitment, bringing to the task enormous energy, great patience, and a flair for the artistic coupled with an appreciation for new technology. Without these great co-workers, this effort would not have been possible.

Many people contribute to the success of the annual symposium, not least of whom is Kay Lawyer at the Holiday Inn Gettysburg Battlefield and her fine professional staff. Professor Gabor Boritt of Gettysburg College, together with the staff of the Civil War Institute that he directs, have been unflagging friends and supporters of the Forum from the beginning. And on-the-spot "assembly line" volunteers like Jo Dzombak, Paul Barker, Dale Jirik, Linda Platt, Edith Holzer, Meg Holzer, and my own adored Virginia Williams have cheerfully helped prepare and distribute materials each year for two hundred attendees. Our Lincoln Forum "community" never ceases to amaze and inspire me. Thanks to all.

Each year the group also presents an annual "Richard Nelson Current Lincoln Forum, Award of Achievement" to a worthy contributor to the field. We are particularly proud to have saluted over the years a number of exceptional individuals who have left a strong mark on both history and our daily lives. These distinguished award winners are the following: Lincoln scholar Gabor Boritt (1996); C-SPAN founder Brian Lamb (1997); historian John Hope Franklin (1998); author and political leader Paul Simon (1999); historian David Herbert Donald (2000); and scholar Garry Wills (2001). Add to this stellar roster one more name: Richard Nelson Current himself, the beloved dean of Lincoln scholars, for whom the award was named in 1998, and who earned his own "Current Award" at a special surprise ceremony in 2000. To paraphrase Lincoln: In doing honor to them, we do honor to ourselves.

I must again applaud John Y. Simon and Harold Holzer, this time specifically for assembling this volume and working tirelessly to prepare it for publication. Much published, and much respected, they have brought both credibility and dedication to all of our editorial projects.

Finally, I thank our friends at Fordham University Press for their enthusiasm for the project and their hard work in bringing it to fruition. We are enormously grateful to Saverio Procario, the director of the Press; Anthony Chiffolo, the managing editor; and Loomis Mayer, the production manager. It is especially heartening to have a new partnership with a publisher whose series "The North's Civil War," ably edited by Paul A. Cimbala, has made such an important contribution to the literature.

"We cannot escape history," Abraham Lincoln argued in 1862. Many of us do not want to. Our hope is that the Lincoln Forum and this volume of essays make our inevitable entrapment in the past both illuminating and irresistible.

Hope Valley, R.I.
February 12, 2002

INTRODUCTION

John Y. Simon and Harold Holzer

THE FIRST TIME THAT Abraham Lincoln was invited to write an autobiographical sketch in 1859, he was able to produce only four meager paragraphs to describe his fifty years of life. He recalled an ancestry of "undistinguished families," a childhood focused relentlessly on the "farm work" that he loathed, and modest successes at the ballot box, in the law, and in a long-forgotten Indian War. He wrote modestly of a history of failures alternating with successes in politics, culminating in his return to public life in 1854, "aroused," as he put it, by the repeal of the Missouri Compromise.

"What I have done since," he concluded, before offering a brief "personal description," was, he believed, "pretty well known." No further details were offered. Sending this slender manuscript on to the supporter who had requested it as a source for journalists who were preparing life stories, Lincoln seemed almost apologetic about the result. "There is not much of it," he sheepishly confided, "for the reason, I suppose, that there is not much of me." That was about to change.

By the time he died at the hands of an assassin less than six years later, Lincoln—and the country he was elected to lead—had endured upheavals so momentous that they all but rewrote American history, which Lincoln came to dominate as the preserver of the Union and the emancipator of the slaves. In less than a decade, he had transformed himself from a prairie politician into the principal hero in the pantheon of national memory.

Understandably, biographers have been expanding on Lincoln's "little sketch" of 1859 ever since, inspired at least in part because Lincoln the writer seldom shed light on Lincoln the man. By now, more books have been written about him than about any other American who ever lived. Every generation since his death has inspired at

least one redefining biography, along with a seemingly endless flood
of titles on specific aspects of Lincoln's public and private lives. And
still the books pour off the presses.

Then why this latest volume?

The Lincoln Forum—a national assembly of Lincoln and Civil War
enthusiasts—has for six years attracted the nation's leading historians
to annual symposia at which they present papers on his life and times.
These presentations have been rich in original scholarship, and precisely directed at areas of the Lincoln story that remain unexplored,
underanalyzed, or subject to unresolved debate. What they have in
common is the ability to analyze, articulate, and intrigue. They contribute to our unending hunger for answers to the questions that
continue to excite interest in the Lincoln theme—that inspire scholars to look afresh at the seminal issues that characterized him, and in
turn become part of the national character as well.

Bringing together papers selected from those delivered at five annual meetings of the Lincoln Forum, these essays represent the diversity of scholarship focused upon an ever-fascinating figure. In an
initial article, James M. McPherson approaches Lincoln as commander in chief by marveling that in the vast Lincoln literature so
little attention has been given the central element of his presidency.
Tracing the evolution of Lincoln's strategic thought through four
stages—from limited war through destruction of Southern resources—McPherson illuminates Lincoln's achievements as military
leader. John Y. Simon follows with a piece that separates the role of
president and commander in chief, illustrated by Lincoln's relationship with Ulysses S. Grant.

Several essays develop the theme of military leadership. Gary Gallagher analyzes Lincoln's reaction to Stonewall Jackson's celebrated
Shenandoah Valley campaign in the spring of 1862. Rather than
reacting in panic, Lincoln showed great skill in organizing and coordinating strategy to meet the threat. Craig Symonds shows that although Lincoln had no experience with the ocean-going navy before
the Civil War, he brought to the task of administering the fleet the
same qualities of versatility, flexibility, and inventiveness he displayed
in military affairs. Especially through his receptivity to new vessels
and weapons, he made his mark in creating a strong and successful
navy.

Had General William Tecumseh Sherman not been in the heart of

Georgia marching toward Savannah on election day in 1864, would he have voted for Lincoln's reelection? John Marszalek explores the tangled relationship between the two men that began awkwardly and explains the process through which Sherman's initial contempt advanced to admiration. In 1863 Lincoln's joyous satisfaction when General George G. Meade repulsed General Robert E. Lee's army at Gettysburg turned into bitter anger when Meade allowed the enemy to retreat to safety. "I could have whipped them myself," Lincoln exclaimed. Gerald Prokopowicz examines this statement and similar expressions to determine whether Lincoln ever contemplated assuming personal command of his army.

J. Tracy Power turns his attention to the effect of the presidential election of 1864 on Confederate morale. Did the potential defeat of Lincoln represent the last hope of the Confederacy? Morale fell in the Army of Northern Virginia in the final months of 1864 following the presidential election, but Power adds to this a number of other factors.

In an intriguing essay on "Lincoln and Women," Frank J. Williams explores the distinction between masculine and feminine traits of behavior and argues that Lincoln developed the capacity to employ both. In a defense of Mary Todd Lincoln, Jean H. Baker answers critics who have made Mary one of the "most detested" First Ladies who ever occupied the White House. Baker argues spiritedly that Mary's display of characteristics that later became fashionable damaged her contemporary reputation, despite her success over adversity as wife, mother, and widow.

Iver Bernstein draws upon Lincoln's comparison of slavery and cancer for an innovative look at the nineteenth-century interpretation of the body politic. In Lincoln's metaphor Bernstein discerns the emergence of organicism applied to political behavior. Simultaneously, the metaphor reflects changing views of medicine. Barry Schwartz takes a fresh look at changing interpretations of the Gettysburg Address, discussing how these have varied and metamorphosed across time to reflect current needs and preoccupations. Even in such apparently simple and direct language lies the raw material for transformation in collective memory.

Nearly sixty years ago, J. G. Randall, the most respected Lincoln authority of his day, published an essay on "The Unpopular Mr. Lincoln," discussing copious abuse heaped upon the president. In response, Hans Trefousse explores the other side of the equation with an essay cataloging comments made by Lincoln's admirers. The chorus of praise gradually increased; near the end of his life many of his countrymen compared him to George Washington, anticipating the apotheosis after Lincoln's assassination. He had become a secular saint and inspired acquisition of relics. In a concluding essay, Harold Holzer discusses Lincoln collectors past and present. By amassing books and manuscripts, they both satisfied their acquisitive instincts and contributed to Lincoln scholarship. By adding yet another Lincoln book to groaning shelves, the editors aspire to gratify modern Lincoln collectors, admirers, and scholars.

February 12, 2002

The Lincoln Forum

1

Lincoln as Commander in Chief

James M. McPherson

WHEN WE THINK about the positive legacy of our greatest presidents, what comes most readily to mind are their constructive political and legislative achievements: setting the republic on a firm foundation during George Washington's administrations; the broadening of democracy under Thomas Jefferson and Andrew Jackson; the Square Deal of Theodore Roosevelt and the New Deal of Franklin D. Roosevelt; the Civil Rights Act pushed through Congress by Lyndon Johnson. When we think about Abraham Lincoln, what comes most readily to mind is preservation of the Union and the abolition of slavery. We remember him for the Emancipation Proclamation, the Gettysburg Address, and the closing lines of his Second Inaugural Address about binding up the nation's wounds with malice toward none and charity for all. Our most vivid image of Lincoln's presidency is the tragedy at Ford's Theatre on that fateful evening of April 14, 1865.

What does *not* occur so readily to us, perhaps, is that all of these impressions of Lincoln are connected directly with his role as commander in chief of the army and navy. Every one of these memorable achievements or events—preservation of the Union, the abolition of slavery, the Gettysburg Address, the Second Inaugural, the assassination—were consequences of the Civil War. Without the war, and without Union victory in the war under Lincoln's hands-on leadership as commander in chief, none of these things would have happened. Without the war, we would probably remember Lincoln—if we remembered him at all—as one of the obscure nineteenth-century presidents, in the same category, say, with Franklin Pierce or Benjamin Harrison.

War is not a pleasant topic. Lincoln himself referred to it this way back in 1848, when he was a member of Congress during the Mexican War: "Military glory [is an] attractive rainbow that rises in show-ers of blood—that serpent's eye that charms to destroy." Lincoln also mocked his own military record as a militia captain during the Black Hawk War in 1832. "Did you know I am a military hero?" he said on the floor of the House. "I fought, bled, and came away" after "charges upon the wild onions" and "a good many bloody struggles with the mesquitoes [sic]."

One of Lincoln's more endearing qualities was his self-mocking sense of humor. But his actions as commander in chief from 1861 to 1865 were deadly serious. We must not forget that he was a war president. His election set in train the events that led to war. His entire tenure in office was bounded by the parameters of war—the only president in our history of whom that is true. Military matters required more of Lincoln's time and energy than did anything else during his presidency. As he said, also in his Second Inaugural Ad-dress: on "the progress of our arms . . . all else chiefly depends." That is why Lincoln spent more time in the War Department telegraph office than anywhere else except the White House. He rarely left Washington except to visit the Army of the Potomac at the front, which he did eleven times during his presidency, for a total of forty-two days with the army. During crucial military operations, Lincoln often stayed all night at the telegraph office in the War Department, reading and sending dispatches and snatching a few hours of sleep on a cot. He probably wrote the first draft of the Emancipation Proc-lamation in that office while awaiting news from the front. That was quite appropriate, because the legal justification of the proclamation was Lincoln's war powers as commander in chief to seize enemy property—slaves—being used to wage war against the United States.

Some historians in earlier generations recognized and appreciated the centrality to Lincoln's presidency and to his historical reputation of his achievements as commander in chief. Back in the 1920s the British historian Colin Ballard entitled his book on the strategy of the American Civil War *The Military Genius of Abraham Lincoln.* In 1952 the American historian T. Harry Williams wrote, in his book *Lincoln and His Generals,* that Lincoln was "a better [strategist] than any of his generals. He was in actuality as well as in title the com-mander in chief who, by his larger strategy, did more than Grant or any other general to win the war for the Union."

I am inclined to agree, though I might not put it quite so strongly.

But judging from the thrust and emphasis of more recent books, historians and biographers of Lincoln now consider Lincoln's role as commander in chief less salient than other aspects of his career. The best reference work on Lincoln, Mark E. Neely's *The Abraham Lincoln Encyclopedia,* published in 1982, devotes less than 5 percent of its space to military matters. Of the seventeen collected essays on Lincoln published in 1987 by the late Don E. Fehrenbacher, one of the foremost Lincoln scholars of our time, not one deals with the president as a military leader. On the 175th anniversary of Lincoln's birth, Gettysburg College hosted a conference on recent Lincoln scholarship. There were three sessions on psychobiography, two on the assassination, two on Lincoln's image in photographs and popular prints, one each on his economic ideas, religion, humor, Indian policy, and slavery. But there were no sessions on Lincoln as commander in chief—a remarkable irony, given the site of the conference. In 1994 the historian Merrill Peterson published his splendid study *Lincoln in American Memory,* highlighting 130 years of the sixteenth president's image in American historiography and popular culture. There are chapters on Lincoln and the South, religion, politics, Reconstruction, civil rights, and several other themes, but no chapter on Lincoln and the army. The most recent study of Lincoln's presidency, by Phillip Shaw Paludan, and the most recent biography, by David Herbert Donald (published in 1994 and 1995, respectively), give less attention to Lincoln as commander in chief than to politics, slavery, and emancipation.

This relative neglect of Lincoln's hands-on connection with the actual war reflects broader trends in mainstream academic historical scholarship, in which military history is held in rather low regard. But we need to take seriously Lincoln's own insistence that on "the progress of our arms . . . all else chiefly depends." Most of the things that historians do consider important in nineteenth-century American history—the fate of slavery, the structure of society in both North and South, the direction of the American economy, the destiny of competing nationalisms in North and South, the definition of freedom, the very survival of the United States—rested on the shoulders of those men who wore the blue and of their commander in chief in the Civil War. If the North had lost the war, Lincoln might well have gone down in history as one of our weakest presidents instead of one of our greatest.

Lincoln himself was painfully aware in 1861 that his Confederate adversary in Richmond was much better qualified as a military leader. Jefferson Davis had graduated from West Point, commanded a regiment in the Mexican War, and served four years during the 1850s as an outstanding secretary of war, whereas Lincoln's only military experience was his combat with mosquitoes in the Black Hawk War. To remedy his deficiencies, Lincoln borrowed books on military strategy from the Library of Congress and burned the midnight oil reading them. His experience as a largely self-taught lawyer and his analytical mind (for mental exercise he had mastered Euclidean geometry on his own) stood him in good stead. By 1862 his orders and dispatches demonstrated a sound grasp of strategic principles.

One book Lincoln did not read was the classic treatise *On War* by the Prussian military theorist Karl von Clausewitz, because that book was not yet translated into English in Lincoln's time. But Lincoln had an intuitive understanding of one of Clausewitz's central ideas: that war is the continuation of politics by other means. Lincoln would also have recognized the distinction that modern military theorists make between two kinds of strategy: *national* strategy, or the shaping and defining of a nation's political goals in time of war; and *military* (or operational) strategy, the use of armed forces to achieve those goals. As president, Lincoln shared the power to determine national strategy with Congress and his cabinet. As commander in chief he shared power with his top generals to shape military strategy.

In both capacities, however, Lincoln believed himself ultimately responsible. Like Harry Truman eighty years later, he knew that the buck stopped on the president's desk. Lincoln thus made sure to hold the final decision on important matters in his own hands, especially on questions of national strategy. Secretary of State William H. Seward initially aspired to be the so-called "premier" of Lincoln's administration. In Seward's notorious memorandum of April 1, 1861, he proposed to abandon Fort Sumter and pick a quarrel with European nations as a way to defuse passions in the South and reunite the country against a foreign foe. "Whatever policy we adopt," wrote Seward, "it must be somebody's business to pursue and direct it." He left little doubt whom he had in mind. Lincoln ignored Seward's advice about provoking a foreign incident, stated that he intended to resupply Fort Sumter, and concluded firmly that whatever was done, "*I* must do it."

Later that year, when General John C. Frémont issued a military order emancipating the slaves of Confederate supporters in Missouri, Lincoln rescinded it. He did so because his national strategy of keeping the border slave states—Delaware, Maryland, Kentucky, and Missouri—in the Union was then balanced delicately on a knife edge. He feared that these states would join the Confederacy if Frémont's order stood. He might well have been right; in any case he could not take the risk at this stage of the war. As Lincoln put it in September 1861, "I think to lose Kentucky is nearly the same as to lose the whole game. Kentucky gone, we can not hold Missouri, nor, as I think, Maryland. These all against us, and the job on our hands is too large for us. We would as well consent to separation at once, including the surrender of this capitol." Eight months later, in May 1862, General David Hunter issued a similar emancipation edict in his military district embracing Union-occupied regions along the south Atlantic coast. Stating angrily that "no commanding general shall do such a thing, upon my responsibility, without consulting me," Lincoln rescinded Hunter's order. But he also warned that, as a matter of national strategy, he might soon find it necessary to exercise his war powers to declare the slaves in Confederate states free. Several months later, of course, he did just that.

These examples concern matters of national strategy—of the nation's war *aims,* the political goals to be achieved by military means decided upon by the president as commander in chief. On the narrower but perhaps equally important questions of military strategy, Lincoln at first deferred to the professionals. The consummate professional at the beginning of the war was General in Chief Winfield Scott, the conqueror of Mexico fourteen years earlier. Scott formulated what the press labeled the "Anaconda Plan." A Virginian, Scott wanted to defeat the Confederacy at the lowest possible cost in lives and property. He proposed to "envelop" the South with a blockade by sea and a fleet of gunboats supported by soldiers moving down the Mississippi River to seal off the Confederacy from the outside world and thus "bring them to terms with less bloodshed than by any other plan."

Lincoln initially supported this military strategy. It was consistent with his national strategy in 1861 of a limited war to *restore* the Union as it had existed before the secession of eleven states. That national strategy in turn was grounded on a belief, widespread in the North at this stage of the war, that a silent majority of the Southern people were Unionists at heart, but had been swept into the Confederacy by the passions of the moment. In his first message to Congress, on July 4, 1861, Lincoln questioned "whether there is to-day, a majority of the legally qualified voters of any state, except perhaps South Carolina, in favor of disunion." Once the federal government demonstrated its firmness and determination by sealing off the Confederacy with the Anaconda Plan, those presumed legions of Unionists would regain control of their states and resume their old place in the Union. That is why, in Lincoln's initial call for militia on April 15, 1861, he defined the conflict not as a war but as a domestic insurrection— "combinations too powerful to be suppressed by the ordinary course of judicial proceedings" were the words Lincoln used—and declared that in suppressing this insurrection the federalized militia would avoid "any devastation, any destruction of, or interference with, property, or any disturbance of peaceful citizens."

The Anaconda Plan would eventually be carried out. The blockade slowly tightened around the Confederacy, and the Mississippi was sealed off from Confederate use by 1863. In the meantime, however, Lincoln's national and military strategies had both evolved a long way from the limited war of 1861.

The first step in that evolution occurred along the banks of the sluggish stream of Bull Run in July 1861. This was a battle that Scott, distrustful of his ninety-day militia, had not wanted to fight. But Northern opinion clamored for a push "Forward to Richmond!" Lincoln concurred with Quartermaster General Montgomery Meigs that "we would never end the war without beating the rebels" in a battle. Such a battle was consistent with the limited-war national strategy, for a Union victory would embolden that presumed silent majority of Southern Unionists. When the field commander of Union forces, Irvin McDowell, protested that he needed more time to train his raw troops, Lincoln reportedly told him, "You are green, it is true; but they are green, also; you are all green alike."

The defeat at Bull Run sobered Lincoln. But it did not change his purpose or lessen his determination. The next day he signed a bill for the enlistment of 500,000 three-year volunteers in the Union army. Three days later he signed a second bill authorizing another 500,000. He called George B. McClellan, who had won minor victories in western Virginia, to become commander of the Army of the Potomac.

(Lincoln sat down and wrote a memorandum outlining a proposal for simultaneous advances in Virginia against the railroad junctions of Manassas and Strasburg, an advance into eastern Tennessee, and a campaign against Memphis on the Mississippi River once the new three-year men were trained.) And Lincoln, having seen what could happen to green troops, initially granted McClellan's pleas for plenty of time to train them. Even after McClellan replaced the aged and infirm Scott as general in chief on November 1, 1861, and began treating with disdain Lincoln's desire to be kept informed about military plans, Lincoln had only this to say: "I will hold McClellan's horse if he will only bring us success."

Lincoln's faith in a silent majority of Southern Unionists began to wear thin after Bull Run. He now realized that the Confederates would have to be beaten into submission, probably in several battles and campaigns. But his military strategy in early 1862 focused mainly on seizing crucial Confederate transport hubs and territory as a way of weakening the enemy. He urged McClellan to move forward and relayed similar wishes to Brigadier General Don Carlos Buell and Major General Henry W. Halleck in the West during the winter of 1861–62. For one reason or another, each of them replied that he was not ready yet. Lincoln's frustration level with his top commanders, which would last until Grant came east in the spring of 1864, began at this time its rise in temperature. On the back of a letter he received from Halleck explaining why he could not move against the Confederate defenses at Columbus, Kentucky, Lincoln wrote in January 1862, "It is exceedingly discouraging. As everywhere else, nothing can be done."

Halleck's explanation is a revealing one: "To operate on *exterior* lines against an enemy occupying a central position, will fail, as it always has failed, in ninety-nine cases out of a hundred. It is condemned by every military authority I have ever read." By this time Lincoln had read some of those same authorities in his own cram course on strategy. But not being bound by the same tunnel vision as the pedantic Halleck, Lincoln drew a different conclusion from his analytical skills and common sense. He recognized that by the very geography of the situation, Union forces *had* to operate on exterior lines from points around the perimeter of the Confederacy. Lincoln grasped, sooner than many of his generals, the strategic concept that modern military theorists define as "concentration in time." Because their overall strategy was one of defending the territory that lay behind their front, the Confederates had the advantage of "interior lines." That advantage enabled them to shift reinforcements from inactive to active fronts—concentration in *space*—unless the Union used its superior numbers to attack on several fronts at once—concentration in *time*. On January 13, three days after reading Halleck's warning against operating on exterior lines, Lincoln wrote to General Buell (who had made a similar point):

> I state my general idea of this war to be that we have *greater* numbers, and the enemy has *greater* facility of concentrating forces upon points of collision; that we must fail, unless we can find some way of making our advantage an overmatch for *his;* and that this can only be done by menacing with superior forces at *different* points, at the same time; so that we can safely attack, one, or both, if he makes no change; and if he weakens one to strengthen the other, forbear to attach the strengthened one, but seize, and hold the weakened one, gaining so much.

Napoleon himself could scarcely have expressed it better. But not for more than two long years would Lincoln have a general in chief who understood this idea. That person, Ulysses S. Grant, began his rise in Lincoln's estimation with his campaign in February 1862 that resulted in the capture of Forts Henry and Donelson on the Tennessee and Cumberland rivers, opening those avenues of invasion into the Confederate heartland. These successes started a string of remarkable Union victories at several locations in the winter and spring of 1862: along the south Atlantic coast from North Carolina to Florida; the battles of Pea Ridge, Arkansas, and Shiloh, Tennessee; occupation of Nashville, Corinth, Mississippi, New Orleans, Memphis, and indeed the whole Mississippi River Valley except the two hundred miles between Vicksburg and Port Hudson. Even McClellan got off the mark and moved the Army of the Potomac up the Virginia Peninsula to within hearing distance of Richmond's church bells by May. The Confederate capital seemed doomed, and the Union military strategy of capturing important *places* and controlling vast stretches of Confederate *territory*—at least fifty thousand square miles of it by June 1862—seemed to be a spectacular success.

But then the Union war machine went into reverse. By September 1862 Confederate counteroffensives in Virginia, Tennessee, and Kentucky took Southern armies from the verge of defeat all the way across the Potomac River into Maryland and north almost to the Ohio River. Robert E. Lee, Stonewall Jackson, and Nathan Bedford Forrest emerged during this period as the most effective and brilliant Confederate commanders and architects of some of these successes. The reversal of the fortunes of war during the summer of 1862 stunned Northerners. But Lincoln did not falter. He issued a new call for volunteers and declared that "I expect to maintain this contest until successful, or till I die, or am conquered, or my term expires, or Congress or the country forsakes me."

Lincoln also took the next step in the evolution of his concept of military strategy, from the conquest of territory to the destruction of enemy armies. Union forces *had* conquered railroad junctions, enemy ports and cities, and those fifty thousand square miles of territory in the winter and spring of 1862, yet by September of that year the North was no closer to winning the war—indeed, perhaps farther from winning—than a year earlier. From August 1862 to June 1863 Confederate armies reconquered much of the territory they had lost, inflicted punishing defeats on Union forces, and twice invaded the North. Clearly, the conquest and occupation of Southern territory would not win the war so long as enemy armies remained capable of reconquering it. Lincoln grasped this truth sooner than most of his commanders did. As early as April 1862, after reluctantly acceding to McClellan's plan to flank the Confederate defenses in northern Virginia by going all the way down the Chesapeake Bay to make his thrust toward Richmond via the peninsula between the York and James rivers, Lincoln told McClellan that no matter which invasion route he took, he was going to have to fight the enemy army instead of merely laying siege to *places.* "Let me tell you," Lincoln wrote to McClellan on April 9, 1862,

> It is indispensable to *you* that you strike a blow. . . . You will do me the justice to remember I always insisted, that going down the Bay in search of a field, instead of fighting at or near Manassas, was only shifting, and not surmounting, a difficulty—that we would find the same enemy, and the same, or equal, entrenchments, at either place. The country will not fail to note—is now noting—that the present hesitation to move upon an intrenched enemy, is but the story of Manassas repeated. . . . I have never written you, or spoken to you, in greater kindness of feeling than now, nor with a fuller purpose to sustain you. . . . *But you must act.*

McClellan, however, seemed constitutionally unable to act, only to react. He yielded the initiative in the Peninsula campaign to Lee. From the Seven Days' battles at the end of June 1862 until the invasion of Maryland in September, it was the Confederates who sought to destroy the Union armies. But Lincoln saw a great opportunity in Lee's invasion of Maryland, to cut the Confederate army off from its base of supplies and strike a crippling blow. "Destroy the rebel army," Lincoln wired McClellan on September 15. But McClellan fumbled away the opportunity at Antietam. For a month after that battle, Lincoln repeatedly urged McClellan to follow up the ambiguous victory there with a real one that would cripple Lee's army, not merely drive it back toward Richmond. "Cross the Potomac and give battle," read one telegram to McClellan. On another occasion Lincoln wrote to him, "We should not operate as to merely drive him away. If we can not beat the enemy where he now is [near Harpers Ferry], we never can. . . . If we never try, we shall never succeed."

But McClellan didn't try, and Lincoln finally grew tired of trying "to bore with an augur too dull to take hold," as he told one of McClellan's supporters, and removed him from command in November 1862. There followed seven months of frustration for Lincoln in the Virginia theater, as Generals Ambrose Burnside and Joseph Hooker led the Army of the Potomac to disastrous defeats at Fredericksburg and Chancellorsville. When Lee used his victory at Chancellorsville as a springboard for another invasion of the North, Lincoln saw this as an opportunity rather than a threat. He told Hooker that this invasion "gives you back the chance that I thought McClellan lost last fall" to cripple the enemy far from his base. As Lee headed north, however, Hooker proposed to cut in behind him to take Richmond. Lincoln threw up his hands in frustration: "Lee's *Army,* not *Richmond,* is your true objective point," he wired Hooker. But that general seemed reluctant to fight Lee again, so on June 28, which turned out to be the eve of the Battle of Gettysburg, Lincoln accepted Hooker's resignation and appointed General George Meade as commander of the Army of the Potomac. Meade skillfully directed a defensive victory at Gettysburg. When word arrived almost simultaneously in Washington of this victory and of General Ulysses S. Grant's capture of Vicksburg on July 4, 1863, Lincoln was elated. "Now," he declared, "if General Meade can complete his work, so gloriously prosecuted thus far, by the literal or substantial destruction of Lee's army, the rebellion will be over."

But there was the rub. Meade seemed satisfied with his repulse of Confederate assaults at Gettysburg. In Lincoln's eyes, he threw away a great opportunity by failing to follow up this success with a vigorous pursuit to trap and destroy the crippled Army of Northern Virginia before it could escape back across the Potomac. On July 4 Meade had issued a congratulatory order to his troops, adding that "our task is not yet accomplished, and the commanding general looks to the army for greater efforts to drive from our soil every vestige of the presence of the invader." "Great God!" exclaimed Lincoln when he read these words. "This is a dreadful reminiscence of McClellan," who had proclaimed a great victory after Antietam because the enemy retreated across the river. "Will our Generals never get that idea out of their heads? The whole country is our soil." That was, after all, the point of the war! To his private secretary John Hay, the president lamented, a week after Lee had gotten his army over the swollen Potomac, "Our Army held the war in the hollow of their hand & they would not close it." So frustrated was Lincoln that when he sat down to write Meade a letter of congratulation for his victory at Gettysburg, the letter soon took on a tone the opposite of congratulation. "My dear general," Lincoln wrote, "I do not believe you appreciate the magnitude of the misfortune involved in Lee's escape. He was within your easy grasp, and to have closed upon him would, in connection with our other late successes, have ended the war. As it is, the war will be prolonged indefinitely. . . . Your golden opportunity is gone, and I am distressed immeasurable because of it."

As he blotted the ink dry and reread this letter, Lincoln decided not to send it, for to do so would surely have provoked Meade's resignation. Lincoln couldn't afford yet another change in the command of the Army of the Potomac, especially when it was basking in public acclaim for Gettysburg. So Lincoln filed the letter away in his papers. But he didn't change his mind about the magnitude of Meade's missed opportunity. Two months later, as the opposing armies in Virginia were maneuvering and skirmishing again over the devastated land between Washington and Richmond, Lincoln declared in exasperation that "to attempt to fight the enemy slowly back to his entrenchments in Richmond . . . is an idea I have been trying to repudiate for quite a year. . . . If our army can not fall upon the enemy and hurt him where he is, is plain to me that it can gain nothing by attempting to follow him over a succession of intrenched lines into a fortified city."

It was this kind of strategic thinking that caused the historian T. Harry Williams to conclude that Lincoln was "a better strategist than any of his generals." But by 1863 there *was* one Union general who measured up to Lincoln's expectations. At the same time that Lincoln wrote his unsent letter to Meade after Gettysburg, he also wrote to General Grant congratulating him on "the almost inestimable service you have done the country" by capturing a whole Confederate army at Vicksburg. To an associate in Washington, Lincoln declared: "Grant is my man and I am his the rest of the war." On other occasions, Lincoln made it clear that the main reason for his support of Grant through the thick and thin of criticism and opposition to that general from many quarters during 1862 and early 1863 was that he and Grant agreed on how to win the war: fight the enemy and capture or cripple his armies—something that Grant did with much greater frequency and success than any other general in the Civil War. "I can't spare this man; he fights," said Lincoln of Grant on one occasion; in response to another demand that he get rid of Grant as a drunk and a failure, Lincoln said that "what I want is generals who will fight battles and win victories. Grant has done this, and I propose to stand by him." One of Lincoln's greatest contributions to victory as commander in chief was to stand by Grant when few others did so, until the whole North came to share Lincoln's opinion of Grant by the time Lincoln brought him to Washington as general in chief in March 1864.

Lincoln finally had a commander who saw eye to eye with him on military strategy. Grant said that in the past, Union armies on various fronts had "acted independently and without concert, like a balky team, no two ever pulling together." This had enabled the Confederates to use their interior lines to shift troops from one point to another to meet the most pressing danger of the moment—as they had done by sending General James Longstreet with two divisions from Virginia to Chickamauga in September 1863. Grant planned a campaign in 1864 for five Union armies stretched over a front of a thousand miles to undertake coordinated offensives. The two principal armies were those commanded by Meade in Virginia and William T. Sherman in Georgia. "Lee's army will be your objective point," Grant told Meade. "Wherever Lee goes, there you will go also." (He made no mention of capturing Richmond.) To Sherman, Grant sent orders "to move against Johnston's army, to break it up and to get into the interior of the enemy's country as far as you can, inflicting all the damage you can against their war resources."

Lincoln was impressed. He told his private secretary Hay that Grant was carrying out his "old suggestion so constantly made and as constantly neglected, to Buell & Halleck, *et al*, to move at once upon the enemy's whole line so as to bring into action to our advantage our great superiority of numbers"—in other words, concentration in *time* to counteract the Confederacy's use of interior lines to concentrate in *space*. The smaller Union armies, even if they did not beat the Confederate units in their front, could at least pin them down and prevent reinforcements from being sent to Lee and to General Joseph Johnston in Georgia. As Lincoln put it, "Those not skinning can hold a leg." Grant liked this phrase so much that he used it in official orders. As matters turned out, the leg holders (Nathaniel P. Banks, Benjamin F. Butler, and Franz Sigel) did not do their job, enabling the Confederacy to hold out for another year. But in the end the skinners—Grant, Meade, Sherman, Sheridan, and George H. Thomas—took off the South's hide.

This did not happen until Lincoln's conception of both military and national strategy had evolved to a fourth stage. To review, the first stage had been restoration of the old Union, the Union as it was before 1861, by a limited war to encourage Southern Unionists to bring their states back in. The second stage was to conquer enough Southern territory to force the Confederates to give up. The third stage was to cripple or destroy Confederate armies. But even this did not prove sufficient, for after one Confederate army was captured at Vicksburg and another crippled at Gettysburg, the South kept fighting, and for a time in the summer of 1864 the Northern people almost seemed ready to throw in the towel and quit paying the terrible price of victory. Even before 1864 Lincoln, like Sherman, had become convinced that this civil war was not just a war between whole societies, between peoples, in which the economy and resources of the home front and the will of the civilian population to sustain the war were as important as the fighting power of the armies. Thus it was necessary to destroy Confederate resources used to wage war.

This was the conviction that underlay the Emancipation Proclama-

tion, for the slaves were one of the most important Southern resources. "We must free the slaves or be ourselves subdued," Lincoln
told his cabinet in July 1862. "The slaves are undeniably an element
of strength to those who have their service, and we must decide
whether that element should be with us or against us. . . . Decisive
and extensive measures must be adopted. . . . We wanted the army
to strike more vigorous blows. The Administration must set an example, and strike at the heart of the rebellion"—slavery. This was the
principle on which the administration also decided to enlist former
slaves in the Union army on a large scale, thus converting their labor
power for the Confederacy into military manpower for the Union. By
August 1863, Grant could tell Lincoln that "by arming the negro we
have added a powerful ally. . . . This, with the emancipation of the
negro, is the heaviest blow yet given the Confederacy."

Emancipation therefore became part of the Union's military strategy. But it was more than that; it also became central to Lincoln's
national strategy, the political goals for which the war was fought, to
cleanse the nation of an institution that Lincoln had more than once
branded as an evil and a "monstrous injustice." Thus Lincoln issued
the Emancipation Proclamation not only as an act of "military necessity," but also as "an act of justice." And at Gettysburg, Lincoln said
that the Union soldiers who gave the last full measure of devotion
there did so not only to preserve the nation but also to give it "a new
birth of freedom."

The Civil War converted slave property into free human beings. It
also converted much other Southern property into ashes. Lincoln's
conception of the strategy necessary to win the war had come a long
way since his statement in April 1861 that the national armies he then
called into being would avoid "any devastation, any destruction of, or
interference with, property, or any disturbance of peaceful citizens."
Now devastation of property and disturbance of civilians who supported the Confederate war effort were the order of the day. As Sherman wrote in reply to Confederate civilians who called him a
barbarian, a commander "may take your house, your fields, your everything, and turn you all out, helpless, to starve. It may be wrong,
but that don't alter the case. . . . Our duty is not to build up; it is
rather to destroy both the rebel army and whatever of wealth and
property it has founded its boasted strength upon." On other occasions, Sherman said that war is cruelty; you cannot refine it. And

fifteen years after the end of the Civil War, he warned the younger generation against glorifying war: War is hell, he told them. Lincoln made the same point, most notably in a speech at Philadelphia in June 1864: "War, at the best, is terrible, and this war of ours, in its magnitude and in its duration, is one of the most terrible." But Lincoln did not shrink from the consequences, and in his Second Inaugural Address on March 4, 1865, he even suggested that this terrible war might be God's punishment of his almost chosen people for the sin of slavery: "Fondly do we hope—fervently do we pray—that this mighty scourge of war may speedily pass away. Yet, if God wills that it continue, until all the wealth piled by the bond-man's two hundred and fifty years of unrequited toil shall be sunk, and until every drop of blood drawn with the lash, shall be paid by another drawn with the sword, as was said three thousand years ago, so still it must be said 'the judgments of the Lord, are true and righteous altogether.'"

In the same address, Lincoln placed responsibility for the war where most Americans believed it belonged, and stated that disunion would have been worse than even the enormous cost of the war. Back in 1861, he said, one side "would make war rather than let the nation survive; and the other would accept war rather than let it perish." And Lincoln would not accept peace, either, except on the terms of unconditional surrender of both independence and slavery by the Confederacy. By 1864 this had become the core of his national strategy. Through the flurry of peace feelers during that terrible summer, when the war seemed to be going badly for the North, unconditional union and emancipation remained Lincoln's terms for ending the war. Just as adamantly, Davis insisted on Confederate independence. As Lincoln put it in December 1864, Davis "does not attempt to deceive us. He affords us no excuse to deceive ourselves. He cannot voluntarily reaccept the Union; we cannot voluntarily yield it. Between him and us the issue is distinct, simple, and inflexible. It is an issue which can only be tried by war, and decided by victory."

Four months later it *was* decided by victory, and no one deserved more credit for that achievement, and thus for the survival of the United States as one nation, indivisible and free, than Abraham Lincoln, commander in chief.

2

Commander in Chief Lincoln and General Grant

John Y. Simon

LIKE GOLDILOCKS, Abraham Lincoln and Ulysses S. Grant is a fable that everyone vaguely remembers. Lincoln initially chose generals who failed to save the Union—one was too timid, another too rash; Henry W. Halleck was too scholarly, Ambrose E. Burnside too stupid. After a string of failures, Lincoln found Grant, who was *just right* to win the war. Like other fairy tales, simplified truth hardly explains complex human events, yet there is often a kernel of insight. Lincoln sought to unite war and politics, Grant sought to keep them separate. Grant was a military marvel, Lincoln a political genius. Once they agreed upon spheres of activity and learned to trust and defer, they formed a triumphant partnership. To reach that point, however, took time. Grant knew what was expected of him as general before he took command. Lincoln, however, virtually invented the role of commander in chief.

The Constitution is relatively brief, concise, and vague when discussing the powers and responsibilities of the president. Article II, section 1, provides that he shall hold "executive Power," and section 2 that he "shall be Commander in Chief of the Army and Navy of the United States and of the Militia of the several States, when called into the actual Service of the United States." When President George Washington took office, he acquired a small army led by Lieutenant Colonel Josiah Harmar. Washington appointed as secretary of war Henry Knox, who, as major general, had succeeded Washington himself as army commander. As Indian warfare loomed, Washington replaced Harmar with Major General Arthur St. Clair, who led his forces to disastrous defeat by the Indians, then replaced him with Major General Anthony Wayne, victor at the Battle of Fallen Timbers.

When threatened with actual insurrection in western Pennsylvania, in what was christened the Whiskey Rebellion, Washington summoned the militia of Pennsylvania, New Jersey, Maryland, and Virginia into federal service and personally commanded a force of some fifteen thousand against the rebels, who generally dispersed without bloodshed. At Washington's urging, Congress tripled the size of the regular army, although this force remained barely adequate to garrison and protect western forts. When war with France threatened in 1798, President John Adams appointed Washington commander in chief, the Senate confirmed the appointment, and Washington prepared to act under this title. When war threats subsided, Washington returned to his cherished retirement.

In consequence, the United States entered the nineteenth century with some uncertainty about the nature of the commander in chief's powers and the issue of who would command the nation's armies. Presidents began to extend and test war powers, beginning with Thomas Jefferson, who sent naval vessels into the Mediterranean to protect American ships against the pirates of Tripoli, and only later informed Congress of his action. When President James Madison called out militia for the War of 1812 and three New England governors refused to comply, the Supreme Court sustained Madison. On grounds of self-defense, President James Monroe ordered General Andrew Jackson into Spanish Florida in 1818 to pursue hostile Seminoles, but Jackson himself, when in the White House, sought congressional approval before employing force to suppress the South Carolina Ordinance of Nullification against the tariff of 1832. While most presidents tended to extend their war powers, President James Buchanan retreated from joining European powers in enforcing their will upon China, explaining that he could not do so "without usurping the warmaking power, which, under the Constitution, belongs exclusively to Congress."[1]

President James K. Polk, however, had already extended such powers by ordering troops into Texas and beyond with the expectation of provoking war with Mexico, then announcing to Congress that hostilities had already commenced. Polk also used his authority to appoint

---

[1] Dorothy Schaffter and Dorothy M. Matthews, *The Powers of the President as Commander in Chief of the Army and Navy of the United States,* 84th Congress, 2nd Session, House Doc. 443, 4.

commanders in Mexico, chosen with an eye toward future presidential politics. Despite his hope that Whigs Zachary Taylor and Winfield Scott would cancel each other out as presidential candidates, they received successive Whig nominations.[2] As a one-term congressman, Lincoln questioned Polk's justification for the war by challenging him to name the "spot" where Polk alleged that American blood had been shed on American soil. Since the war had already proved a glorious success before Lincoln criticized its origin, Lincoln returned to Springfield with a clouded reputation and the odious nickname of "spotty Lincoln" or, even more damning, "ranchero spotty."[3]

While presidents explored the extent of their powers as commander in chief, the army developed its own leadership structure. The military academy at West Point annually graduated classes of trained officers who gradually ascended ranks in either field or staff lines. At commencement, most could not be accommodated into the limited slots for officers and were appointed brevet second lieutenants. Brevet meant honorary, and young officers awaited the death or retirement of a superior officer, an event that would move up anyone inferior in rank in that regiment or staff department. From the viewpoint of an ambitious young West Point graduate, lack of provision for military retirement combined with a lack of warfare meant frustratingly long waits for promotion.[4]

Brevet Second Lieutenant Grant, an 1843 military academy graduate, waited for a regular slot for two years. Grant's regiment, the Fourth Infantry, went to Louisiana when storm clouds gathered over Texas. When the regiment assembled in New Orleans, elderly Colonel Josiah Vose took command of battalion drill, soon dismissed the troops, and promptly dropped dead from unexpected exertion. With mixed emotions, young officers regretted the death of the admirable old colonel yet immediately recognized that everyone else moved up one notch. As Grant recalled his services in the war with Mexico, he

---

[2] Leonard D. White, *The Jacksonians: A Study in Administrative History, 1829–1861* (New York: Macmillan, 1954), 50–66.

[3] David Herbert Donald, *Lincoln* (New York: Simon & Schuster, 1995), 124–25.

[4] Edward M. Coffman, *The Old Army: A Portrait of the American Army in Peacetime, 1784–1898* (New York: Oxford University Press, 1986), 99; William B. Skelton, *An American Profession of Arms: The Army Officer Corps, 1784–1861* (Lawrence: University Press of Kansas, 1992), 215. Both authors mention Colonel John DeB. Walbach, who still commanded the Fourth Artillery when he died in 1857, more than ninety years old.

had gone into the battle of Palo Alto in May, 1846, a second lieutenant, and I entered the city of Mexico sixteen months later with the same rank, after having been in all the engagements possible for any one man and in a regiment that lost more officers during the war than it ever had present at any one engagement. My regiment lost four commissioned officers, all senior to me, by steamboat explosions during the Mexican war. The Mexicans were not so discriminating. They sometimes picked off my juniors.[5]

Grant's services in the Mexican War won him brevet promotion to first lieutenant and captain, but although he moved up to first lieutenant in September 1847, there was no vacancy for captain in his regiment until an elderly officer died in 1854. When accepting this commission on the Pacific Coast, Grant, frustrated, ill, and lonely, also submitted his resignation. Like other officers trapped in this stagnant system, he anticipated a better life as a civilian. Captain Halleck submitted his resignation the next day. Because Grant resigned as of July 31 and Halleck as of August 1, bureaucrats quibbled over Grant's pay for July for decades but presumably promptly paid the more astute Halleck. Other promising officers, including George B. McClellan and William T. Sherman, resigned for roughly the same reasons. Halleck became senior partner in the leading law firm in San Francisco; Grant failed as a Missouri farmer. Grant had left the army to reunite his family and never expressed regret about his resignation. None of his classmates who remained in service had advanced beyond captain seven years later when the Civil War began.

At the apex of the regular army sat the general in chief or commanding general. Scott, a brigadier general in the War of 1812 and a brilliant field commander in the Mexican War, had held the office for twenty years when the Civil War began. He had reached the age of seventy-five and frequently could not rise from his bed. Of four brigadier generals, John E. Wool was two years older than Scott; David E. Twiggs was forced to resign after surrendering U.S. forces in Texas to Confederates without even a token show of resistance; William S. Harney negotiated with rebels in Missouri and was pushed to the sidelines; and Quartermaster General Joseph E. Johnston, the only general young enough to command effectively in the field, resigned

[5] *Personal Memoirs of U. S. Grant,* 2 vols. (New York: Charles L. Webster, 1885–86), 1:162–63.

to serve the Confederacy. Officers ultimately capable of winning the war for the Union lay mired at low rank or had resigned from the peacetime army.

Since the general in chief was also commanding general of the army, the titles were frequently conflated as commander in chief of the army. Since the latter title could be separated from the constitutionally mandated commander in chief of the army *and navy*, the misleading title remained in use through the Civil War, and in a letter to Scott on April 25, 1861, seven weeks after taking office, Lincoln referred to Scott as commander in chief.[6] This was, however, the only time Lincoln misused the title.

As president of a nation sundered by war, Lincoln was acutely conscious of his status as commander in chief. Scott retained the position of general in chief for eight months, rendering Lincoln valuable service. Scott drew on his long tenure and intimate knowledge of the officer corps to provide sound advice, and he had attempted to persuade fellow Virginian Robert E. Lee to stand by the flag. Scott advised Lincoln that Fort Sumter, militarily indefensible, must be abandoned, advice ultimately ignored for Lincoln's more successful strategy. Nonetheless, Scott remained a sound thinker, however much his assistance was impaired by his steadily declining physical condition.

Ready or not, Lincoln had to take charge after war erupted when Fort Sumter fell. As commander in chief, he proclaimed a blockade of the rebellious states, summoned troops to suppress the insurrection, suspended the writ of habeas corpus in areas close to the capital, and called Congress back into session on the Fourth of July, a date that fell after the Kentucky elections. He had taken actions controversial at the time and since, invoking war powers; yet only in the proclamation concerning volunteers had he actually used the words *commander in chief,* words that he used sparingly throughout the remainder of the Civil War.

One of the most interesting examples of Lincoln's use of the phrase came in a proclamation of May 19, 1862, revoking orders issued by Major General David Hunter, Department of the South, imposing martial law in the states of Florida, Georgia, and South

[6] Roy P. Basler et al., eds., *The Collected Works of Abraham Lincoln,* 9 vols. (New Brunswick, N.J.: Rutgers University Press, 1953–55), 4:344.

Carolina. "Slavery and martial law in a free country are altogether incompatible," Hunter announced; all slaves "are therefore declared forever free."[7] In response, Lincoln as president, stated that he had no knowledge of Hunter's intention to issue such an order, nor did he know that it was genuine, nor had he authorized any commander to free slaves, so he declared the order "altogether void." "I further make known," Lincoln continued, "that whether it be competent for me, as Commander-in Chief of the Army and Navy, to declare the Slaves of any state or states, free, and whether at any time, in any case, it shall have become a necessity indispensable to the maintainance of the government, to exercise such supposed power, are questions which, under my responsibility, I reserve to myself."[8]

President Lincoln had revoked Hunter's orders, whereas Commander in Chief Lincoln reserved the right to issue such orders himself. This he did four months later, and in both the preliminary Emancipation Proclamation of September 22, 1862, and the Final Proclamation of January 1, 1863, he invoked the powers of commander in chief. On September 13, in responding to a petition of "Chicago Christians" urging emancipation, Lincoln admitted that "as commander-in-chief of the army and navy, in time of war, I suppose I have a right to take any measure which may best subdue the enemy."[9]

What is surprising is how frequently Lincoln used the title commander in chief in relationship to emancipation compared to how rarely he used it elsewhere. In proclamations suspending habeas corpus or in additional draft calls, for example, where those words might be expected, he frequently omitted them. Perhaps he reserved the title for emancipation because he knew he was entering an uncharted constitutional area. Yet any conclusion that Lincoln might have been wary of using the power of the commander in chief during the Civil War is unwarranted, and no wise general should ever have forgotten the power of the chief executive.

The first to forget was McClellan. Brought to Washington to take command following the disastrous Union defeat at Bull Run, McClellan was overwhelmed by attention he received from Washington officials. McClellan viewed Lincoln and Scott with contempt. He

[7] Ibid., 5:222.
[8] Ibid.
[9] Ibid., 5:421.

expected to train, discipline, and reinforce his Army of the Potomac until he was assured of victory over the enormous force of rebels that threatened Washington. McClellan was wrong about enemy numbers, cruel in his treatment of Scott (whom he forced into retirement and superseded as general in chief), and misjudged Lincoln's patience and forbearance. After half a year of delay, Lincoln seized control and forced McClellan into action. On January 27, 1862, Lincoln issued "President's general War Order No. 1" designating February 22 as "the day for a general movement by the Land and Naval forces of the United States against the insurgent forces."[10] Never implemented, the order nonetheless announced Lincoln's intention to manage the war, preferably by coordinating Northern strength against the rebellion.

As McClellan embarked on his Peninsular campaign against Richmond in the spring of 1862, Lincoln reaffirmed his authority by withholding an entire corps for the defense of Washington and by removing McClellan from the post of general in chief. For the latter, he had precedent: Scott did not command the entire army for the period when he campaigned in Mexico. Richmond was much closer than Veracruz, however, and the telegraph kept McClellan in immediate contact with Washington. Lincoln had sent a different message. McClellan expected to resume the post of general in chief after capturing Richmond. He wavered at the gates of Richmond, while Lincoln personally commanded an expedition that captured Norfolk.

Meanwhile, Lincoln had become exasperated enough to employ the phrase so often neglected. "If you could know the full pressure of the case, I am confident you would justify it—even beyond a mere acknowledgment that the Commander-in-chief, may order what he pleases."[11] Finding McClellan becalmed at Harrison's Landing, Lincoln appointed Halleck to the post of general in chief. Halleck had been Scott's original choice as his successor, and Halleck had made aggressive noises while commanding in the West. Lincoln expected Halleck to force McClellan to advance against Richmond or to face removal, and by doing neither, Halleck set the stage for Union defeat at Second Bull Run. Thereafter, Lincoln thought, Halleck performed merely as a clerk—and a fairly obnoxious one at that. Halleck's con-

[10] Ibid., 5:111.
[11] Lincoln to McClellan, March 31, 1862, ibid., 5:175–76.

tinuing value as general in chief consisted of his role in transmitting Lincoln's orders, becoming a mechanism through which unsuccessful generals were sacked.[12]

Every commander of the Army of the Potomac came to hate Halleck, although he still retained friends in the West, most notably Grant and Sherman. Grant recognized Halleck's friendship when challenged by John A. McClernand. During the Vicksburg campaign, Halleck proved to be Grant's staunchest ally in curbing that overly ambitious subordinate. Yet when Vicksburg fell, a military achievement of such magnitude that Grant's assignment to the Army of the Potomac loomed as a real possibility, he regarded the prospect with dismay, recognizing that this commander fell under the immediate supervision of the commander in chief and Secretary of War Edwin M. Stanton.

As Grant expressed his concerns, he feared becoming "McClellanized," by which he meant having his military actions closely scrutinized, criticized, and potentially directed at three levels of control: commander in chief, secretary of war, and general in chief.[13] Grant knew that Lincoln had burdened McClellan with advice and orders, given his army to John Pope, and destroyed his military career. Grant's independence in the West, which had brought him dazzling success, had already cost him the jealous displeasure of Halleck. Grant remembered that Lincoln had furthered the unseemly ambitions of McClernand, whom Grant had removed from command three weeks before Vicksburg surrendered. Politically, only the fall of Vicksburg justified the fall of McClernand.

Lincoln understood from the outbreak of the war that success required the support of Democrats, in part acquired through their visibility in command. Democrats included West Pointers, few of whom favored the Republicans, and uniformed politicians such as Benjamin F. Butler. Political appointments of Democrats to command needed the balance of equally prominent Republicans like Nathaniel P. Banks. Lincoln further needed the support of ethnic groups, especially Germans, who were gratified by appointments like that of Franz Sigel. Lincoln later explained that promotion of General Peter

[12] John Y. Simon, "Lincoln and Halleck," in Charles M. Hubbard, ed., *Lincoln and His Contemporaries* (Macon, Ga.: Mercer University Press, 1999), 69–85.

[13] John M. Schofield, *Forty-six Years in the Army* (New York: Century, 1897), 361–62.

J. Osterhaus was based "on what we thought was high merit, and somewhat on his nationality."[14] Grant shared with Halleck an aversion to appointments based primarily on political or ethnic grounds, even though he admired the conduct of subordinates John A. Logan, a proslavery Democrat, and Frank Blair, a Republican exemplar, both of whom would ultimately switch parties.

Grant's reprieve from eastern command proved temporary. In July 1863 General George G. Meade had repulsed Lee's last desperate charge at Gettysburg the day before Vicksburg surrendered. Grant and Meade received broad public acclaim. Meade's failure to pursue Lee dismayed and angered Lincoln, controversy erupted among Meade's subordinates, and the fall campaigns of the Army of the Potomac were lackluster at best. In November Grant's dramatic victory at Chattanooga elevated him to a class by himself; Congress recognized this when it passed legislation to create the rank of lieutenant general, a rank held previously only by Washington.

When the bill became law, however, Lincoln hesitated. At the beginning of a presidential election year, he feared that Grant might receive the Republican nomination, and before promoting Grant, Lincoln required assurances that he would not become a candidate. Grant's friends gave such assurances readily and wholeheartedly. Grant had unequivocally rebuffed Democratic overtures and carried a deep distaste for politics into the White House.

Nearly three years of Civil War, with the end beyond sight and even the outcome in doubt, accounted for Lincoln's concern about his renomination and reelection. Some Republican radicals nominated John C. Frémont as a protest candidate, and others already looked to Grant. At the Union convention in June, Lincoln received every first ballot vote except twenty-two Missouri votes for Grant, later switched to make the nomination unanimous. By the summer of 1864, Grant almost certainly could have received the Democratic nomination for president or could have mounted a strong threat to Lincoln as a Republican.

Grant had voted for Democrat James Buchanan in 1856 and favored Stephen A. Douglas in 1860. On the other hand, the Republican governor of Illinois commissioned him as colonel, and he owed

---

[14] Lincoln to Maj. Gen. William T. Sherman, July 26, 1864, in *Collected Works of Lincoln,* 7:463.

appointment as brigadier general to his local Republican congress-man. Lincoln also knew that Grant had followed administration pol-icy, especially with regard to the enlistment of black troops.

Lincoln wanted a general in chief who would hurl the superior numbers of the Union armies against the Confederacy. The president needed assurance that Grant would not desert the army for political office. Lincoln saw Grant as a potential political rival, as possibly another McClellan, that former military savior headed toward the Democratic nomination for president. Grant remembered that Lin-coln had given Sherman's command to McClernand, whose ambi-tions included toppling Grant. Before Grant came east, Lincoln needed abundant reason to believe that Grant posed no political threat. Grant needed equal assurance that Lincoln posed no military threat. Even after the bargain was struck, both needed reassurance.

Lincoln met Grant for the first time on March 8, 1864, at a crowded White House reception. To gratify public curiosity, Grant had to stand on a crimson sofa in the East Room. Later Lincoln explained to Grant the ceremony scheduled for the following day. In the presence of the entire cabinet, Lincoln intended to present Grant with his commission as lieutenant general and to make a brief speech, expecting him to reply with something that would allay the jealousy of other generals and put him on "good terms" with the Army of the Potomac. Grant's brief written remarks, three sentences to Lincoln's four, touched neither point directly, yet seemed entirely appropriate: "I accept the commission with gratitude for the high honor confered. With the aid of the noble armies that have fought on so many fields for our common country, it will be my earnest endeavor not to disap-point your expectations. I feel the full weight of the responsibilities now devolving on me and know that if they are met it will be due to those armies, and above all to the favor of that Providence which leads both Nations and men."[15]

General in Chief Halleck, now outranked by his former subordi-nate, stepped down. Higher rank required Grant to assume overall command. Grant resolved this problem by arranging Halleck's ap-pointment as chief of staff, leaving him in Washington to coordinate orders, freeing Grant to establish headquarters wherever he wished.

---

[15] John Y. Simon, ed., *The Papers of Ulysses S. Grant,* 24 vols. (Carbondale: South-ern Illinois University Press, 1967–), 10:195.

Halleck's new post separated strategic command from administration, a crucial innovation in modern warfare. Grant avoided the position of military adviser to Lincoln and Secretary of War Stanton, a role congenial to Halleck, but one intolerable to Grant, who intended to remain a commander rather than a courtier and to distance himself from politicians. Halleck became Grant's intermediary. Grant expected "to exercise actual command of all the armies, without any interference from the War Department."

Grant then visited Meade, who had expected Grant to replace him with a veteran of the western armies. When Meade said that he would willingly relinquish command to another, Grant promptly decided to retain him. Grant established headquarters with the Army of the Potomac, not displacing Meade but coordinating command from a point with the largest and most prominent of all armies, remaining close to Washington without becoming caught in its political eddies, and entrusting western command to Sherman.

By the time he returned to Washington, Grant was ready to return west. He canceled dinner at the White House, an invitation he had already accepted, telling Lincoln that he had endured enough of "this show business."[16] Besides, he explained, "a dinner to me means a million dollars a day lost to the country."

Grant visited Washington for three days. During that time he spent little time with Lincoln and much of that in the presence of the cabinet. In their first private meeting, as Grant recalled it, Lincoln said that "he had never professed to be a military man or to know how campaigns should be conducted, and never wanted to interfere in them: but that procrastination on the part of commanders, and the pressure from the people at the North and Congress, *which was always with him,* forced him into issuing his series of 'Military Orders,'"[17] some of which he conceded were mistaken. By implication, Lincoln indicated that he would not treat Grant as he had treated McClellan. Lincoln added that "while armies were sitting down waiting for opportunities to turn up which might, perhaps, be more favorable from a strictly military point of view, the government was spending millions of dollars every day; that there was a limit to the sinews of war, and a time might be reached when the spirits and

---

[16] Horace Porter, *Campaigning with Grant* (New York: Century, 1897), 22.
[17] *Personal Memoirs of Grant,* 2:122.

resources of the people would become exhausted."[18] He simply wanted someone to "take the responsibility and act,"[19] something Grant assured him that he would do.

Whether Lincoln abdicated his control of the war has since been disputed, but Grant thought that Lincoln did so. Facing the uncertainties of an election year, remembering that no incumbent had been reelected since Jackson, Lincoln dared not risk responsibility for military setbacks. Grant's spring campaign opened with an exchange of formal letters with Lincoln. "The particulars of your plan I neither know, or seek to know," wrote Lincoln.[20] "Should my success be less than I desire, and expect," Grant responded, "the least I can say is, the fault is not with you."[21]

Although Lincoln wrote that he did not know the "particulars" of Grant's plan, Lincoln had heard overall strategy explained in sufficient detail to understand that Grant intended to use all armies in a coordinated offensive. No longer could Confederates use interior lines to counter sporadic attacks. Every army would perform some role in the grand offensive. "Those not skinning can hold a leg," Lincoln observed to Grant.[22] In devising this plan, Lincoln said privately, Grant had implemented a strategy that Lincoln had always urged. Grant controlled five major armies; in addition to those under Grant himself and Sherman, their commanders were Republican Banks, Democrat Butler, and German Sigel. Grant shelved all three during the next year, not without a struggle, and Butler survived until after the election.

On May 4 Grant plunged across the Rapidan and led his armies into the Wilderness, suffering tremendous casualties. Moving on his left flank, he encountered Lee again at Spotsylvania, at the North Anna, then at Cold Harbor, where the second assault proved singularly disastrous. Undaunted, Grant launched a brilliant flanking maneuver that bewildered Lee and took the Army of the Potomac south of the James River and Richmond to the thinly held Confederate

---

[18] Porter, *Campaigning with Grant*, 26.

[19] *Personal Memoirs of Grant*, 2:122.

[20] Lincoln to Grant, April 30, 1864, in *Collected Works of Lincoln*, 7:324.

[21] Grant to Lincoln, May 1, 1864, in *Papers of Grant*, 10:380.

[22] Michael Burlingame and John R. Turner Ettlinger, eds., *Inside Lincoln's White House: The Complete Civil War Diary of John Hay* (Carbondale: Southern Illinois University Press, 1997), 194.

lines at the vital rail center of Petersburg. Only then did Lincoln break six weeks of public silence about Grant's strategy and tactics. "I begin to see it. You will succeed. God bless you all."[23]

Grant's brilliant movement across the James River to Petersburg had been followed by federal folly, incompetence, and timidity as thinly held Confederate lines stalled an assault of tenfold more troops. Grant had lost the momentum for a smashing victory and faced Lee's veterans in the Petersburg trenches. Furthermore, Jubal Early's corps, sent to stop David Hunter's threat to Lynchburg, had driven federal forces into West Virginia and could look down the Shenandoah Valley toward Washington. Gradually Grant grasped the dismal implications of those missed opportunities and settled into a siege. Meanwhile, he underestimated Early's threat, detaching troops only after Early reached Harpers Ferry. By the time Confederate troops reached the outskirts of Washington, enough of Grant's tardily sent troops had reached the forts to discourage more than a skirmish. Yet Early's corps remained intact, threatening numerous important transportation and supply centers while weakening Northern morale. To coordinate the pursuit of Early, Grant first had suggested William B. Franklin. On July 25 he recommended placing Meade in charge, for reasons he did "not care to commit to paper."[24]

Smoldering animosities blazed in the Army of the Potomac, fanned by William F. Smith, the commander who deserved blame for the June 15 failure at Petersburg, but who blamed everyone else. Relentless in charges against both Meade and Butler, Smith implicated Grant himself in failure. Both Meade and Butler reacted vigorously to criticism, Meade by loudly losing his temper, Butler by quietly plotting against his foes.

To break the Petersburg siege, coal miners of the 48th Pennsylvania dug a tunnel beneath Confederate lines, filled the end with explosives, and detonated a devastating blast. Union troops failed to exploit the opening and were repulsed with heavy losses, a battle Grant called the "saddest affair I have witnessed in this war. Such opportunity for carrying fortifications I have never seen and do not expect again to have."[25]

---

[23] Lincoln to Grant, June 15, 1864, in *Collected Works of Lincoln*, 7:393.
[24] Grant to Lincoln, July 25, 1864, in *Papers of Grant*, 11:309.
[25] Grant to Halleck, Aug. 1, 1864, ibid., 11:361.

The day after the Battle of the Crater, with Early still a threat to Northern cities, Lincoln arrived at Fort Monroe for a five-hour conference with Grant. Grant had been slow and ineffective in meeting Early's threat and had not yet coordinated a unified pursuit. After leading his army on the bloody road to Petersburg, he had not harvested the strategic rewards. If Grant had entered the Wilderness with any misconception that Lincoln had delegated management of the war, Grant received the necessary correction. Lincoln took control.

As in 1862, when McClellan was as close to Richmond as Grant was two years later, the result of Early's raid might have been a detachment of troops from offensive to defensive deployment. Before Lincoln arrived, Grant had ordered a division of cavalry to Washington. After the conference, he sent General Philip H. Sheridan to take command of all troops in the area and "to put himself south of the enemy and follow him to the death."[26] When Lincoln read the telegram, he responded that such action would "neither be done nor attempted unless you watch it every day, and hour, and force it."[27] Grant hurried to Washington to organize the pursuit of Early.

In effect Lincoln had told Grant where to go and what to do, and had at least hinted what might happen if he failed. With twice as many troops as Lee, Grant had settled into a protracted siege and had allowed himself to become "McClellanized." If Lincoln's intervention had been painful, it was timely and necessary. He had withheld intervention until the case for defending Washington was unmistakable. Even Grant recognized the necessity for an offensive in the Shenandoah Valley.

The fall of Atlanta in September came in time to counter Democratic claims that the war was a failure. Sherman then planned a march to the sea, a move so daring that even Grant hesitated before giving approval. Chief of Staff John A. Rawlins vigorously opposed the expedition and, as Grant recalled, persuaded authorities in Washington to delay Grant's approval. Stanton telegraphed on October 12 that the president expressed "much solicitude" about the plan and hoped that "it will be maturely considered."[28] Grant had already wired his approval. Sherman's celebrated Christmas gift of Savannah to Lincoln was equally Grant's triumph.

---

[26] Ibid., 11:358.

[27] Lincoln to Grant, Aug. 3, 1864, in *Collected Works of Lincoln*, 7:476.

[28] *Papers of Grant*, 12:303.

By the end of 1864, after Lincoln's reelection, Sherman's capture of Savannah, and General George H. Thomas's smashing victory at Nashville, the end of the war loomed. Efforts to negotiate peace during 1864, sometimes bizarre and always doomed, at least uncovered the two basic Confederate demands: independence and slavery. When hope for independence waned, that for slavery persisted. Confederates believed that Northerners might sacrifice emancipation for peace and reunion. Under such circumstances, Lincoln stood for unconditional surrender and wondered whether Grant would stand firm.

As a professional soldier, Grant shared the conservatism of the peacetime army. Fifteen years in the army starting at West Point had provided him with close friends now commanding rebel forces. Marriage into a family of border state slaveholders strengthened his Southern ties, including those to his wife's cousin James Longstreet, also Grant's old army friend. Grant had demanded unconditional surrender when he had no practical alternative. How would he respond to peace initiatives and offers of negotiation?

That test came at the end of January 1865, when Confederate emissaries arrived at City Point requesting permission to visit Washington to confer with Lincoln about the "existing War," and "upon what terms it may be terminated."[29] Lincoln sent an emissary to pose conditions: unless the commissioners discussed a "common country," no conference could take place. Grant, who had served dinner to the commissioners, now realized that he had blundered through cordiality. To underscore the point, Lincoln told Grant to allow "nothing which is transpiring, change, hinder, or delay your Military movements, or plans."[30]

In a telegram to Stanton, Grant asserted that the commissioners had shown him "that their intentions are good and their desire sincere to restore peace and Union."[31] Grant forced Lincoln's hand. "Induced by a despatch of Gen. Grant," he wired Secretary of State Seward, "I join you at Fort-Monroe so soon as I can come."[32] The conference itself, to which Grant was not invited, proved entirely unproductive. Lincoln demanded reunion and emancipation; Jeffer-

---

[29] Grant to Lincoln, Jan. 31, 1865, ibid., 13:333.
[30] Lincoln to Grant, Feb. 1, 1865, in *Collected Works of Lincoln*, 8:252.
[31] Grant to Stanton, Feb. 1, 1865, in *Papers of Grant*, 13:345.
[32] Lincoln to William H. Seward, Feb. 2, 1865, in *Collected Works of Lincoln*, 8:256.

son Davis had empowered his emissaries to concede neither but only to urge a hare-brained scheme to unite in an expedition to drive the French from Mexico. Lincoln gained nothing by conferring and would not have gone without Grant's urging, a point he emphasized in reporting to Congress.

In February conversations between Edward O. C. Ord and Longstreet on political prisoners veered toward peace negotiations. Longstreet asserted that Lee believed the Southern cause to be hopeless while Davis insisted on continuing the war. Ord suggested that Lee threaten to resign so as to force Davis to negotiate for compensation for lost slaves "and an immediate share in the Gov't."[33] When Lee requested a meeting with Grant to discuss matters further, Grant forwarded the message to Washington and received an unequivocal reply from Stanton:

> The President directs me to say to you that he wishes you to have no conference with Gen Lee unless it be for the capitulation of Lees army, or on solely minor and purely military matters[.] He instructs me to say that you are not to decide, discuss, or confer upon any political question: such questions the President holds in his own hands; and will submit them to no military conferences or conventions—mean time you are to press to the utmost, your military advantages.[34]

In January Grant had discussed with Lincoln the awkward status of the president's son Robert, a student at Harvard College and Law School during a war to which his father had sent so many other sons. "Please read and answer this letter as though I was not President, but only a friend," wrote Lincoln.

> [Robert] wishes to see something of the war before it ends. I do not wish to put him in the ranks, nor yet to give him a commission, to which those who have already served long, are better entitled, and better qualified to hold. Could he, without embarrassment to you, or detriment to the service, go into your Military family with some nominal rank, I, and not the public, furnishing his necessary means? If no, say so without the least hesitation, because I am as anxious, and as deeply interested, that you shall not be encumbered as you can be yourself.[35]

[33] John Y. Simon, "Grant, Lincoln, and Unconditional Surrender," in Gabor S. Boritt, ed., *Lincoln's Generals* (New York: Oxford University Press, 1994), 193.
[34] Stanton to Grant, March 3, 1865, in *Papers of Grant,* 14:91.
[35] Lincoln to Grant, Jan. 19, 1865, in *Collected Works of Lincoln,* 8:223.

Grant responded that he would "be most happy to have him in my Military family." Rank, he continued, would be

> immaterial but I would suggest that of Capt. as I have three Staff officers now, of conciderable service, in no higher grade. Indeed I have one officer with only the rank of Lieut. who has been in the service from the begining of the war. This however will make no difference and I would still say give the rank of Capt.[36]

The next day Robert wrote that he needed to return to Cambridge and then wanted to attend his father's second inauguration, so he asked Grant's "kind indulgence" before reporting.[37] His father had already formally nominated him for a commission as captain. If Robert's princely status and aristocratic airs annoyed Grant, he gave no indication of displeasure. He remembered the power of the commander in chief. Robert's staff appointment, so unwarranted a favor, cemented a personal relationship between Grant and Lincoln.

Robert's prolonged civilian life and military sinecure probably owed much to his mother's increasing emotional deterioration. After her son Willie's death in February 1862, her behavior grew steadily more irrational and intolerable. Perhaps unaware of the extent of the problem, Grant invited Lincoln to visit in March, thinking that he would want to see Robert but would not do so without a formal invitation. Besides, Robert had no staff role greater than escorting his parents. Accompanied by Mary and Tad, Lincoln arrived at City Point on March 24 for a visit that lasted a fortnight. Jealous of Grant's growing fame, Mary almost immediately insulted Grant's wife Julia. On two carriage rides to inspections, Mary launched into hysterical outbursts that embarrassed everybody. Julia later insisted that the Grants decline an invitation to Ford's Theatre that her husband might have accepted since it came from Lincoln.

With the end of the war finally in sight, Lincoln, Grant, Sherman, and Admiral Porter met on March 28 on the president's boat, the *River Queen,* to plan the future. Sherman and Porter remembered that Lincoln was ready to recognize existing Southern governments whenever the war ended, with "liberal views" toward rebels, and "peace on almost any terms."[38] Both Sherman and Porter, however,

---

[36] Grant to Lincoln, Jan. 21, 1865, in *Papers of Grant,* 13:281.

[37] Ibid., 13:282.

[38] *Memoirs of Gen. W. T. Sherman, Written by Himself,* 2 vols. (New York: Charles L. Webster, 1891), 2:329.

sought to justify Sherman's overly generous terms to Confederate General Johnston, given after Lincoln died and quickly disavowed by President Johnson and by Stanton. Sherman had negotiated the surrender of all Confederate armies, had provided that their weapons could be taken to their state arsenals, and had stipulated that the United States would recognize the authority of these state governments and the political and property rights of their citizens. Had Sherman's terms received approval, slavery might well have survived the war when former Confederate states refused to ratify the Thirteenth Amendment.

If Sherman had been overwhelmed by the congratulatory and harmonious mood in the cabin of the *River Queen,* Grant remembered the harsh tone of the rebuke he received after he proposed a military convention with Lee. He also remembered Lincoln's preconditions for negotiation presented to Confederate commissioners in February: that "the Union should be preserved" and that "slavery should be abolished."[39] Porter, who unconvincingly claimed to remember the conversation on the *River Queen* in great detail, reported that Grant sat quietly smoking throughout, speaking only once, to ask about Sherman's destruction of railroads.

Had Lincoln lived, Sherman insisted, the surrender terms to Johnston would have received presidential approval. Grant knew better. He made excuses for Sherman and embraced Sherman's quarrels with Stanton and Halleck without deviating from the central principle that Sherman had no right to offer terms beyond those given to Lee at Appomattox.

In writing and speaking in later years, Grant frequently succumbed to the sentimentality of the age. He created the impression that mutual harmony and respect had existed from their first meeting and persisted until Lincoln's death. In reality, however, Grant and Lincoln forged an effective partnership despite initial uneasiness. General in Chief Grant had to act vigorously within the military sphere, tread softly in the political sphere, and understand the blurry border between them. Success depended upon never forgetting that Lincoln always retained the power of the commander in chief.

---

[39] *Memoirs of Grant,* 2:514.

3

"You Must Either Attack Richmond or Give Up the Job and Come to the Defence of Washington": Abraham Lincoln and the 1862 Shenandoah Valley Campaign

Gary W. Gallagher

ABRAHAM LINCOLN REACTED ADMIRABLY to Major General Thomas J. "Stonewall" Jackson's famous Shenandoah Valley Campaign of May and June 1862. Far from panicking when Jackson advanced toward the Potomac during the last week of May, Lincoln used the rebel threat in an effort to force Major General George B. McClellan to attack the Confederate army protecting Richmond. He manifested a sure grasp of Union and Confederate strategy, an understanding of his generals' personalities, and a resolute determination to prod—almost to will—his commanders to act in such a way as to forge victories outside Richmond and in the Shenandoah Valley.

Lincoln dealt with Jackson's movements within a strategic picture that during the first five months of 1862 witnessed a string of fabulous Union successes. In the Western Theater, United States forces captured Forts Henry and Donelson, won the Battle of Shiloh, and took control of Nashville, much of Middle Tennessee, New Orleans, and the upper and lower reaches of the Mississippi River. A huge army under Major General Henry W. Halleck was closing in on Corinth, a vital rail center in northern Mississippi, by the end of May. In the Trans-Mississippi arena, the Battle of Pea Ridge on March 7–8 ensured unquestioned Union control of Missouri and opened the way for further operations into Arkansas.

The Eastern Theater offered an equally dismal picture for the Confederacy. Although historians too often read backward from Union defeat during the Seven Days' battles to paint a problematic picture in the East during the spring and early summer, it is more useful to focus on the Northern successes preceding that failure. McClellan's Army of the Potomac, the Union's largest military force, took Yorktown on May 3 and Williamsburg three days later. Confederates evacuated Norfolk on May 9, scuttling the *C. S. S. Virginia* on May 11 as they fell back up the peninsula toward Richmond. The loss of the *Virginia,* a powerful ironclad that had raised Southern hopes for an end to the blockade just two months earlier, proved especially devastating for many Confederates. By May 23 McClellan's host had come within a few miles of Richmond. Other important Union forces under Generals Irvin McDowell, Nathaniel P. Banks, and John C. Frémont stood at Fredericksburg, in the Shenandoah Valley, and in western Virginia, respectively. In short, prospects for a Union military victory scarcely could have been better as the end of May approached.

The first glimmer of good news for the Confederacy during this period came from Stonewall Jackson in the Shenandoah Valley. Few episodes of the Civil War are more dramatically charged than Jackson's operations in May and early June 1862. They reenergized the Confederate home front and catapulted Jackson to national and international fame.

The campaign's outline is well known. The daring Jackson pushed his seventeen thousand men relentlessly during a month of brisk action. Following a strategic blueprint laid out by Robert E. Lee (who held a desk job in Richmond as Jefferson Davis's principal military adviser), Jackson sought to tie down Frémont and Banks, denying their manpower to McClellan's investing army on the peninsula below Richmond. He accomplished his task brilliantly. He opened the campaign in the Allegheny Mountains west of Staunton, where he defeated an advance element of Frémont's force at the Battle of McDowell on May 8. He then hastened back to the Shenandoah Valley proper, marched rapidly northward, and at New Market veered east to cross the Massanutten Range into the Luray Valley. Moving north again, Jackson's force captured a Union garrison at Front Royal on May 23, defeated Banks at the Battle of Winchester on May 25, and pursued the fleeing Federals all the way to Harpers

Ferry on the Potomac. Exposed in the lower reaches of the valley, he hurried southward to the vicinity of Harrisonburg and won a pair of victories at Cross Keys and Port Republic on June 8–9. He then left the valley to join the main Confederate army near Richmond in time for the Seven Days' battles.[1]

Jackson's effort in the valley typically is seen as one of the greatest military campaigns in U.S. history. Most writers have pronounced it a fantastic operation carried out against long odds that immobilized thousands of Union soldiers and sent tremors through the North. Lincoln often appears as a sort of foil to Jackson's cunning generalship in the valley. Those who rhapsodically portray Jackson as an elusive genius cast him as a master manipulator who not only flummoxed Frémont, Banks, and other Federal generals, but also scared Lincoln into issuing a series of misguided presidential directives. Lincoln at first joined Secretary of War Edwin M. Stanton and other top Republicans in thinking only of Washington's safety, goes a common argument, wringing his hands in frustration, and massing troops to deal with Jackson. Only later, his fear having abated, did Lincoln try to orchestrate a pursuit of the wily Confederate general.

Although most historians know that Lincoln quickly turned his thoughts to striking Jackson while the Confederate Army of the Valley lay near Harpers Ferry, a common perception persists that he exhibited at least a mild case of panic in the wake of Jackson's victory over Banks at the Battle of Winchester. The crucial document on this point is Lincoln's communication to McClellan on May 25. The Confederates were driving Banks north as well as menacing Leesburg and the Manassas Gap Railroad, stated Lincoln, in what numbers remained unclear. "I think the movement is a general and concerted one," added the president, "such as could not be if he was acting upon the purpose of a very desperate defence of Richmond. I think the time is near when you must either attack Richmond or give up the job and come to the defence of Washington. Let me hear from you instantly."[2]

---

[1] For an overview of the 1862 Valley Campaign, see Robert G. Tanner's *Stonewall in the Valley: Thomas J. "Stonewall" Jackson's Shenandoah Valley Campaign, Spring 1862* (1976; rev. ed., Mechanicsburg, Pa.: Stackpole Books, 1996). An older but still useful study is William Allan's *History of the Campaign of Gen. T. J. (Stonewall) Jackson in the Shenandoah Valley of Virginia. From November 4, 1861, to June 17, 1862* (1880; reprint, Dayton, Ohio: Morningside, 1987).

[2] Roy P. Basler et al., eds., *The Collected Works of Abraham Lincoln*, 9 vols. (New Brunswick, N.J.: Rutgers University Press, 1953–55), 5:235–36.

Many historians have seen in this letter a jittery Lincoln suggesting that McClellan might have to abandon his campaign against Richmond in order to save Washington. A few examples will suggest the tenor of many accounts. In his biography of Lincoln, David Herbert Donald remarked that Banks's defeat caused many Northerners to fear that "Jackson might cross the Potomac and threaten Washington itself." The president "at one point believed the Confederates were planning to take the national capital" and warned McClellan he might have to abandon the Peninsula. Stephen B. Oates, in an earlier biography of Lincoln, described how, on May 24–25, Washington received "shattering news from the Shenandoah Valley, where rebel columns under Stonewall Jackson were on a rampage." With Stanton's support, wrote Oates, Lincoln responded by ordering McDowell to guard Washington and telling McClellan that he might have to return to the capital.[3]

Jackson's biographers often have sketched an even more nervous Lincoln. Just as McClellan closed in on Richmond with the prospect of reinforcement by McDowell, wrote Byron Farwell in language typical of many other biographies, news of Banks's reverse at Winchester derailed everything: "[T]o the utter dismay of McClellan and McDowell, Lincoln, alarmed by reports from the Shenandoah, changed everything in a twinkling." British author G. F. R. Henderson, whose 1898 biography of Jackson has wielded more influence than any other, employed more dramatic language. "Terror had taken possession of the nation," he observed regarding Northern reaction to news from the valley, and "Lincoln and Stanton were electrified even more effectually than Banks."[4]

Some participants and observers rendered similar verdicts at the time. Charles W. Trueheart, a soldier in Jackson's command, sent a strongly upbeat account to his father on July 4, 1862. After the victory at Winchester, averred Trueheart, "we marched to the Ferry to make a demonstration at crossing into Md., and going towards Washington. And it had the desired effect. Yankeedom trembled in its boots. Lin-

---

[3] David Herbert Donald, *Lincoln* (New York: Simon & Schuster, 1995), 355; Stephen B. Oates, *With Malice toward None: The Life of Abraham Lincoln* (New York: Harper & Row, 1977), 301.

[4] Byron Farwell, *Stonewall: A Biography of General Thomas J. Jackson* (New York: W. W. Norton, 1992), 298; G. F. R. Henderson, *Stonewall Jackson and the American Civil War*, 2 vols. (1898; 1 vol. reprint, New York: McKay, 1961), 263.

coln immediately called on the Yankee Govs. to send on the State Militia to protect the 'Capitol.'" From Washington on May 26, Secretary of the Treasury Salmon P. Chase spoke of how Jackson's force had "endangered Harpers Ferry & even Washington, & menaced Maryland." "To repel it & if possible capture or destroy the invaders became a prime necessity," remarked Chase: "To this end two of McDowells divisions were ordered to the support of Banks & Fremont."[5]

McClellan answered Lincoln by telegraph at 5:00 P.M. on the 25th. Thinking first of himself as usual, "Little Mac" insisted—correctly as it turned out—that the object of Jackson's movement "is probably to prevent reinforcements being sent to me." Information gathered from observation balloons, Confederate deserters, and African Americans who had fled to Union lines, continued McClellan, suggested that most of the rebel army remained at Richmond. The most important part of McClellan's message reported that "the time is very near when I shall attack Richmond." Two Union corps had crossed the Chickahominy River and reached a point within six miles of Richmond, and the rest of the army stood ready to cross as soon as engineers completed bridges. McClellan thus promised the major Union offensive on the Richmond front that Lincoln desperately desired.[6]

That desire had ripened during months of frustrating relations with McClellan. By late May 1862, McClellan had been in command of the Army of the Potomac for about eight months and had yet to fight a big battle. He consistently had asked for more men, more animals, more guns, more supplies—more of everything—before he could attack. Lincoln had lost patience with this behavior, and I believe he seized upon Jackson's movement toward the Potomac as a pretext to force McClellan to take the offensive or risk abandonment of his cherished movement toward Richmond. That threat was implicit in the message he sent McClellan on May 25, and McClellan's response

[5] Edward B. Williams, ed., *Rebel Brothers: Civil War Letters of the Truehearts* (College Station: Texas A&M University Press, 1995), 60–61; John Niven et al., eds., *The Salmon P. Chase Papers,* 5 vols. (Kent, Ohio: Kent State University Press, 1993–98), 3:204. Although Chase's letter was dated May 24, the editors note that its content suggests it "was probably written on or about Monday, May 26."

[6] Stephen W. Sears, ed., *The Civil War Papers of George B. McClellan: Selected Correspondence, 1860–1865* (New York: Ticknor & Fields, 1989), 276.

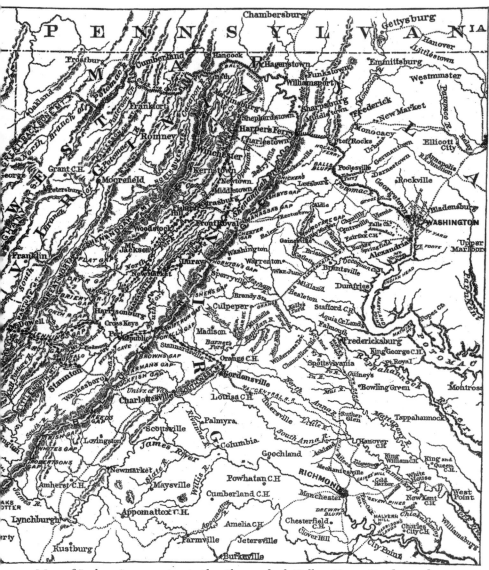

Map of Jackson's campaign in the Shenandoah Valley. From *Battles and Leaders of the Civil War*. The crossed line and arrows indicate Jackson's movements in the valley.

probably signaled to Lincoln that the threat had served its purpose. (McClellan's telegram claimed that he had planned the offensive before Lincoln's message came to hand.) To reiterate, I see the May 25 correspondence not as evidence of panic on Lincoln's part growing out of fear for the safety of Washington, but of an effort to get McClellan to apply offensive pressure against the rebel force defending Richmond. Lincoln's instructions to generals Frémont and McDowell on May 24 lend credence to my interpretation. They also demonstrate that Lincoln hoped to inaugurate an offensive against Jackson from the outset rather than take defensive measures to save Washington.

Lincoln received word from Frémont on May 24 of Jackson's attack at Front Royal the previous day. That modest clash had cost the Union about one thousand prisoners and isolated Banks in the lower valley. "General Banks informs me this morning of an attack by [the] enemy" wrote Frémont. "This is probably by Jackson, who marched in that direction some days since. [Maj. Gen. Richard S.] Ewell's force with him. General Banks says he should be re-enforced immediately." Lincoln ordered Frémont to march southeastward toward Harrisonburg in an effort to cut Jackson off: "The exposed condition of General Banks makes his immediate relief a point of paramount importance. You are therefore directed by the President to move against Jackson at Harrisonburg and operate against the enemy in such a way as to relieve Banks." In a telegram sent late that afternoon, Frémont promised to "move as ordered & operate against the Enemy in such way as to afford prompt relief to genl Banks." That evening, the president thanked Frémont for his prompt response but believed it necessary to emphasize the need for immediate implementation of the presidential order: "Much—perhaps all—depends upon the celerity with which you can execute it. Put the utmost speed into it. Do not lose a minute."[7]

At 5:00 P.M. on the 24th, Lincoln ordered McDowell to contribute twenty thousand men to the effort against Jackson. McClellan had hoped McDowell's forty thousand men, massed near Fredericksburg, would soon swell the ranks of the Union force at Richmond. On May

---

[7] *The War of the Rebellion: A Compilation of the Official Records of the Union and Confederate Armies,* 128 vols. (Washington, D.C.: Government Printing Office, 1880–1901), ser. I, 12, pt. 1:642–43; *Collected Works of Lincoln,* 5:230–31.

23 Lincoln and Stanton had visited McDowell's force at Fredericksburg and agreed that it would advance toward Richmond three days
hence. Jackson's appearance in the lower valley prompted Lincoln's
new instructions to McDowell: "Gen Fremont has been ordered by
Telegraph to move from Franklin on Harrisonburg to relieve Gen
Banks and capture or destroy Jackson & Ewell's force. You are in-
structed laying aside for the present the movement on Richmond to
put twenty thousand men (20000) in motion at once for the Shenandoah moving on the line or in advance of the line of the Manassas
Gap R Road. Your object will be to capture the forces of Jackson &
Ewell." McDowell acknowledged receipt of the order and said it was
"in process of execution." But he also manifested his disappointment
by declaring, "This is a crushing blow to us."[8]

Lincoln's orders to McDowell conveyed a decidedly offensive message. If fear for Washington's safety stood paramount, McDowell
could have marched directly toward the city to man its defenses.
The destruction of Jackson's army, not the protection of the capital,
dominated Lincoln's thinking. Anticipating that McDowell might
balk at pressing the action without cooperation from Banks and Frémont, Lincoln stipulated that "it is believed that the force with which
you move will be sufficient to accomplish the object alone." Lincoln
understood that both McDowell and McClellan preferred that the
old orders be carried out. He probably blanched when McDowell,
after stating that he obeyed Lincoln's orders immediately, listed a
number of obstacles to success. "I beg to say," observed the rotund
general, "that co-operation between General Frémont and myself to
cut Jackson and Ewell there is not to be counted upon, even if it is
not a practical impossibility. Next, that I am entirely beyond helping
distance of General Banks; no celerity or vigor will avail so far as he
is concerned." Moreover, it would take "a week or ten days" to shift
his soldiers to the valley by a route that afforded ample food and
forage, "and by that time the enemy will have retired." But McDowell also stated that he would send Brigadier General James Shields's
division toward Strasburg along the route of the Manassas Gap Railroad. "I have ordered General Shields to commence the movement
by to-morrow morning," McDowell assured Lincoln, and a "second

---

[8] Ibid., 232–33; *Chase Papers*, 1:345; *Official Records*, ser. I, 12, pt. 3:220.

division will follow in the afternoon." Lincoln chose to focus on the positive elements in McDowell's communications. "I am highly gratified by your alacrity in obeying my order," he wrote after receiving the general's initial response. "The change was as painful to me as it can possibly be to you or to any one. Every thing now dependes upon the celerity and vigor of your movement."[9]

Lincoln knew Secretary of the Treasury Chase, who maintained close ties with McDowell, preferred that the latter's command not be diverted from a march to reinforce McClellan. He knew as well that McDowell hoped to discuss the campaign with Chase on the evening of the 24th, and Lincoln took time to tell his cabinet officer that he hoped the new deployments would yield an offensive success. "It now appears that Banks got safely in to Winchester last night," the president explained to Chase, "and is, this morning, retreating to Harper's Ferry. . . . I think it not improbable that Ewell Jackson and [Edward "Allegheny"] Johnson, are pouring through the gap they made day-before yesterday at Front-Royal, making a dash Northward. It will be a very valuable, and very honorable service for Gen. McDowell to cut them off. I hope he will put all possible energy and speed into the effort."[10]

Lincoln took these aggressive steps despite alarmist messages from Banks, Brigadier General John White Geary, who was stationed along the Manassas Gap Railroad, and other Federal commanders about the size and intentions of the Confederate forces in the lower valley. Geary behaved almost hysterically, exaggerating Confederate numbers, claiming the rebels had moved well east of the Blue Ridge Mountains, and otherwise complicating Lincoln's effort to grasp the nature of Jackson's movements.[11]

Over the next several days, Lincoln sought unsuccessfully to coordinate the efforts of McDowell and Frémont. On May 26 he asked McDowell, who remained at Falmouth, just up the Rappahannock from Fredericksburg, "Should not the remainder of your force except sufficient to hold the point at Frederick'sburg, move this way—to

[9] *Collected Works of Lincoln*, 5:232–33; *Official Records*, ser. I, 12, pt. 3:220–21.
[10] *Collected Works of Lincoln*, 5:234–35.
[11] On the welter of information reaching Lincoln, see ibid., 5:234–40. See also William Alan Blair and Bell I. Wiley, eds., *A Politician Goes to War: The Civil War Letters of John White Geary* (University Park: Pennsylvania State University Press, 1995), 45–47.

Manassas junction, or to Alexandria? As commander of this Department, should you not be here? I ask these questions." The next day he telegraphed Frémont. "I see you are at Moorefield [due west of Strasburg]," stated the exasperated president. "You were expressly ordered to march to Harrisonburg[.] What does this mean?" A testy Frémont replied, through Stanton at 6:00 A.M. on May 28, that his troops suffered from short rations and were in no condition to undertake more marching. The general also assumed he had discretion to follow a line of march that seemed most appropriate, but if ordered to do so he would literally follow Lincoln's directions. On Lincoln's instructions, Stanton telegraphed three more times on May 28, urging Frémont to "move against the enemy." In replying to one of these messages from Washington, Frémont stated that the "President's order will be obeyed accordingly."[12]

On May 28 Lincoln exchanged messages with McClellan. The latter reported a victory by Union corps commander Fitz John Porter near Richmond and clearly wanted more men. "There is no doubt that the enemy are concentrating everything on Richmond," claimed McClellan, who then lectured his commander in chief about priorities: "It is the policy and duty of the Government to send me by water all the well-drilled troops available. I am confident that Washington is in no danger." Lincoln promised to do what he could but reminded McClellan of dangers at other points. Conflicting reports about the size and disposition of Jackson's forces had reached Washington from different Union commanders. Some sources placed the rebels east of the Blue Ridge, others raised alarms about Confederate movements west of the Blue Ridge, and still others indicated that rebel reinforcements were marching from north of Richmond to reinforce Jackson. "I am painfully impressed with the importance of the struggle before you," stated Lincoln, choosing words that reflected his discomfiture with McClellan's failure to deliver a telling blow against the enemy at Richmond, "and I shall aid you all I can consistently with my view of due regard to all points."[13]

On the Shenandoah front, Lincoln grew impatient with the absence of strong movements by either McDowell or Frémont. "You say Gen. Geary's scouts report that they find no enemy this side of

[12] Collected Works of Lincoln, 5:240, 243.
[13] Ibid., 5:244–45.

the Blue Ridge," he commented sarcastically to McDowell at 4:00
P.M. on May 28. "Neither do I. Have *they* been *to* the Blue Ridge
looking for them?" Later that day another message, sent by Lincoln
through Stanton, went to McDowell: "There is very little doubt that
Jackson's force is between Winchester and Charlestown. His troops
were too much fatigued to pursue Banks. A large body of rebel cavalry is near Charlestown now. Jackson and Ewell were near Bunker
Hill yesterday at noon. Of this there is no doubt." McDowell answered this last message at 7:20 P.M. Regarding the positions of Jackson and Ewell, McDowell replied, "I beg leave to report that I am
pushing Generals Shields and [E. O. C.] Ord upon Front Royal with
all expedition possible."[14]

Perhaps the most famous of Lincoln's messages during the Valley
Campaign also carried a date of May 28. Impatient with his commanders in the valley, and utterly convinced that Jackson lay in a
precarious position far from possible reinforcements, he wrote to
McDowell. "I think the evidence now preponderates that Ewell and
Jackson are still about Winchester," commented the president. "As-
suming this, it is, for you a question of legs. Put in all the speed you
can. I have told Fremont as much, and directed him to drive at them
as fast as possible." The president could not resist getting in a dig at
Frémont. "By the way," he told McDowell, "I suppose you know,
Fremont has got up to Moorefield, instead of going to Harrisonburg."
McDowell responded in a message received in Washington at 11:18
P.M. "I beg to assure you," he said, "that I am doing everything which
legs and steam are capable of to hurry forward matters in this quarter." "I shall be deficient in wagons when I get out of the way of
the railroad for transporting supplies," McDowell added by way of
preparing Lincoln for further bad news, "but shall push on nevertheless."[15]

May 29 and 30 brought further frustration to Lincoln. Reports left
no doubt that Jackson had reached Harpers Ferry. Lincoln reasoned
that while positioned there, at the northern end of the Shenandoah
Valley, the Confederates should have offered easy pickings for the
converging columns of McDowell, moving from the east toward
Front Royal and Strasburg, and Frémont, located west of Strasburg

---

[14] Ibid., 5:246; *Official Records*, ser. I, 12, pt. 3:269.
[15] *Collected Works of Lincoln*, 5:246; *Official Records*, ser. I, 12, pt. 3:270.

in the vicinity of Moorefield. Banks lay at Williamsport, whence he also could join the effort. At noon on May 29, Lincoln wrote Banks (virtually the same message also went to Frémont and McDowell): "Gen McDowell's advance should & probably will be at or near Front Royal at 12. M to-morrow. Gen. Fremont will be at or near Strasburg as soon. Please watch the enemy closely, and follow & harass and detain him, if he attempts to retire." Here Lincoln sought yet again to wring an aggressive performance out of one of his generals. It was not enough that Jackson retreated; Lincoln wanted Banks to engage him in such a manner as to allow Frémont and McDowell to cut off his route southward up the valley. Once isolated north of Strasburg and Front Royal, Jackson might be vulnerable to a decisive Union blow.[16]

Banks answered Lincoln at 3:30 P.M., employing a tone frequently adopted by his fellow Union commanders engaged in the valley drama. "My command is much disabled," he said, "but we will do what we can to carry out your views." McDowell weighed in with his own somewhat gloomy report, received in Washington at 5:45 P.M., that General Shields faced problems with the railroad in Thoroughfare Gap. Shields first estimated that repairs might take twenty-four hours, but McDowell sent him "the President's telegram, and he reports he will make such arrangements that will enable him to be in Front Royal before 12 o'clock m. to-morrow, with his other two brigades within 4 miles of the town by the same hour." Mustering what for him amounted to unbridled sanguinity, McDowell closed with the observation that "[e]verything seems to be getting along well now, notwithstanding this morning's trouble."[17]

Frémont offered nothing to offset Lincoln's doubts about Banks and McDowell. A telegram sent by Frémont on May 30 from Moorefield, which arrived in Washington at 11:30 A.M., raised the specter of thirty to sixty thousand rebels under Jackson near Winchester. Long accustomed to McClellan's grotesque overestimates of Confederate strength, Lincoln tersely, and accurately, replied that the number "cannot be more than twenty probably not more than fifteen thousand." Frémont's location bothered the president at least as much as his projection of numbers. "Where *is* your force?" Lincoln inquired

---

[16] *Collected Works of Lincoln*, 5:247–48.
[17] *Official Records*, ser. I, 12, pt. 1:533, pt. 3:277.

sharply. "It ought this minute to be near Strasburg. Answer at once." Lincoln sent another communication to Frémont at 9:30 P.M. With a message in hand that indicated Jackson was near Harpers Ferry, Lincoln tried to summon optimism in pressing Frémont to hurry. "I send you a despatch just received from Gen. [Rufus] Saxton at Harper's Ferry," stated the president. "It seems the game is before you. Have sent a copy to Gen. McDowell." Informed by Frémont soon thereafter that a "[h]eavy storm of rain most of yesterday and all last night" had left the roads in terrible condition, Lincoln could not have hoped for a rapid march to sever Jackson's line of march up the valley. Could McDowell retrieve the situation? "I somewhat apprehend that Frémont's force, in it's present condition, may not be quite strong enough in case it comes in collision with the enemy," Lincoln had written at midmorning on the 30th. "For this additional reason, I wish you to push forward your column as rapidly as possible." It is difficult to imagine Lincoln's believing McDowell would surge boldly ahead—though he took the time to let his general know that he expected him to do all possible to bring Jackson to bay.[18]

There is no need to analyze correspondence between Lincoln and his generals over the next few days to support my basic point. Throughout this period in late May, Lincoln strove to get offensives in both the lower valley and outside Richmond. He failed in both instances. Jackson escaped a prospective Union trap, beating both Frémont and Shields's advance element of McDowell's force to Strasburg and escaping up the valley. For his part, McClellan repulsed Confederate attacks in the Battle of Seven Pines or Fair Oaks on May 31 and June 1 but launched no aggressive movement of his own. When "Little Mac" reported on June 18 that intelligence suggested a deployment of ten to fifteen thousand Confederate troops from Richmond to reinforce Jackson in the valley, Lincoln immediately pressed his cautious general to attack. "If this is true," the president pointed out, "it is as good as a reinforcement to you of an equal force. I could better dispose of things if I could know about what day you can attack Richmond, and would be glad to be informed, if you think you can inform me with safety."[19]

A date for Union attacks never arrived, and within two weeks

---

[18] *Collected Works of Lincoln,* 5:250–52; *Official Records,* ser. I, 12, pt. 1:648–49.
[19] *Collected Works of Lincoln,* 5:276.

McClellan had suffered a major defeat at the Seven Days' battles. He had withstood Lincoln's untiring efforts to coax a forward-moving victory from him. So also had the collection of generals who commanded in the valley during May and early June 1862.

Lincoln had done all that was possible from his post in Washington. Never really unnerved by Jackson's movements, he had tried to exploit Jackson's presence in the lower valley to prod McClellan into action at Richmond. Lincoln sought at the same time to concentrate Frémont's and McDowell's forces to smash Jackson's little army. As he contemplated failure in both directions, Lincoln must have entertained thoughts similar to those expressed by his Attorney General when it still seemed possible to capture or destroy Jackson's force. "It is shamefully true that the enemy's officers are vastly superior to ours in boldness, enterprise and skill, while our troops almost constantly beat theirs, with any thing like equal numbers and a fair field," wrote Edward Bates in his diary on June 4, 1862. "If our Genls. now allow Jackson to escape, they ought to lose the public confidence, for obvious lack of enterprise and action."[20]

On the evening of May 25, McClellan wrote his wife about Lincoln's suggestion that the Army of the Potomac should attack or be withdrawn to Washington. Lincoln was "terribly scared about Washington," observed McClellan, "& talks about the necessity of my returning in order to save it! Heaven save a country governed by such counsels! . . . It is perfectly sickening to deal with such people. . . . I get more sick of them every day—for every day brings with it only additional proofs of their hypocrisy, knavery & folly— . . . [W]ell, well, I ought not to write this way," added a Little Mac obviously pleased with himself, "for they may be right & I entirely wrong, so I will drop the subject."[21] Although McClellan did not mean these last words, Lincoln *had been right* in his handling of Union military forces in response to Jackson's movements. It was a crisis that showed how far the president had come in just more than a year as commander in chief.

---

[20] Howard K. Beale, ed., *The Diary of Edward Bates 1859–1866* (1930; reprint, New York: Da Capo Press, 1971), 261.

[21] *Civil War Papers of McClellan*, 275.

4

Men, Machines, and Old Abe: Lincoln and the Civil War Navy

Craig L. Symonds

IN ADDITION TO HIS HISTORICAL PERSONA as the Great Emancipator, Abraham Lincoln has also been extolled as an effective manager of war, both as a strategist and as a commander in chief. This is particularly noteworthy in light of the fact that he had virtually no background in things military when he took office, and, indeed, it is one of the measures of Lincoln's genius that he could preside over a great war so successfully given his meager military background. Characteristically, Lincoln was quick to poke fun at himself in this respect, satirizing his own brief stint as a militia captain in the Black Hawk War. But despite his disavowals, every student of the Civil War knows that Lincoln had an intuitive understanding of military affairs, and that his understanding grew with each passing week. He had always been a voracious reader, and, moreover, a reader who chose subjects for their pragmatic utility rather than their entertainment value. He had read a bit about the great captains of war in his youth, and he read much more after Fort Sumter, eventually becoming conversant with military terminology as well as strategic principles. It is a tribute to his agile brain that he could transform himself so quickly from a novice into an authority. But if Lincoln had to start nearly from scratch in his effort to absorb the principles and the terminology of land warfare, his knowledge of that medium was positively voluminous when compared with his understanding of naval matters.

Lincoln was a product of the American West. In Roy Basler's eight volumes of Lincoln's collected speeches and writings—nearly five thousand pages—there is only one reference to Lincoln's having even mentioned the navy prior to 1861. That one reference, by the way, was in 1848 during his single term as a U.S. congressman, when he criticized James K. Polk for his veto of the Whig appropriation bill. Polk objected to the bill on the grounds that the internal improvements urged by the Whigs were local rather than national. Lincoln took him to task for such an assertion. The novice congressman admitted that the proposed navy appropriations offered some local financial benefit to particular cities—New York and Charleston among them—but the benefits of the institution itself, he insisted, were primarily national. It would be foolish, he declared, to refuse to make a national improvement simply because some of the benefits might fall unevenly on the various sections of the country. Here is Lincoln the pragmatist, Lincoln the Whig nationalist, even Lincoln the Unionist, if you would. But his reference to the navy in this case is only in passing, as one example of a national institution that benefits the whole people. Beyond that, his interest did not go. Not until the Fort Sumter crisis thirteen years later did Lincoln write or speak another public word about naval matters.[1] When he took office in March 1861, navies and naval affairs were as foreign to Lincoln as Chinese politics, maybe more so. And yet as president, he would preside over the development and deployment of the greatest national armada of the century, one that would not be eclipsed in size or numbers until the First World War, a half century later. In doing so, Lincoln demonstrated once again the mental prowess to grasp new issues with instinctive understanding, to embrace new ideas and new technologies, and a willingness, even an eagerness, to seize upon common sense solutions to complicated problems. It may be going a bit too far to suggest that Lincoln became a naval expert, but he did become more than superficially adept at managing the elements of naval power.

Three things made Lincoln successful as a manager of naval warfare in the nation's only experience with total war. The first was an unwillingness to be hamstrung by established doctrine concerning the limited role of government. Lincoln believed in an activist government, so long as its activities served the community as a whole and not merely some privileged segment of it. Because the Civil War created a number of unprecedented problems for government to solve, it provided him with nearly infinite opportunities to exercise

---

[1] Speech on Internal Improvements, June 20, 1848, in Roy P. Basler et al., eds., *The Collected Works of Abraham Lincoln,* 9 vols. (New Brunswick, N.J.: Rutgers University Press, 1953–55), 1:483.

his pragmatic approach to problem solving. In nearly every case he responded with a practical solution unfettered by concerns for how it had always been done before. As he wrote to Governor Edwin D. Morgan of New York, he believed that "[W]e are in no condition to waste time on technicalities." Lincoln was no scofflaw; he revered the law. It was simply that he believed that laws were the creatures of society, not the other way around. Intelligent men of goodwill could—and should—find ways to do the things that would benefit society.[2] A second factor that proved critical in Lincoln's success was his knack for making sound judgments about those whom he assigned to positions of responsibility. This is not to say that he did not make mistakes. Every student of the Civil War can recall unhappy appointments that would come back to haunt Lincoln: from Simon Cameron as secretary of war to generals George McClellan, David Hunter, or Franz Sigel. But many of Lincoln's unfortunate appointments were themselves the product of political necessity, and he was willing to correct his errors, if errors they proved to be. On the whole, Lincoln allowed those who served the country—or in our case the navy—to stand or fall based on their achievements. It was an eminently reasonable yardstick, and for the most part Lincoln applied it even handedly. When officers performed, they got promoted; when they did not, they found themselves eased out of the way to make room for those who could. It mattered less if these individuals caused him personal grief or political embarrassment, the key issue was: Did they get the job done?

A third factor in Lincoln's makeup that proved critical in his success was his inventiveness when confronted by unfamiliar problems. As noted above, Lincoln was utterly innocent of any expertise in naval affairs. Soon after he took office, he confessed apologetically to his secretary of the navy, "I know but little about ships."[3] But his was a naturally creative mind that could bend itself to the solution of all sorts of issues, including the application of new technologies. Back in 1849 when Lincoln was returning to Chicago from Washington at the

---

[2] Lincoln to Morgan, May 20, 1861, in *Collected Works of Lincoln*, 4:375. For a longer discussion of this issue, see Craig L. Symonds, "An Improvised Army at War, 1861–1865," in Kenneth J. Hagan and William R. Roberts, *Against All Enemies: Interpretations of American Military History from Colonial Times to the Present* (Westport, Conn.: Greenwood Press, 1986).

[3] Lincoln to Welles, May 14, 1861, in *Collected Works of Lincoln*, 4:370.

end of his one and only term as a U.S. congressman, the steamboat on which he was traveling had difficulty getting over and around the shifting shoals in the Ohio River. Taking note of this, once he was back in Illinois, Lincoln put pencil to paper and sketched out a device that he called "adjustable buoyant chambers" designed to lift river vessels over the shoals. He even got a patent for it. This example of Lincoln's interest in the technology of river transport is illuminating. He may not have been a naval expert, but he was a man who was fascinated by gadgets. During the Civil War, he would become fascinated by the gadgetry of warfare, and not incidentally, naval warfare. Eventually he would become an advocate—and a knowledgeable one—of ironclads, floating mortar platforms, and advanced naval ordnance.[4]

Before offering examples of how Lincoln applied these characteristics in his management of both the men and the machines of the U.S. Navy during the Civil War, it is necessary first to profile the navy over which he would preside. The U.S. Navy in 1861 was not a particularly impressive institution, especially by European standards. It consisted of 571 naval officers (captains, commanders, and lieutenants) and 7,600 men. There were no admirals; that rank was not created by Congress until late in 1862. The reason for the absence of flag officers, quite simply, is that although Congress had always thought of the national army as a kind of expanded militia—that is, as a reflection of America itself—it conceived of navies as tools of empire. In part this derived from British tradition; ever since the English Civil War, the ground troops in England have been called the *British* Army, whereas the sea service is called the *Royal* Navy. In the same spirit, Congress deliberately avoided establishing the rank of admiral in the U.S. Navy out of a conviction that admirals and democracies simply did not go together.

Of the 571 naval officers listed in the U.S. Navy Register in 1861, some 253 of them (that is, 44.3 percent) were Southern born, and of those, almost exactly half (126) resigned to go with the South. That left the Union navy with a cadre of some 445 trained professionals to officer the wartime navy, though of course the dramatic expansion

---

[4] David Herbert Donald, *Lincoln* (New York: Simon & Schuster, 1995), 156. The patent is dated March 10, 1849, and was granted May 23, 1849. I thank Budge Weidman for a copy of the original patent request.

necessitated by the war would bring hundreds more into the service and lead in due course to the appointment of more than a dozen admirals. Virtually all of this expansion within the upper levels of the officer corps came about by elevating those officers already in service, often by several grades. Lieutenants became captains; commanders became flag officers and eventually admirals. Only in the lower command levels of the navy hierarchy did men straight in from civilian life obtain commissions as volunteer officers. As a result, there was no nautical counterpart to what historians generally call "political generals." In addition, Lincoln issued a call for eighteen thousand new sailors, thus more than tripling the size of the navy.[5] Ships were a more serious problem. On paper, the U.S. Navy in 1861 consisted of ninety warships. But of those, fully half were out of commission for one reason or another, and of the forty-two ships that were in commission, many were elderly sailing ships whose primary function was to cruise back and forth on distant station patrol to show the U.S. flag overseas. In the secession spring of 1861, the U.S. Navy had only eight warships armed and ready to assume active operations in home waters. Still, that was eight more than the Confederacy had. Moreover, with the exception of Norfolk, the Union had control of most of the important naval yards where new ships might be built and where merchant ships might be converted to military use. In time, the Union would produce hundreds of new ships and convert more than four hundred more from commercial use to military use. The Confederacy could not hope to match such an effort.

Lincoln's success in applying this ad hoc, patched-together navy in the pursuit of national victory in the Civil War would depend on his ability to manage successfully the two key elements of naval power: the men who organized, officered, and manned the fleet, and the machines of war that they would employ.

First the men. At the top of the navy hierarchy was the secretary of the navy. Gideon Welles was a bit of an eccentric, even within Lincoln's eclectic cabinet. At age fifty-eight, the former Hartford, Connecticut, editor was almost completely bald, though he imperfectly disguised that fact by wearing a long, curly, dark-gray wig that

---

[5] William S. Dudley, *Going South: U.S. Navy Officer Resignations & Dismissals on the Eve of the Civil War* (Washington, D.C.: Naval Historical Foundation, 1981), 12–20.

clashed jarringly with his snow-white beard and that, moreover, often fell askew whenever he lifted his hat. Though Welles did have some claim to naval expertise, having served for three years as chief of the Bureau of Provisions and Clothing under President Polk, it was less for that than for his political credentials that Welles found himself on Lincoln's cabinet. As chairman of the Connecticut delegation at the 1860 Chicago convention, Welles had played a key role in halting William H. Seward's apparent coronation as the Republican candidate, and to achieve regional representation, Lincoln needed a New England Democrat to help balance his cabinet between former Whigs and former Democrats. Indeed, though Welles was pretty sure he was going to get a cabinet post, he did not know whether it was to be that of navy secretary or postmaster general until Lincoln made the formal announcement to the Congress.[6]

Welles's tenure in the navy bureaucracy back in the 1840s (where he had played a minor role in the mobilization of the fleet for the war with Mexico) did give him some appreciation of the problems likely to be encountered with civilian contractors and naval agents. Alas, while this experience prepared him to study procurement contracts with a keen eye, it did not prepare him to think about the strategic use of the navy. For that he relied on the professionals, and in particular on Navy Captain Gustavus Vasa Fox, who became the nation's first assistant secretary of the navy. The creation of such a post made sense. Indeed, it was probably essential given the unprecedented administrative duties that would have to be borne by those managing a navy that would soon expand from forty-two active-service ships to over 650. Curiously, however, the appointment resulted not from a reasoned consideration of the circumstances, but from more political deal-making. Welles wanted one of his old newspaper cronies, William Faxon, for the job as the Navy Department chief clerk. But the Blairs, Francis and Montgomery (father and son), a politically influential family from Missouri, insisted that the job go to their friend Fox, then a retired navy lieutenant who had served for many years as a captain of U.S. mail ships. Lincoln initially told Welles that he could give the post to Faxon so long as he provided Fox with a good sea command. But the Blairs complained, and Lincoln asked

---

[6] John Niven, *Gideon Welles: Lincoln's Secretary of the Navy* (New York: Oxford University Press, 1973), 304.

Welles to reconsider, urging him not to allow "any ordinary obstacle prevent his appointment." Welles was reluctant: he had already promised the job to Faxon. In the end Lincoln's solution was to ask Congress to create the post of assistant secretary for Fox, and allow Faxon to remain in the chief clerk's job. It was a typical example of Lincoln's pragmatism concerning political matters, and in the end it proved to be inspired.[7]

If Welles resembled a tipsy Neptune with his white beard and unreliable toupee, Fox (whose ancestry was Swedish) resembled a Chinese mandarin in a business suit. Although he also had a receding hairline, Fox eschewed a wig and combed his thin dark hair straight back. An equally dark beard surrounded his mouth and chin (though he shaved his cheeks), and his lank mustache drooped in a Fu Man-chu style. Fox proved to be a perfect foil for Welles. His job consisted of translating strategic decisions into professional orders. As a navy captain he could provide insight about personalities, ship types, ord-nance, logistics, steam plants, and all the other technical elements of a modern navy in the nineteenth century. He supervised operational planning, fleet movements, and communication with the blockade commanders. In effect, he performed all the jobs that today are the provenance of the Chief of Naval Operations, a job that would not be created officially for another half century. Below Welles and Fox were the professional serving officers. And the key word here is "pro-fessional." Though Lincoln was besieged by office seekers through-out his presidency, few such claimants sought positions as naval officers. There was simply too much technical knowledge necessary for a former congressman or judge to claim that he had a right to command a ship by virtue of his position in society. Nevertheless, Lincoln did have has share of problems with difficult or precipitous ship captains, professionals though they might have been.

In November 1861 the actions of an overzealous navy captain named Charles Wilkes cast Lincoln's administration into the most serious diplomatic crisis of the war. Wilkes was a career navy officer who had commanded the round-the-world exploring expedition in 1838–42 and collected the materials that comprised the initial hold-ings of the Smithsonian Institution. Promoted to captain upon the

---

[7] Ibid., 351–53; Lincoln to Welles, May 8, 1861, in *Collected Works of Lincoln*, 4:363.

outbreak of war, he was in command of the steam frigate *San Jacinto* in November 1861 when he took it upon himself to stop the British packet steamer *Trent* on the high seas and remove from that ship the Confederate commissioners to England and France, James M. Mason and John Slidell. His action sent an electric thrill through the American public, which overwhelmingly approved of his bold action. Twisting the British lion's tail was always good for a round of huzzahs at home, and doing so while capturing a couple of traitors was even better. Northern newspapers vied with one another to lionize Wilkes. By a vote of 109–16, the House passed a resolution calling upon Lincoln to support Wilkes and thus uphold the honor of the United States.[8] Unsurprisingly, Wilkes's action provoked a very different reaction in England. There, the newspapers expressed outrage that the Americans had violated the British flag, an outrage mirrored in the British cabinet. Lord Palmerston (the prime minister) and Lord John Russell (the foreign secretary) insisted that this insult to the national honor must not be tolerated. Within days the Royal Navy began to fit out its ships, work in the shipyards proceeding around the clock, and the British cabinet issued what amounted to an ultimatum. In an instruction to its minister in Washington, Lord Lyons, the cabinet insisted that the United States must disavow Wilkes's action, offer an immediate apology, and return Mason and Slidell to British protection. If the United States did not accept these demands within seven days, Lord Lyons was authorized to request his passport, an act tantamount to breaking off diplomatic relations. These instructions, dispatched to Queen Victoria for her signature, were rewritten by Albert, the prince consort, who took it upon himself to add (in his words) "a hope that the American captain had not acted under instructions," thus suggesting a way out for the Americans. It was practically Albert's last official act in life, for he died a few days later. Lord Lyons presented the amended note to Secretary of State Seward on December 23.[9] Lincoln's dilemma was obvious: if he acceded to the British demand and surrendered Mason and Slidell, he would dampen war enthusiasm at home and alienate some of his most devout supporters. It would discourage naval officers from aggressively

---

[8] Norman B. Ferris, *The Trent Affair: A Diplomatic Crisis* (Knoxville: University of Tennessee Press, 1977), 171.

[9] Ibid., 52; Gordon H. Warren, *Fountain of Discontent: The Trent Affair and Freedom of the Seas* (Boston: Northeastern University Press, 1981), 179–80.

prosecuting the blockade. Worse, it might fragment the precarious coalition of Republicans and War Democrats that sustained his administration. In light of that, Lincoln's first instinct is illuminating. When Wilkes stopped at the White House to pay his respects, Lincoln received him enthusiastically and offered his congratulations. Wilkes was entirely unapologetic, saying that "I felt I had done nothing more than my duty and should do it again if placed under similar circumstances." Lincoln apparently agreed, telling Wilkes that (as Wilkes later put it) "he intended to stand by me and rejoiced over the boldness, as he said, of my act."[10]

Moreover, Lincoln was also inclined to reject the British ultimatum. When Seward read him the note that Lord Lyons delivered, Lincoln shook his head and said, "No." On the other hand, if Lincoln did reject the ultimatum, he risked a war with Britain, and possibly with France as well, and in the midst of an ongoing civil war (a war that so far was going rather badly), British belligerence, with or without French support, might very well mean defeat. There was no good option here.[11] Lincoln eventually found his way out of this crisis by linking the release of Mason and Slidell to an age-old Anglo-American dispute about neutral rights at sea. It was not Lincoln's purpose to resolve, finally, the question of neutral rights, so much as it was to find a practical resolution to the immediate crisis that would allow him to steer a safe course between the twin shoals of British hostility and American chauvinism. Mason and Slidell were returned to the British, the European powers remained neutral in the war, and Lincoln's administration survived the half-hearted protests that followed. Significantly, Wilkes found himself promoted to rear admiral and Lincoln personally saw to it that he got a squadron command. The outcome of this crisis suggested that Lincoln was likely to be more forgiving of officers who exceeded their orders by aggressive action than he was of officers who erred on the side of caution and did nothing.[12]

Nor was Lincoln's response to Wilkes's act an isolated case. A simi-

---

[10] Charles Wilkes, *Autobiography of Rear Admiral Charles Wilkes, U.S. Navy, 1798–1877* (Washington, D.C.: Naval History Division, Department of the Navy, 1978), 775–76.

[11] Warren, *Fountain of Discontent*, 181.

[12] Gideon Welles, *The Diary of Gideon Welles*, 3 vols. (New York: W. W. Norton, 1960), 1:73.

lar incident involving another overzealous navy captain took place not quite two years later in October 1863 in the neutral harbor of Bahia, Brazil. There, Captain Napoleon Collins, commanding the screw steamer *Wachusett,* found the Confederate raider *Florida* safely resting at anchor in that neutral port. The British-built *Florida* was one of the most effective commerce raiders in the Confederate service and had been responsible for the destruction of over sixty U.S. merchant ships. (The *Florida* captured thirty-nine vessels herself; two of those prizes she converted to commerce raiders that captured twenty-two more.) Collins had been searching for her for months, and here she was, peacefully at anchor, in Bahia harbor. When Collins's ship entered the harbor and anchored nearby, local authorities sought from him a commitment that he would do nothing to violate Brazilian neutrality, and Thomas Wilson, the U.S. consul, assured the Brazilians that Collins would behave himself—though Collins himself kept silent.

At three o'clock the next morning, with two-thirds of the *Florida*'s crew on shore leave, Collins's *Wachusett* got underway and rammed the *Florida,* sending a boarding party over the bulwarks and taking the ship as a prize. Collins then towed the wounded *Florida* out of the harbor and into international waters, eventually taking it back to Washington. Once again the popular response in the Union States to this bold act was enthusiastic support. Confederate cruisers like the *Florida* and the *Alabama* had wreaked havoc on Union merchant shipping, and the public was cheered to hear that one of them had been seized. And once again the response from overseas was much more hostile. Brazil demanded restitution and the return of the *Florida.*

This time there could be no doubt about a misunderstanding of orders. Collins knew he had violated the law, and he freely confessed as much. At his court martial, he summarized his defense in a single sentence: "I respectfully request that it may be entered on the records of the court as my defense that the capture of the *Florida* was for the public good."[13]

---

[13] *Official Records of the Union and Confederate Navies in the War of the Rebellion* (Washington, D.C.: Government Printing Office, 1894–1922), ser. I, 3:268; hereafter cited as *ORN.* For a discussion of this incident as a reflection of officer values, see Llewellyn Lewis, "For the Public Good," undergraduate history honors papers, U.S. Naval Academy, 1990.

Apparently Lincoln agreed. Though the military court recommended Collins's dismissal from the service, Welles overturned the conviction and not only reinstated Collins, but promoted him to captain. He could not, and would not, have done so without Lincoln's approval. Though Welles officially informed all ship captains that it was their duty to maintain "a strict observance of the rights of neutrals," in this particular case, as in many others, he, and the administration he served, weighed the gain against the cost in assessing their response to violations of neutrality.[14] Success was Lincoln's yardstick. But even when success was lacking, he was more inclined to forgive overzealousness than excessive caution. He found it easier to forgive Ambrose E. Burnside for Fredericksburg or Ulysses S. Grant for Cold Harbor, for example, than he did to excuse McClellan or George G. Meade for failing to pursue Robert E. Lee aggressively after Antietam or Gettysburg. That same instinct—transferred to a nautical medium—made it easier for him to forgive Wilkes for stopping the *Trent* or Napoleon Collins for seizing the *Florida,* than to excuse Samuel F. Du Pont for refusing to give Charleston another try after his initial repulse in April 1863. Indeed, Lincoln compared Du Pont to McClellan, seeing him as a man who was unwilling to take a risk, to grapple with his enemy using every instrument at hand, and to pursue him aggressively until he was run to ground. In short, Lincoln preferred men who erred on the side of action, to those who feared to err at all.

In addition to handling the legal and diplomatic consequences of some of his captains at sea—*the men*—Lincoln also involved himself in the nuts and bolts of naval warfare—that is, *the machines.* One authority has suggested that although Lincoln had been born in a log cabin and raised on a farm, there was more Eli Whitney in him than Henry David Thoreau. Actually there was quite a bit of both. But there is no doubt that, from the first days of the war, Lincoln demonstrated a genuine and persistent interest in the gadgetry of war, including—maybe even especially—naval warfare. As was evident in his invention of "adjustable buoyant chambers" in 1849, machines intrigued him, and what were warships, after all, with their steam plants, navigational devices, and naval guns, but intricate machines of

[14] Welles to Bailey, May 12, 1863, in *ORN,* ser. I, 17:426; Lewis, "For the Public Good," 28.

war?[15] Barely two months into his presidency, Lincoln began making regular trips to the Washington Navy Yard. It was a habit that began innocuously enough. On May 9, 1861, the president attended a musical concert at the Yard, listening to a lengthy program of military marches and sentimental ballads by the band of the 71st New York regiment. Before leaving, he asked the Yard's commanding officer, John A. Dahlgren, if he could witness the firing of one of the new eleven-inch naval guns of Dahlgren's own design.

It was a spectacular demonstration. The gun crew fired three times, and hit the target three times. John Hay, who was accompanying the president, recorded the event in his diary. The thunderous crash, the brilliant muzzle flash, the leaping rebound of the massive gun, followed instantly by the sight of the eleven-inch shell skipping across the water "throwing up a 30 ft column of spray at every jump" toward the target— it was, wrote Hay, a scene both "novel and pleasant." Almost as an afterthought, he added: "The Prest. was delighted."[16]

So delighted, in fact, that Lincoln began to make trips to the Navy Yard as part of his regular weekend routine. A typical Saturday morning would find him riding in his carriage from the White House to the Navy Yard to witness the testing of some new weapon or another, and as often as not he would stay to have lunch with Captain Dahlgren. Very quickly, Lincoln and Dahlgren became fast friends. Welles, who was perhaps jealous of their close relationship, referred to Dahlgren as "a courtier" and suspected him of trying to take advantage of the president's friendship to promote himself.[17] The origins of Lincoln's close relationship with Dahlgren date back to the first chaotic days of the war. In April, in the desperate days just after Fort Sumter, the Navy Yard had been under the command of Maryland resident Franklin Buchanan, a forty-five-year navy veteran who had been the founding superintendent of the Naval Academy fifteen years before. (The superintendent's quarters at the Naval Academy

[15] Robert V. Bruce, *Lincoln and the Tools of War* (Indianapolis: Bobbs-Merrill, 1956), 10.

[16] Hay Diary, May 9, 1861, in Michael Burlingame and John R. Turner Ettlinger, eds., *Inside Lincoln's White House: The Complete Civil War Diary of John Hay* (Carbondale: Southern Illinois University Press, 1997), 22. See also Robert J. Schneller, Jr., *A Quest for Glory: A Biography of Rear Admiral John A. Dahlgren* (Annapolis: Naval Institute Press, 1996), 185.

[17] Welles, *Diary*, 1:62.

is still called Buchanan House.) But Buchanan was suffering a crisis of conscience in the secession spring of 1861. Shocked by the bloodshed in the streets of Baltimore when the 6th Massachusetts had marched through the city en route to Washington, Buchanan determined that he could no longer serve an administration that trampled so egregiously on the rights of its citizens, and he resigned both his command and his commission, turning the Navy Yard over to Dahlgren, then only a commander. Lincoln was grateful to Dahlgren for stepping into the breach (so to speak), and when Dahlgren asked for a promotion to captain commensurate with his new duties, Lincoln gratified him. Soon afterward, Lincoln began his regular trips to the Navy Yard to visit with this officer-inventor.[18]

Lincoln and Dahlgren had little in common besides the fact that they were virtually the same age (though Lincoln looked at least a decade older). What drew them together was their mutual love of technology. Dahlgren was an ordnance expert who in the 1850s had developed a new-style naval gun that was thickened at the breach so that it could withstand heavier charges. This gun has been shown in numerous photographs; many contemporaries noted its resemblance to a soda bottle. The eleven-inch Dahlgren gun, which Lincoln had asked to see fired after the concert in early May, was standard on many U.S. Navy warships by the time of the Civil War. Indeed, the Civil War took place at a time when the western world was going through a technological revolution. The invention of the minie ball in the 1850s had made rifled muskets a deadly weapon on Civil War battlefields, and other inventions—including the Dahlgren gun— would likewise revolutionize naval warfare. Rifled ordnance, the use of exploding shell over solid shot, steam propulsion, the screw propeller, even mines and submarines—all made their appearance in the Civil War. Perhaps the most notable innovation in this regard was the appearance of the ironclad warship.

The idea of an armored warship was not new. The French already had one in service, the *Gloire,* and the British had one under construction. Recognizing the onset of another technological revolution, the Union had established a board—commonsensically called the Ironclad Board—to evaluate various designs for armored warships.

---

[18] Craig L. Symonds, *Confederate Admiral: The Life and Wars of Franklin Buchanan* (Annapolis: Naval Institute Press, 1999), 143–46.

This was the origin of the vessel that eventually became the *Monitor*. The Ironclad Board surveyed dozens of models, and built several of them, but the one that captured both Lincoln's imagination, and a place in history, was the *Monitor*. John Ericcson, the ship's Swedish-born designer, wrote to Lincoln suggesting that "The time has come . . . when our cause will have to be sustained, not by numbers, but by superior weapons. By a proper application of mechanical devices alone you will be able with absolute certainty to destroy the enemies of the Union." Ericcson even suggested that by relying on superior technology, "you can destroy the enemy without enlisting another man."[19] Here is the essence of what Russell Weigley would later call "the American Way of War": the application of machinery as a force multiplier to inflict punishment on the enemy without risking American lives. Ericcson's prediction proved premature by a couple of generations, but the notion of it appealed to the mechanically inclined Lincoln.[20]

When a representative from Ericcson approached Lincoln with a model of the revolutionary-looking vessel, Lincoln examined it with interest and joked that, although he did not know much about ships, he had an affinity for this one since he had worked on a Mississippi River flat boat, and because this vessel was "as flat as needs be," he understood it well enough. Lincoln referred the proposal to the Ironclad Board, but significantly, he personally attended the meeting at which it was discussed. Many of the senior officers present were skeptical of the seaworthiness of the odd little craft, but they listened to the briefing and then looked to Lincoln to see what kind of response the president might have. Lincoln ensured the project's success when he remarked, with characteristic jocularity, "All I have to say is what the girl said when she put her foot into the stocking: 'It strikes me there's something in it.' "[21]In March, the *USS Monitor* steamed down to Hampton Roads to take on the *Virginia* (formerly the *Merrimack*). It was armed, incidentally, with two eleven-inch Dahlgren guns. Alas for Dahlgren's reputation as an ordnance expert,

[19] Bruce, *Lincoln and the Tools of War*, 68.

[20] Ibid.; Russell F. Weigley, *The American Way of War: A History of United States Military Strategy and Policy* (New York: Macmillan, 1973).

[21] Bruce, *Lincoln and the Tools of War*, 172; James Tertius deKay, *Monitor: The Story of the Legendary Civil War Ironclad and the Man Whose Invention Changed the Course of History* (New York: Walker, 1997), 76.

those eleven-inch guns on the *Monitor* failed to penetrate the thick armor plate of the *Virginia* in their classic duel, and as a result, Welles asked Dahlgren to design some fifteen-inch guns and even a twenty-inch gun! The weapons that resulted were huge—iron monsters that dwarfed their gun crews. Welles wrote his wife that seeing a fifteen-inch Dahlgren and comparing it to others was like seeing an elephant surrounded by lesser quadrupeds, thus suggesting a whole new meaning to the phrase "seeing the elephant."[22]

Quite a few fifteen-inch guns were placed on U.S. warships. One of them successfully smashed through the thick armor pate of the Confederate ironclad *Tennessee* in the Battle of Mobile Bay in August 1864. Only one twenty-inch gun was ever built, and it never saw active service. Even so, it earned a place in history for being the largest naval gun ever built, easily surpassing the fifteen-inch guns of the German *Bismarck,* the sixteen-inch guns of the American *Iowa* class battleships, and even the 18.1-inch guns of the Japanese super-battleships *Yamato* and *Musashi.*

To Lincoln, this ordnance revolution was fascinating. A tinkerer by instinct, he involved himself in all sorts of technological undertakings in addition to his public interest in Dahlgren guns and ironclad monitors. He was enthusiastic about mortar boats, or bomb ships, which were capable of lofting rounds of heavy ordnance on a high trajectory to rain down on both ships and land forces alike. As with Dahlgren's guns, bigger was better, as far as Lincoln was concerned. He lobbied hard for a whole squadron of river vessels that would carry thirteen-inch mortars. In January 1862 one officer reported to Navy Flag Officer Andrew H. Foote that Lincoln "is stirring up the army ordnance with a sharp stick about mortars." Lincoln told this officer, Henry Wise, "I am going to devote a part of every day to these mortars and I won't leave off until it fairly rains Bombs." In the end, Lincoln got his way. His bomb vessels were instrumental in the fight for New Orleans when David G. Farragut's fleet ran past forts Jackson and St. Philip, at Vicksburg, and in most of the major battles of the Mississippi River.[23] Lincoln was occasionally thwarted in his endeavors by the entrenched bureaucracy. James W. Ripley, the army's chief of

[22] Du Pont to Sophie du Pont, October 22, 1862, in John D. Hayes, ed., *Samuel Francis Du Pont: A Selection from His Civil War Letters,* 3 vols. (Ithaca, N.Y.: Cornell University Press, 1969), 2:258.

[23] Henry Wise to Foote, January 23, 1862, in *Collected Works of Lincoln,* 5:108.

ordnance, routinely referred all proposed new innovations to a committee of inquiry, where, more often than not, the idea died of mal-
nourishment.[24] The navy was slightly more open-minded, but even it
could be hidebound about the adoption and implementation of new
technology, and true to his character, Lincoln often attempted to
circumvent established routine by involving himself personally in the
testing of new weapons: for the army as well as for the navy.

On one occasion as he was leaving Captain Dahlgren's office after
a lengthy lunch, he noticed a group of men test firing a breach-load-
ing rifle. He stopped to watch, asked if he could try it, and putting
the gun to his shoulder, he fired a round at the target. On another
occasion, Lincoln urged Dahlgren to test a repeating rifle that had
been invented by a Frenchman named Raphael. Bringing both
Edwin M. Stanton and Welles with him to the Navy Yard, as well as
a reporter from the New York *Tribune,* Lincoln and his coterie
watched for hours as technicians tested the weapon. Closely following the ensuing discussion about the importance of allowing gas to
escape from the breach between shots, Lincoln with a twinkle in his
eye and a glance at the *Tribune* reporter, asked the technicians if they
had "heard of any machine, or invention, for preventing the escape
of 'gas' from newspaper establishments."[25] Like many of his jibes,
Lincoln's arch reference to the media was not entirely without a
point. Very likely, one of the reasons he escaped so frequently to the
Navy Yard was to avoid the hundreds of office seekers and special
interest pleaders that besieged him every day at the White House.

Eventually Lincoln's navy fulfilled the role assigned to it by Winfield Scott's much-maligned Anaconda Plan: it blockaded the southern coast—imperfectly, perhaps, but enough to ensure that life
became just that much more difficult for the citizens of the Confederacy; it played a major role in the seizure of the western rivers,
including the Tennessee and Cumberland rivers as well as the Mississippi; and it cooperated with Union armies in a number of important
campaigns from the Virginia peninsula to Vicksburg. At war's end it
numbered some 671 vessels, including over fifty monitors and as
many mortar vessels. Those ships hovered off the southern coast and
plied the western rivers. The Confederate navy attempted to counter

---

[24] Bruce, *Lincoln and the Tools of War,* 22–36; Donald, *Lincoln,* 431.
[25] Schneller, *Quest for Glory,* 185; Donald, *Lincoln,* 432.

the overwhelming Union superiority in numbers with innovations of their own: ironclads like the *Virginia*, submarines like the *Hunley*, and those dreaded "infernal machines" that today we call mines. They sought to exploit the legal loopholes of the blockade declaration and the diplomatic crisis spawned by the *Trent* incident. But in the end, the blockade became tighter and tighter, the rivers were lost to them one by one, and despite their technological innovations, the Union navy matched them, and then out-produced them, to ensure the maintenance of Union naval superiority. In much of this, Lincoln was an active player. He picked good men—or at least he tried to— and then he measured them by their achievements. And if they did not always reach the mark, he preferred those who overreached to those who feared to reach at all. He advocated and lobbied for technological innovations such as the seagoing monitors and the river-bound mortar vessels. In all of this, his practical side dominated. Unwilling to be hamstrung by protocol or bureaucracy, he sought solutions that were both realistic and effective. Protocol was valuable only if it contributed to an effective solution. Otherwise it was mere pettifoggery. As he had written to a nervous state governor back in 1862, "We are in no condition to waste time on technicalities."

5

Abraham Lincoln and William T. Sherman: The Cause Was Union

John F. Marszalek

IF HE HAD EVER MET ABRAHAM LINCOLN before the coming of the Civil War, William T. Sherman never mentioned it. No doubt he had heard of him, though. His foster father Thomas Ewing was a leading member of the Whig party, to which Lincoln also belonged, and Ewing must have talked about the Illinois lawyer and politician, one time or another. Sherman himself kept a close eye on politics, so he must have known about Lincoln's anti–Mexican War position, his near–vice presidential nomination during the 1856 Republican national convention, and his well-publicized debates with Stephen A. Douglas in the 1858 Illinois senatorial race. Still, Sherman was more enthralled with Henry Clay than he was with a lesser-known politician like Lincoln.[1] Similarly, Lincoln had never heard of Sherman, his banking, military, and civilian careers in California and Louisiana hardly the stuff of public fame.

During the four years beginning in 1861, Lincoln and Sherman still did not come to know each other all that well, actually being together only a small part of five widely separated days. Yet they impacted on each other and the nation in a significant way. Though totally different personalities, they shared one basic belief, and that was the cause. And, to both of them, the cause was Union.

Sherman first began to pay serious attention to Lincoln during the 1860 election. His foster father, now his father-in-law, Ewing, was one of the Whig members of the Constitutional Union party, which nominated John Bell of Tennessee for the presidential office. Sherman supported Bell too because he thought his election would give

---

[1] John F. Marszalek, *Sherman, A Soldier's Passion for Order* (New York: Free Press, 1993), 83–84.

the nation time to solve the slavery issue, but he let it be known at the
time that he would leave his post as superintendent of the Louisiana
Military Seminary if the state ever left the Union.[2]

Then Ewing complicated Sherman's life by switching his support
from Bell to Lincoln, causing Sherman to worry about the reaction
in Louisiana. Sherman maintained his support for Bell, but, in exasperation, he decided not to vote in the election, thus raising some
eyebrows. Since Lincoln was not on the Louisiana ballot at all, suspi-
cion arose that Sherman was abstaining because he was not able to
vote for the Republican. Sherman stubbornly stood his ground, and
Lincoln's election and the resulting secession of South Carolina took
attention away from his refusal to vote. When Louisiana seceded in
January 1861, Sherman waited as long as he could, but, in February,
he called the Military Seminary cadets and faculty together and sadly
bid them goodbye, weeping as he left. He knew that he was leaving
behind friends, the best job he had ever had, and his greatest hope
for future success.[3]

Sherman did not blame Lincoln and the Republicans for his problems; he blamed his friends in Louisiana and throughout the South
for destroying the Union that he saw as the only hope for the nation.
When he reached Washington on his way home to Ohio, however, he
quickly turned against Lincoln. He found the nation's capital in turmoil, displaying little serious response, he believed, to Southern secession. When his brother, the new senator from Ohio, took him to
see the recently inaugurated president, he became even more upset.
John Sherman spent the first several minutes discussing patronage
with Lincoln, and then he finally said: "Mr. President, this is my
brother, Colonel Sherman, who is just up from Louisiana, he may
give you some information you want." "Ah!" Lincoln responded.
"How are they getting along down there?" "I think they are getting

---

[2] Ibid., 125–26; Robert G. Gunderson, *Old Gentlemen's Convention: The Washington Peace Conference of 1861* (Madison: University of Wisconsin Press, 1961),
15; William T. Sherman (WTS) to Daniel French Boyd, September 16, 1860, Sherman Family Papers, University of Notre Dame Archives (SFP, UNDA); WTS to
Ellen Sherman (ES), November 23, 1860, SFP, UNDA.

[3] WTS to John Sherman, October 3, 1860, William T. Sherman Papers, Library of
Congress (WTSP, LC); G. Mason Graham to WTS, November 5, 1860, WTS to ES,
November 10, 1861, SFP, UNDA; David French Boyd, "William Tecumseh Sher-
man, First Superintendent of the Louisiana State Seminary, Now the Louisiana State
University," [LSU] *Alumnus* 5 (October 1909): 11.

along swimmingly," Sherman answered. "They are preparing for war." "Oh, well!" Lincoln said. "I guess we'll manage to keep house."[4]

Sherman was stunned and shocked into an uncharacteristic silence. As soon as he and John were alone, however, he blasted his brother and all politicians, obviously including Lincoln. "You have got things in a hell of a fix, and you may get them out as you best can," he sputtered. He refused to join the army or in any way tie his future to Lincoln and an administration that he believed was so unprepared for war and so unconcerned about it. He left for St. Louis to take a position as president of a street railway company.[5]

Only after Ewing family pressure changed his mind, did Sherman, on May 14, 1861, become colonel of the 13th Regular Infantry Regiment. After a series of transfers, he became a brigade commander in Daniel Tyler's 1st Division in Irvin McDowell's army. He participated in the Union defeat at First Bull Run, distinguishing himself despite the Federal loss. The chaos of this battle and its aftermath only convinced him further that Lincoln and his administration were indeed not taking the crisis seriously.[6]

After Bull Run Sherman tried to restore order and discipline in his brigade, only to find that an uncomfortably high number of men had had enough of war and wanted to go home. An officer even challenged his authority in front of the troops, telling him that he was going to New York because his ninety days were up. Sherman stood his ground. "If you attempt to leave without orders, it will be mutiny," he said, "and I will shoot you like a dog!" The men scattered, and the officer skulked away.

That same July 1861 day, Lincoln paid a visit to Sherman's brigade. Sherman saw him at a distance, riding in an open horse-drawn carriage. He ran out to meet the party, and Lincoln invited him into the carriage to direct the driver. As they proceeded, Sherman noticed that Lincoln was "full of feeling, and wanted to encourage our men." He asked the president if he intended to make a speech. Lincoln nodded yes. Sherman then asked him "to please discourage all cheer-

---

[4] WTS to Maria (Minnie) Sherman, December 15, 1860, William T. Sherman Papers, Ohio Historical Society; WTS, *Memoirs of General William T. Sherman*, 2 vols., notes by Charles Royster (New York: Library of America, 1990), 1:185–86.

[5] WTS, *Memoirs*, 1:186.

[6] Marszalek, *Sherman, A Soldier's Passion for Order*, 152.

ing, noise, or any sort of confusion; that we had had enough of it before Bull Run to ruin any set of men, and that what we needed were cool, thoughtful, hard-fighting soldiers—no more hurrahing, no more humbug."

When Lincoln arrived at the camp, he stood up in the carriage and gave what Sherman described as "one of the neatest, best, and most feeling addresses" he had ever heard. The soldiers began to yell, but the president stopped them. "Don't cheer, boys. I confess I rather like it myself, but Colonel Sherman here says it is not military; and I guess we had better defer to his opinion."

Lincoln made the same speech to all the regiments in Sherman's brigade, ending each talk with an offer that the men appeal to him if they ever had a complaint. As Sherman watched, the officer who had talked of leaving for New York worked his way to the front of the listening soldiers. "Mr. President, I have a cause of grievance," he intoned. "This morning I went to speak to Colonel Sherman, and he threatened to shoot me." Lincoln, tall man that he was and standing in the carriage, literally towered over the complaining officer. Stooping down and pretending to whisper but speaking loud enough for all to hear him, Lincoln said, "Well, if I were you, and he threatened to shoot [me], I would not trust him, for I believe he would do it."[7]

Sherman now had a much more favorable view of Lincoln, and apparently Lincoln was also impressed with Sherman, his relationship to John Sherman and Ewing certainly no detriment. Still, Sherman continued to worry about the Union war effort. Lincoln's favorable impression of Sherman and Sherman's concern about the war in the East merged when Robert Anderson, the hero of Fort Sumter, needed a deputy in the Department of the Cumberland, headquartered in Louisville, Kentucky. Sherman, Anderson, and Lincoln met in late August 1861 to discuss the position, and Sherman demonstrated his continued unwillingness to take a leading part in a war he thought the Union was botching. He agreed to become Anderson's assistant but asked Lincoln to promise he would never give him command. Lincoln agreed, joking that "his chief trouble was to find places for the too many generals who wanted to be at the head of affairs."[8]

---

[7] WTS, *Memoirs,* 1:206–8; WTS, Speech, in *Proceedings of the 7th Annual Reunion of the Army of the Cumberland,* September 17, 18, 1873, 98–99.
  [8] WTS, *Memoirs,* 1:210.

Arriving in Kentucky in early September 1861, Sherman's concern about Union unpreparedness surfaced for all to see. He believed that the Confederates were on the verge of overwhelming inadequate Union forces there, and that no one in authority was doing anything about it. At least, he thought, he did not command in Kentucky, and he had Lincoln's assurance that he never would. On October 8, 1861, however, Anderson resigned because of physical and mental stress, and an unhappy and concerned Sherman had to take over by virtue of his rank.[9]

Sherman became so upset at this unexpected turn of events that he wrote directly to the White House, repeating his complaints and worries, and even bluntly ending one letter to the president "Answer." When Secretary of War Simon Cameron and Adjutant General Lorenzo Thomas arrived in Kentucky on October 17, accompanied by reporters, Sherman's anxieties and demands frightened everyone who heard him. He said he only had eighteen thousand men and needed sixty thousand for defense and 200,000 to go on the offensive. Sherman's naturally eccentric personality had already caused concern to those around him, and this latest statement only cinched the case. Word had been spreading of Sherman's feverous pacing in the hall of his hotel every night and of his disheveled appearance all the time. Rumors now circulated that he was crazy, and on December 11, 1861, the Cincinnati *Commercial* headlined "GENERAL WILLIAM T. SHERMAN INSANE," opening an all-out press attack on his sanity.[10]

The Ewing family was outraged at this slur, none more so than Sherman's wife, Ellen. She grew so upset at the attacks on her husband that, like him, she wrote directly to the president "appeal[ing] in confidence . . . for some intervention . . . and vindication." When a week passed without a response, she traveled to Washington with her father to see Lincoln herself. She repeated her concerns to him, and Lincoln's response calmed her. He praised her husband, pointing out that his behavior in Kentucky had been strange, but that he was

---

[9] WTS to Lorenzo Thomas, October 8, 1861, WTSP, LC; Thomas to WTS, October 10, 1861, in *The War of the Rebellion: A Compilation of the Official Records of the Union and Confederate Armies*, 128 vols. (Washington, D.C.: Government Printing Office, 1880–1901), ser. I, 4:299–300.

[10] WTS to Abraham Lincoln (AL), October 10, 14, 1861, *Official Records*, ser. I, 4:300; WTS, *Memoirs*, 1:218–21; Lorenzo Thomas to Simon Cameron, October 21, 1861, *Official Records*, ser. I, 3:548–49.

certainly not crazy. Ellen was satisfied. She continued to believe in an army-press conspiracy against her husband, but she never included the president in her roster of villains. Lincoln had charmed his way out of a difficult situation. Sherman was unhappy that his wife had gone to see the president, but he had to be pleased at Lincoln's statement of support. Lincoln's patience and his support had helped Sherman survive a major crisis in his life.[11]

It was Sherman's heroic performance on the Shiloh battlefield in April 1862 that proved to be the turning point in his Civil War career. From this point on, he steadily grew in military stature. He participated in the capture of Corinth, Mississippi, in late May 1862, successfully governed Memphis, Tennessee, and, despite being repulsed at Chickasaw Bayou in December 1862, played a key role in Ulysses S. Grant's July 4, 1863, capture of Vicksburg, Mississippi. He helped Grant lift the Confederate siege of Chattanooga in late 1863 and in early 1864 conducted the Meridian Mississippi Campaign, the dress rehearsal for his later destructive activities in Georgia. He captured Atlanta in September 1864, marched to the sea in November and December, and then marched through the Carolinas as the war ended. Throughout, Lincoln's patient handling of the obstreperous general and his agreement with Halleck's and Grant's promotion recommendations paid huge dividends.

Despite Lincoln's steady support, Sherman continued to cause the president problems throughout the war. When Lincoln issued his preliminary Emancipation Proclamation in September 1862, for example, Sherman vociferously opposed it, continuing to believe in slavery. When a newspaper reporter resurrected the insanity charge as part of his criticism of Sherman's rebuff at Chickasaw Bayou in December 1862, Sherman displayed his anger and the power he held over noncombatants within his military jurisdiction by court martialing the New York *Herald's* Thomas W. Knox and sending him packing. Some of his reporter colleagues, fearing a precedent, appealed the sentence directly to the president. Lincoln amiably greeted the delegation of reporters and defused the situation by allowing Knox back into Sherman's army, *but* only if Grant agreed. Grant, following Lincoln's lead, said he would allow Knox back *but* only with Sher-

---

[11] ES to AL, January 10, 1862, copy, ES to WTS, January 29, 1862, WTS to ES, January 16, 1862, SFP, UNDA.

man's consent. With great glee, Sherman blasted the reporter, and the matter ended there. But Sherman was unhappy at Lincoln's intervention, considering it political interference. Similarly, when in 1862–63 Lincoln supported John McClernand, an Illinois congressman, for command of a Vicksburg expedition, Sherman saw it as more political meddling and expressed unhappiness with Lincoln.[12]

He was also irritated at the president for attempting to convince him to change one of his orders. As he prepared for the campaign that was to result in the capture of Atlanta, Sherman announced in no uncertain terms that he wanted no reporters, nurses, or chaplains encumbering his supply vehicles, especially the trains. These groups resisted so vociferously that Lincoln felt it necessary to write Sherman one of his classic letters, asking for a softening of his exclusion order. Sherman refused, telling the president, "I beg of you to be satisfied that the clamor is partly humbug." To Sherman's pleasure, Lincoln deferred to him and let the matter drop.[13]

Later in the Atlanta campaign the president made another request of his general. Excited at the progress Sherman was making against General Johnston, Lincoln became concerned about Sherman's harsh handling of the recruiters sent from Northern states to enlist freed slaves into the Union army. Sherman saw these agents as another civilian nuisance and put obstacles in their way every chance he had. Lincoln asked for his cooperation, and Sherman reluctantly agreed. Later, however, his true feelings came out. He believed it ridiculous to include any blacks in the army, insisting insultingly that "all the Psalm-singing on earth" would not make blacks equal to whites.[14]

Though once again displeased with Sherman's attitude, Lincoln kept quiet. After all, he was in the middle of a hard presidential campaign, and he could not afford to antagonize his successful general. Where previously Sherman had needed Lincoln, now the president needed the general. If Sherman were successful in Georgia,

---

[12] John F. Marszalek, *Sherman's Other War, The General and the Civil War Press,* rev. ed. (Kent, Ohio: Kent State University Press, 1999), 131–67.

[13] WTS to Charles A. Dana, April 21, 1864, in Charles A. Dana, *Recollections of the Civil War,* reprint (New York: Collier Books, 1963), 153–54; AL to WTS, May 4, 1864, WTS to AL, May 5, 1864, *Official Records,* ser. I, 38, pt. 4:25, 33–34.

[14] Edwin M. Stanton to WTS, May 20, 1864, Edwin M. Stanton Papers, Library of Congress; WTS to J. A. R., September 12, 1864 in *Historical Magazine* 21 (February 1872): 113.

Lincoln's presidential reelection hopes would receive a boost. If Sherman became bogged down in front of Atlanta, the way Grant seemed to be stymied in front of Richmond, a war-weary North might turn to Democratic party candidate George B. McClellan. Or so Lincoln thought. In September 1864, Atlanta fell to Sherman's soldiers, and Lincoln was ecstatic. Whether Sherman's capture of the Georgia capital ensured Lincoln's electoral victory in November will perhaps never be known for sure and will long be debated, but clearly this triumph boosted the president's candidacy.[15]

Something significant had indeed happened. The president and the general, whose relationship had begun in the rockiest manner, were now tied together in battling for the survival of the Union. As Grant and Robert E. Lee locked in a stalemate in Virginia, Lincoln was able to look to the West and to Sherman for the success that buoyed his spirit and the attitude of the people. At the same time, Sherman, though against emancipation and determined to fight the war in his own way, was beginning to view Lincoln much more favorably too.

But problems continued to appear. In a process that is too complicated to discuss here, Sherman decided on undertaking what became his march to the sea, his path of destruction from Atlanta to Savannah, the initiation of psychological warfare against the citizens of the South in order to end the war with the least loss of life but as quickly as possible. Sherman wanted to turn his back on John Bell Hood and the Confederate Army of Tennessee and institute a war of property destruction instead.

Grant did not like the idea. He wanted Sherman to destroy Hood's army first, then proceed on his march. Secretary of War Edwin M. Stanton had similar concerns, and so did the president. Sherman kept

---

[15] The debate over the impact of Sherman's capture of Atlanta on the election of 1864 is best exemplified in Albert Castel, *Winning and Losing the Civil War: Essays and Stories* (Columbia: University of South Carolina Press, 1996), in which he holds that Atlanta was crucial to the Lincoln victory in 1864 and the continuation of the war, and Larry Daniel, "Atlanta: Was It Really a Turning Point?" *North & South* (February 1998): 44–51, who disagrees. Both historians agree that Lincoln believed that Atlanta was crucial to his reelection hopes. In his book on the battle for Atlanta, Richard McMurry says both Castel and Daniel are correct—"up to and from a point," i.e., depending on how the argument is framed; Richard M. McMurry, *Atlanta 1864: Last Chance for the Confederacy* (Lincoln: University of Nebraska Press, 2000), 207.

insisting, however, that he be allowed to send George H. Thomas with sixty thousand troops after Hood, while he took another sixty thousand men and started across Georgia. He made such a forthright case that Grant reluctantly gave in, and then so did Stanton and Lincoln.

This capitulation to Sherman did not mean that Lincoln, Stanton, and Grant were completely happy with the decision. In fact, they were totally in the dark about Sherman's activities. Sherman stopped all communication with the outside world when he began his march, cutting the telegraph lines and destroying the railroad that had supplied him during his Atlanta campaign. He banned all reporters and had mail for his men sent to Nashville as part of his attempt to confuse the Confederates. He sent the few remaining residents and refugees out of Atlanta and destroyed its military capacity, not, however, burning it to the ground in the tradition of *Gone with the Wind.*[16]

The leadership in Washington had no way of knowing how Sherman's army was faring in Georgia. Even the president and the general's brother were in the dark. One day, while Sherman was marching through Georgia, his brother, Senator John Sherman, asked Lincoln what he knew about Sherman's activities. Lincoln expressed his ignorance, displaying what might best be called confident concern. "Oh no, we have heard nothing from him," Lincoln told John Sherman. "We know what hole he went in, but we don't know what hole he will come out of."[17]

When Sherman reached the Atlantic coast and then captured the key city of Savannah in December 1864, Lincoln became ecstatic at Sherman's telegraphic announcement: "I beg to present you as a Christmas-gift the city of Savannah, with one hundred and fifty heavy guns and plenty of ammunition, also about twenty-five thousand bales of cotton." This telegram reached Washington on Christmas Eve, so the effect was dramatic on the president and on the nation. Lincoln responded warmly, congratulating Sherman profusely: "Many, many thanks for your Christmas-gift—the capture of Savan-

---

[16] Marszalek, *Sherman*, 288–316. This author has completed a book on the march to the sea that will appear in the Campaigns and Commanders Series published by the McWhiney Foundation Press and marketed by the Texas A&M Press.

[17] John Sherman, "An Address Commemorative of General William T. Sherman," New York Commandery, Military Order of the Loyal Legion of the United States, April 6, 1892, 15.

nah," he wrote. He admitted his error in ever doubting Sherman's plan to march through Georgia. "But what next?" Lincoln asked, and then he caught himself. "I suppose it will be safer if I leave Gen. Grant and yourself to decide," he concluded. The bond between the president and the general was now secure.[18]

When Sherman successfully and spectacularly marched through the Carolinas, routing what was left of the Confederate army in the western theater of the war, Lincoln grew even more pleased. He decided it was time, in late March 1865, to meet with his military leaders to plan the war's conclusion. Sherman, Grant, Admiral David Dixon Porter, and the president met on the *River Queen*, a boat in the James River near City Point, Virginia, their meeting resulting in one of the most famous paintings of the Civil War, George P. A. Healy's "The Peacemakers."[19]

Lincoln and Sherman had not seen each other since their meeting in the fall of 1861 before Sherman left for Kentucky to become Anderson's assistant and subsequently suffer the insanity accusation. The forty-five-year-old general looked full of energy, but the fifty-six-year-old president appeared haggard and drawn from the pressures of his office. Unfortunately, Lincoln left no evaluation of Sherman, but the general was obviously impressed with Lincoln, pleased that he "remembered me perfectly, and at once engaged in a most interesting conversation." Sherman was happy to have Lincoln ask him all kinds of questions about his marches and was amused that Lincoln showed especial interest in "the more ludicrous parts—about the 'bummers,' and their devices to collect food and forage."

The next day they had a more serious discussion about the progress of the war. According to Porter's notes, Sherman and Grant both thought that one great battle yet remained before the Confederacy would collapse. This thinking upset Lincoln. He repeatedly lamented the war's bloodshed and called for the avoidance of any further fighting. His generals were not optimistic that this was possible, but they agreed that victory was just over the horizon. Sherman asked Lincoln what his plans were for the defeated Confederacy and its army. The

---

[18] WTS to AL, December 22, 1864, WTS, *Memoirs*, 1:711; AL to WTS, December 26, 1864, in Roy P. Basler et al., eds., *The Collected Works of Abraham Lincoln*, 9 vols. (New Brunswick, N.J.: Rutgers University Press, 1953–55), 8:181–82.

[19] Harold Holzer and Mark E. Neely, Jr., *Mine Eyes Have Seen the Glory: The Civil War in Art* (New York: Orion Books, 1993), 156.

president said he was ready for the postwar period, and all he wanted from his military "was to defeat the opposing armies, and to get the men composing the Confederate armies back to their homes, at work on their farms and in their shops."

As for the Confederate president, Lincoln told one of his stories. "A man once had taken the total-abstinence pledge," Lincoln began. "When visiting a friend, he was invited to take a drink, but declined, on the score of his pledge." The friend then offered him some lemonade, suggesting that he might make the lemonade more tasty by adding some brandy. The teetotaler said that, if the brandy were added "'unbeknown' to him, he would not object." Sherman understood the point. If Jefferson Davis escaped "unbeknown" to Lincoln, the president "would not object" either.[20]

Sherman left Lincoln "impressed by his kindly nature, his deep and earnest sympathy with the afflictions of the whole people." Lincoln's desire to restore the nation to a peacetime footing as quickly as possible and with the least animosity made a strong impression on Sherman, who shared these thoughts. Sherman left his meeting with the president encouraged that he was on the right path with his own hard war, soft peace philosophy. As he departed, he worried about Lincoln's haggard appearance, but he was impressed that Lincoln was "the very impersonation of good-humor and fellowship." The last words Lincoln expressed to him, Sherman remembered, were "that he would feel better when I was back" with the army in North Carolina.[21]

The two men never saw each other again. Lincoln had only a few weeks of life left. Sherman was yet to face public accusations of treason for his generous peace agreement with Johnston, a compact that he always insisted was based on Lincoln's suggestions on the *River Queen.*

Lincoln and Sherman had never been close personally, but they agreed with one another on the need to preserve the Union above all else. Their careers meshed in 1861–65, the success of one depending on the support and the success of the other. A pessimistic Sherman had found the president lacking when they first met in 1861, but like

---

[20] David Herbert Donald, *Lincoln* (New York: Simon & Schuster, 1995), 568, 572; WTS, *Memoirs,* 1:810–13.
[21] WTS, *Memoirs,* 1:813.

most people, he came to respect and admire Lincoln. "Of all the men I ever met," Sherman concluded when he wrote his memoirs, "he seemed to possess more of the elements of greatness, combined with goodness" than anyone Sherman had ever known.[22] The cooperation of Lincoln and Sherman had been instrumental in winning the war and preserving the Union. Sadly, the assassination prevented them from putting their mutual respect to work during the difficult peace that followed. If Lincoln had lived, would he and a pro-Southern Sherman have been able to work together to win the peace as they had cooperated to win the war? This is one of the big "what ifs" of the Civil War years, and we will never be able to answer it in any definitive way. We do know, however, that Lincoln and Sherman had had differences during the 1861–65 period, but that they had worked together anyway because they had a common goal. The cause was Union in 1861–65. It would make sense, therefore, to believe that, despite significant differences over Reconstruction, they would have cooperated once again. After all, in those postwar years, the cause was still Union.

[22] Ibid.

6

"If I Had Gone Up There, I Could Have Whipped Them Myself": Lincoln's Military Fantasies

Gerald J. Prokopowicz

IN JULY 1863, at the Pennsylvania crossroads town of Gettysburg, the Union Army of the Potomac under George Gordon Meade won a momentous victory over Robert E. Lee's Army of Northern Virginia. In three days of intense fighting, Meade's army inflicted twenty-eight thousand Confederate losses, while suffering twenty-three thousand killed or wounded of its own, including three of its seven corps commanders. On the fourth day of the confrontation between the two forces, the battlefield was comparatively quiet. Lee sent a seventeen-mile long wagon train of wounded men back toward Virginia, but defiantly kept the rest of his troops in place on Seminary Ridge, daring Meade to attack him. Meade, however, showed no sign of wanting to continue the fight, and Lee at last ordered the rest of his army off the battlefield. After waiting another day to be certain that Lee was retreating, Meade pursued cautiously.

In Washington, D.C., where reports from Meade's headquarters arrived via a chain of semaphore and telegraph stations, sometimes within the hour, President Abraham Lincoln's elation at reading of the Union victory was mixed with concern that Meade might lose the advantage he had gained. From the moment in June when the Confederates had marched north into Maryland, Lincoln had wanted the Army of the Potomac not simply to chase Lee back to Virginia, but to follow him, attack him, cut him off from his base, and destroy

A version of this essay previously appeared in Gabor Boritt, ed., *The Lincoln Enigma: The Changing Faces of an American Icon* (New York: Oxford University Press, 2001).

him. Now, with Lee's weakened forces trapped between Meade's troops and the rain-swollen Potomac, all this seemed possible. The end of the war was in sight, Lincoln thought, if only Meade would attack. But the president found the tone of his general's dispatches disconcerting, especially when Meade spoke of "efforts to drive from our soil every vestige of the presence of the invader." "Will our Generals never get that idea out of their heads?" Lincoln fumed. "The whole country is *our* soil."[1]

What happened next left Lincoln nearly beside himself with frustration. Meade did not attack, Lee crossed the Potomac safely at Williamsport on July 14, and the war seemed no closer to its end than ever. Major General Henry Wager Halleck, Lincoln's military chief of staff, immediately informed Meade of Lincoln's unhappiness with the result of the campaign, prompting Meade to offer his resignation. To soothe Meade's injured pride, Lincoln sat down that same afternoon to write the general a letter of thanks and apology. "I am very— *very*—grateful to you for the magnificent success you gave the cause of the country at Gettysburg; and I am sorry now to be the author of the slightest pain to you," he began. But even as the words flowed from Lincoln's pen, his emotions overcame him again: "I do not believe you appreciate the magnitude of the misfortune involved in Lee's escape. He was within your easy grasp, and to have closed upon him would, in connection with our other late successes, have ended the war. As it is, the war will be prolonged indefinitely. . . . Your golden opportunity is gone, and I am distressed immeasurably because of it." So distressed was Lincoln that he had begun to wonder aloud about going to the headquarters of the Army of the Potomac and, under his constitutional power as commander in chief, taking personal control of the army in order to complete the pursuit and destruction of Lee's forces. "Nothing I could say or do," he lamented to his secretary John Hay, "could make the Army move. . . . [But] if I had gone up there, I could have whipped them myself."[2]

---

[1] General Orders No. 68, July 4, 1863, in *The War of the Rebellion: A Compilation of the Official Records of the Union and Confederate Armies,* 128 vols. (Washington, D.C.: Government Printing Office, 1880–1901), ser. I, 27, pt. 3:519; Michael Burlingame and John R. Turner Ettlinger, eds., *Inside Lincoln's White House: The Complete Civil War Diary of John Hay* (Carbondale: Southern Illinois University Press, 1997), 62.

[2] Lincoln to George G. Meade, July 14, 1863, in Roy P. Basler et al., eds., *The Collected Works of Abraham Lincoln,* 9 vols. (New Brunswick, N.J.: Rutgers Univer-

Traditionally historians have dismissed this extraordinary sugges-tion as nothing more than an expression of Lincoln's frustration, like an angry baseball fan yelling, "Hey, I coulda caught that one myself" at a $2-million-a-year utility infielder who has dropped an easy pop fly. But there is reason to believe that Lincoln meant what he said. This was not the first time that Lincoln had spoken of taking personal command of the Army of the Potomac. On January 12, 1862, Lincoln had discussed military strategy with an old friend, Illinois Senator Orville H. Browning. Since General in Chief George B. McClellan had typhoid fever and the three main Federal armies were showing no signs of preparing to take aggressive action, Lincoln told Browning that he was "thinking of taking the field himself." After McClellan recovered from his illness, he brilliantly outflanked the rebels by moving the Army of the Potomac by sea to the Virginia peninsula, but there he lost his nerve and advanced so slowly that Lincoln re-portedly said, "If McClellan is not using the Army I should like to borrow it for a while." When Lincoln speculated on July 15, 1863, that he might have led the army to victory after Gettysburg, Hay confirmed in his diary that the president "had that idea" before.[3]

Not only did Lincoln regularly speak of playing a more direct role in the conduct of the war, but on occasion he acted out his fantasy of participating in the fighting. During a visit to McClellan's headquar-ters on the Peninsula in May 1862, Lincoln, accompanied by Secre-tary of War Edwin Stanton and Treasury Secretary Salmon Chase, sailed in a revenue cutter across Hampton Roads toward the Confed-erate-held city of Norfolk. In a moment of surreal adventure, Lincoln and Stanton boarded a smaller boat, sailed to the southern shore, disembarked, and strolled on the Confederate beach for a few dan-gerous minutes. Based on the president's report that the coastline was more navigable than had been supposed, Union infantry went ashore at the same spot the next day and captured Norfolk.

As president, Lincoln traveled little, but when he did leave the

sity Press, 1953–55), 6:327–28; Burlingame and Ettlinger, eds., *Inside Lincoln's White House*, 62–63.

[3] Theodore Calvin Pease and James G. Randall, eds., *The Diary of Orville Hick-man Browning*, 2 vols. (Springfield: Illinois State Historical Library, 1925), 1:523 (January 12, 1862); John G. Nicolay and John Hay, eds., *Complete Works of Abra-ham Lincoln*, 12 vols. (New York: Tandy-Thomas, 1905), 7:141; Burlingame and Ettlinger, eds., *Inside Lincoln's White House*, 63.

White House it was often to get a closer look at the war. He did not have to go far in July 1864, when Jubal Early's rebel raiders approached within shooting distance of Washington. Lincoln took the opportunity to ride out to Fort Stevens on the outskirts of the city to observe the fighting. There he stood on the parapet amid the whistling of enemy bullets while sensible veteran officers took shelter behind the walls; according to legend, one of those officers was the future Supreme Court justice Oliver Wendell Holmes, Jr., who did not recognize the president and yelled at him, "Get down, you damn fool." Lincoln got down, but his appetite for danger was apparently not sated. The following year, during his trip to Ulysses S. Grant's headquarters at City Point in April 1865, he dared to enter the city of Richmond on foot before the embers had cooled from the fires that marked the rebels' withdrawal, and toured the former capital of the Confederacy escorted only by his young son Tad and a few sailors.

These stories raise two questions. First, for what purpose did Lincoln, a lifelong politician with almost no military experience, so consistently seek to participate more directly in the war? Second, what would have happened if Lincoln had gone beyond speculation and observation and assumed the leadership of the Army of the Potomac? The questions are interrelated. Lincoln felt both a personal and public imperative to demonstrate his willingness to share the risks of war, as a matter of honor as well as political leadership. He also saw, as the war went on, that few of the men he was appointing to command were any more qualified or capable than he was. But the particular leadership abilities that made him a great president would not necessarily have made him a great general, or even a good one, and it was fortunate for the Republic that he kept his fantasies in check long enough to allow leaders like Grant and William T. Sherman to emerge and relieve him of the need to imagine himself guiding the Union to victory on the battlefield.

The primary motive for Lincoln to go to war in person was the opportunity to make a public display of his personal bravery. Physical courage, Lincoln knew, was an important aspect of political as well as military leadership in a society that lionized war heroes like George Washington and Andrew Jackson. As a young man, Lincoln had learned first-hand the political value of courage, when he moved to the rough-and-tumble frontier village of New Salem in 1831 and quickly won the respect of the local ruffians by outwrestling their leader, Jack Armstrong. A year later, when the men of New Salem answered the state's call for militia to drive Chief Black Hawk and his people away from their ancestral lands, Lincoln was among the volunteers. So impressive had been his demonstration of courage against Armstrong that Lincoln was elected captain of the New Salem company, a victory that gave him more satisfaction, he wrote in 1860, than any other success in his life.

Lincoln saw no action in the Black Hawk War, but as a congressman in 1848, he used his brief wartime experience to mock Democratic presidential candidate Lewis Cass's pretensions of military heroism. Lincoln took the trouble to attack Cass's military record because he knew that, for many voters, a candidate's bravery in battle seemed to matter more than his views on the issues of the day. This lesson was driven home for Lincoln when his Whig Party won the presidential elections of 1840 and 1848 by nominating former generals William Henry Harrison and Zachary Taylor, whose political qualifications were questionable but whose physical courage was beyond doubt.

If courage was a desirable quality in a leader, honor was indispensable. As Douglas Wilson has persuasively argued, it was Lincoln's interest in, even obsession with, his personal honor that led him to do things in his personal life that otherwise made no sense at all. His 1837 proposal of marriage to Mary Owens, despite her "weatherbeaten" appearance and "want of teeth," was a particularly grotesque example. Lincoln felt obligated by his honor to follow through on what he thought she thought was a promise to marry her if she returned to Springfield from Kentucky, which she did. It was fortunate for all concerned that Owens's common sense exceeded Lincoln's, prompting her to reject his reluctant, honor-driven offer. In his next matrimonial venture, Lincoln found himself engaged to marry Mary Todd, but had second thoughts that led him to break off the engagement. Soon, however, he found the pain of violating his honor (as he perceived it) worse than the prospect of a life with Mary, and so asked for her hand a second time, resulting in marriage in 1842.[4]

A third affair of honor in which Lincoln found himself embroiled, also in 1842, involved Illinois State Auditor James Shields, an adver-

[4] Lincoln to Mrs. Orville H. Browning, April 1, 1838, in *Collected Works of Lincoln*, 1:118.

sary whom Lincoln apparently found a good deal less intimidating
than either Owens or Todd. When Shields challenged Lincoln to a
duel over an insulting newspaper article, Lincoln accepted. Dueling
was illegal in the state, but Lincoln, the lawyer who had preached
"reverence for the laws" as the *"political religion"* of the nation in his
1838 Lyceum address, placed his personal honor above the spirit if
not the letter of the law. He proposed to meet Shields at a location
in Missouri, just across the Mississippi River, where they would fight
using "Cavalry broad swords of the largest size" while standing in a
ten-foot square. Lincoln may have proposed the absurd terms of the
contest in the hopes of turning the whole thing into a joke, but he
was not laughing when he showed up on the appointed day, prepared
to eviscerate the much smaller Shields. At the last moment friends of
the two men found a way to resolve their quarrel. Lincoln was later
embarrassed by the incident and made it a point never to discuss it,
but the fact remained that he had been willing to risk his political
career and his very life rather than compromise his reputation for
personal courage.[5]

One might imagine that as president of the United States, Lincoln
in 1861 could consider his honor validated and his leadership confirmed, without the need to make further displays of his bravery. But
the outbreak of the Civil War changed the definition of leadership,
by elevating the importance of courage. The volunteer armies of both
sides were led largely by amateur officers who found that most of the
skills that had brought them success in civil life were of little use on
the battlefield. These officers may have known how to make grand
speeches, negotiate deals, win friends, fix machines, or raise prize
crops, but most of them could no more maneuver a company across
a pasture than Lincoln could in his Black Hawk War days, when he
once found himself leading his men toward a fence with a gate in the
middle. Unable to remember the proper words of command to send
his line of men endwise through the gate, he ordered them to halt,
fall out, and reform in five minutes, on the other side of the fence.
The typical Civil War volunteer officer, innocent of military training
or experience, could not base his claim to leadership on technical

[5] Address before the Young Men's Lyceum of Springfield, Illinois, January 27,
1838, ibid., 1:108–15, 112; Memorandum of Duel Instructions to Elias H. Merry-
man, [September 19, 1842], ibid., 1:300–301.

competence; only by demonstrating superior bravery could he hope to win the respect of his troops.

President Lincoln was a volunteer captain writ large; his lack of military experience meant that he too had to find a way to demonstrate his fitness as a war leader. His awareness of the importance of courage as an element in wartime leadership was sharpened in February 1861, when he completed his inaugural journey from Springfield to Washington by traveling incognito through Baltimore to avoid a rumored assassination plot. Political cartoonists had a field day with the spectacle of Lincoln sneaking into the capital like a spy rather than a head of state, exaggerating the cloth cap that he wore in place of his characteristic stovepipe hat into a full set of Scottish regalia complete with kilt, or (more humiliating still by the prevailing standards of male honor) portraying him as dressed in women's clothing.

Two other events early in Lincoln's presidency focused his attention on his personal obligations as a war leader. The first was the death of Colonel Elmer Ellsworth at Alexandria, Virginia, on May 24, 1861. Ellsworth, a young Lincoln protégé who had accompanied the inaugural party by train from Illinois, made a profligate display of his bravery by marching his regiment across the Potomac to Alexandria and climbing out onto the roof of a hotel to tear down a Confederate flag that was visible from the White House. For his trouble, Ellsworth was shot by the hotel keeper and became the first Union officer to die in the war.

Lincoln had long used metaphors of combat in his speeches describing the struggle against the expansion of slavery; in Peoria in 1854 he characterized the response of antislavery men to the Kansas-Nebraska Act as a hand-to-hand battle fought with brutal weapons: "[W]e rose each fighting, grasping whatever he could first reach—a scythe—a pitchfork—a chopping axe, or a butcher's cleaver." When he sat to write a moving letter of condolence to the parents of Elmer Ellsworth, killed by a real shotgun rather than a metaphorical farm implement, he must have reflected on his personal responsibility for the consequences of Ellsworth's bravery. Lincoln had never shown any lack of the political courage that he called for in his followers; now that he was asking for much greater sacrifices, what price should he be prepared to pay?[6]

---

[6] Speech at Peoria, Illinois, October 16, 1854, ibid., 2:247–83, 282.

Five months later, at the Battle of Ball's Bluff, Virginia, Lincoln's old political crony Edward Baker was killed in action while leading his troops to defeat. Unlike Ellsworth, Baker was of the same generation as Lincoln. In the 1840s Lincoln, Baker, and John J. Hardin had agreed to support one another in turn in seeking to be the Whig Party candidates for Congress, and in 1846 Lincoln named his second son Edward Baker Lincoln in his friend's honor. That same year Hardin volunteered to serve in the Mexican War, where he was killed at the Battle of Buena Vista, four months after Lincoln was elected to Congress on a platform opposing the war. When Baker fell at Ball's Bluff, Lincoln could not have helped noting that he was the lone survivor of the old Whig leadership of Sangamon County; the others had courageously sacrificed their lives for their country. Moreover, Baker's death was a reminder to Lincoln that his age was no excuse for not serving; his contemporaries were showing themselves quite capable of going to war, and dying, just as nobly as young Colonel Ellsworth.

As president, Lincoln could not very well go to the front at the head of a brigade, as Baker did. But he did do all he could to demonstrate, publicly and privately, that he was as willing as any man to put everything he had, including his life, at risk in the Union cause. After the Scotch cap fiasco, Lincoln swore off any further measures designed to protect him from assassination, and made it his practice to ride alone at night to the Soldier's Home, or walk to the War Department without escort, almost daring his enemies to make attempts on his life. He took irrational risks in the face of the enemy, at Norfolk, Fort Stevens, and Richmond. He accepted the death of his favorite son Willie as a price he had to pay, since he was asking equally painful sacrifices of so many other families, and he overrode his wife's desperate wishes in allowing his oldest boy Robert to join the army, for the same reason. Under the draft law that was enacted midway through the war, conscripted men were permitted to hire substitutes rather than serve in person, and although Lincoln was exempt from the draft (by age as well as occupation) he nonetheless took the trouble to hire a substitute, John Staples of Pennsylvania, to go to war in his place. In sum, he did everything required by the letter of the law and the code of honor that he could do to participate in the war, short of going to the front and taking personal command of the Army of the Potomac.

While that was more than enough for the public and for posterity, it was apparently not enough to satisfy Lincoln's own sense of honor. When he looked at those who were doing the fighting, he must have seen few reasons why he should not be among them. That he was a head of state did not necessarily excuse him from going to war, for although no English king had led his troops into action since George II at Dettingen in 1743, other European monarchs continued to combine military and political leadership throughout Lincoln's lifetime. On June 24, 1859, for example, while attorney Lincoln was engaged in filing legal papers on behalf of his clients, three of the crowned heads of Europe (Napoleon III of France, Franz Josef I of Austria, and Victor Emanuel II of Piedmont) were personally directing their armies in battle at Solferino. Lincoln might have laughed at the idea that he should model his behavior after that of the kings and emperors of the Old World, but he could not so easily dismiss the example set two years later by his Southern counterpart Jefferson Davis, who reacted to news of the battle at Bull Run by riding to the battlefield, eager to inspire his generals and rally his troops with his martial presence.

In 1861 the idea of president-as-general was by no means as outlandish as it would later seem. Washington had ridden into Pennsylvania in 1794 at the head of the militia that he had called from neighboring states to suppress the Whiskey Rebellion, and during the Nullification Crisis of 1832, Jackson had warned South Carolina that he would not hesitate to lead troops into the state and hang John C. Calhoun if necessary to vindicate the authority of the federal government. These examples must have carried weight with Lincoln, for whatever he may have thought of Jackson's politics (or Washington's), he regarded the two men as models of male behavior. He invoked them both in his angry reply to a delegation from Baltimore that urged him to yield to Southern demands in April 1861: "[Y]ou would have me break my oath and surrender the Government without a blow. There is no Washington in that—no Jackson in that—no manhood nor honor in that."[7]

While the demands of manhood and honor pushed Lincoln into making public displays of his courage, the ineffectiveness of his gen-

---

[7] Reply to Baltimore Committee, April 22, 1861, ibid., 4:341.

erals pulled him toward the idea of going to war in person. Physically, he would have been up to the task. He was fifty-two when the war began, younger than Lee and much younger than his own general in chief, Winfield Scott. He was strong, still able to lift an ax by its handle and hold it with his arm outstretched, as he demonstrated one day in the White House to an amused party of onlookers, none of whom could do the same. He had great stamina and relatively good health, and could ride a horse competently if not with elegance. As a youth on the Indiana frontier, he had learned how to endure hardships, and as a lawyer riding the Eighth Judicial Circuit in Illinois, he had regularly traveled great distances in all kinds of weather, lodged in Spartan quarters, eaten poor food, and experienced with his fellow lawyers the camaraderie of an all-male world. Indeed, the relish with which he later recalled his circuit-riding years suggests that he might even have found military campaigning an enjoyable alternative to domestic life in the White House.

Intellectually, Lincoln was no less qualified than many of the generals whom he appointed. He would have been little hampered by his lack of a formal military education, any more than he had allowed his lack of a formal legal education to stop him from becoming the foremost courtroom lawyer in his state. If volunteer officers like John Logan or Nathan Bedford Forrest could command armies successfully without a West Point diploma, there is no reason to suppose that Abraham Lincoln could not have done the same. Lincoln himself sometimes doubted the value of formal educational qualifications for officers. "I personally wish Jacob R. Freese, of New-Jersey to be appointed a Colonel for a colored regiment," Lincoln wrote to Stanton of an officer candidate who had failed a qualifying examination in 1863, "and this regardless of whether he can tell the exact shade of Julius Caesar's hair." The curriculum at West Point before the Civil War was, after all, aimed at turning out junior officers with engineering skills, not at producing leaders of great armies, for which antebellum America had little need. It is widely noted that Lincoln took time during the war's first winter to borrow from the Library of Congress a military textbook written by General Halleck, apparently to teach himself the fundamentals of military science much as he had taught himself law or the geometry of Euclid years earlier. More significant is that Lincoln did not bother to follow up his initial reading with further study, once he realized that army-level strategy is a matter more of common sense and politics than of technical military skill.[8]

That Lincoln had the strategic insight to be a successful general is clear. As the war progressed, he demonstrated an increasingly sure grasp of the basic principles of war. In September 1861 he drafted a "Memorandum for a plan of campaign" that was the closest thing to an overall strategic plan produced by anyone in the Federal administration, with the exception perhaps of Scott's much-derided Anaconda Plan. In his advice to his generals, Lincoln displayed an intuitive understanding of such concepts as the advantage of interior lines and the importance of focusing on the objective. At the outset of the Gettysburg campaign, Lincoln calmly replied to Major General Joseph Hooker's proposal to go south and take Richmond while Lee was invading the North: "I think *Lee's* Army, and not *Richmond,* is your true objective point." When Grant explained his plan for the Union armies in the East and West to act at the same time, either advancing or pinning down the enemy in their front, Lincoln was delighted to find a general who shared his idea that, as he put it, "Those not skinning can hold a leg."[9]

In imagining how Lincoln would have fared as a general, not too much should be made of his skill as a strategist. Unsuccessful generals like McClellan and Hooker were able to conceive of strategic plans no less brilliant than those of Grant or Sherman. It was the character of the plans' authors that determined success or failure, more than the nuances of their strategies. Here again, Lincoln compares favorably with many of his generals. Unlike McClellan, who sullenly blamed the sorry outcome of his cleverly designed Peninsula Campaign on the administration, Lincoln was not afraid to take responsibility for failure as well as success. Unlike the luckless Ambrose Burnside, who in December 1862 relentlessly sent brigade after brigade up Marye's Heights at Fredericksburg long after any chance of victory was gone, Lincoln could admit when he had made a mistake; consider his humble letter to Grant after Vicksburg, in which he confessed that he had doubted Grant's strategy in approaching the city from the south, and then wrote, "I now wish to make the personal

---

[8] Lincoln to Edwin M. Stanton, November 11, 1863, ibid., 7:11.

[9] Lincoln to Joseph Hooker, June 10, 1863, ibid., 6:257; Burlingame and Ettlinger, eds., *Inside Lincoln's White House,* 194.

acknowledgment that you were right, and I was wrong." Unlike Meade, who regularly called councils of war to gain the advice of his generals, Lincoln did not rely overmuch on his advisors and made some of his most important decisions without, or even against, the advice of his cabinet. Unlike Don Carlos Buell (or William Rosecrans, or especially McClellan), Lincoln was neither a procrastinator nor a perfectionist, yet neither was he rash, for he had learned during his long political career how to accept temporary delay and even defeat while pursuing a larger overall goal.[10]

Lincoln's performance in the role of commander in chief provides further evidence of how well he might have done in the field. Early in the war he occasionally usurped the authority of his subordinates and concerned himself with details better left to those on the scene. During the Confederate invasion of Kentucky in 1861, for example, he sent numerous telegrams directing the movements of individual regiments and gunboats. By the summer of 1862 Lincoln had learned to delegate such minutiae and to focus on larger issues, so that when Confederate cavalry raiders again entered Kentucky in August 1862, sowing panic among local authorities, Lincoln responded with a single message to Major General Halleck: "They are having a stampede in Kentucky. Please look to it."[11]

Yet for all of Lincoln's qualifications, it remains almost impossible to picture Honest Abe as a man on horseback. Although he equaled or excelled most of his generals in physical health, mental acuity, strength of character, and ability to learn, he remained a profoundly unmilitary figure. When General Rosecrans complained about some imagined snub he received in the parceling out of promotions, Lincoln answered, "Truth to speak, I do not appreciate this matter of rank on paper, as you officers do." Lincoln did not see the world as his professional officers did, in regard to rank or anything else. His was the world of politics, characterized by compromise, negotiation, persuasion, and deal making, a world in which even those who attained the highest levels of success were still ultimately responsible to and at the mercy of their constituents. The military world, based on hierarchy, obedience, and command, was alien to him. He regarded his brief immersion in it during the Black Hawk War as a

---

[10] Lincoln to Ulysses S. Grant, July 13, 1863, in *Collected Works of Lincoln*, 6:326.
[11] Lincoln to Henry W. Halleck, July 13, 1862, ibid., 5:322.

subject for self-mockery. In an 1852 speech lampooning Democratic presidential candidate Franklin Pierce's claims of military glory, Lincoln described the last muster of the Springfield militia: "Among the rules and regulations, no man is to wear more than five pounds of cod-fish for epaulets, or more than thirty yards of bologna sausages for a sash; and no two men are to dress alike, and if any two should dress alike the one that dresses most alike is to be fined. . . . Flags they had too, with devices and mottoes, one of which latter is, 'We'll fight till we run, and we'll run till we die.'" Lincoln honored those who served the nation in the army and navy, but it is safe to say that the values, ideals, and practices of the military world left Lincoln distinctly unimpressed.[12]

Conversely, many of Lincoln's traits that served him well in the courtroom and on the campaign trail would have been out of place on the battlefield, beginning with his sense of humor. It is difficult to name a funny general, perhaps because the horror and misery of war are not laughing matters. In 1862 Lincoln experienced a public relations debacle after his visit to McClellan's headquarters at Antietam, when a report circulated that he had asked his companion Ward Hill Lamon to sing a comic ditty called "Picayune Butler" while he toured the scene of the recent battle. Anti-Lincoln cartoons pictured the president calling for a funny song, oblivious to the dead and dying soldiers at his feet. Even his own cabinet at times criticized his habit of reading funny stories in moments of national drama, a habit that Lincoln justified as a way of releasing tension and preserving his mental health. Effective though it was as a tool for persuasion or comic relief, Lincoln's humor would have found no safe political outlet while he was leading men to their deaths.

Similarly, Lincoln's fundamental gentleness and mercy, which contributed to his greatness as a president, would have sabotaged him as a military commander. For Lincoln, one of the few reliefs from the cares of office was the opportunity to pardon soldiers who had been convicted of desertion, sleeping on guard duty, and other violations of the articles of war, if he could find any extenuating circumstances. "It makes me rested, after a day's hard work," he told Schuyler Colfax, "if I can find some good excuse for saving a man's life." But if

---

[12] Lincoln to William S. Rosecrans, March 17, 1863, ibid., 6:139; speech to the Springfield Scott Club, August 14 and 26, 1852, ibid., 2:135–57, 149–50.

these pardons rested Lincoln, they made more work for his generals, some of whom claimed that Lincoln's well-known tenderness made it harder for them to enforce discipline. For Lincoln to succeed as a general, he would have had to deny himself the comfort of caring about individuals, and followed instead the example of Sherman, who observed in the summer of 1864: "I begin to regard the death and mangling of a couple thousand men as a small affair, a kind of morning dash. And it may be well that we become so hardened."[13]

Generals like Sherman, Grant, Thomas, Lee, Jackson, and the other great commanders of the war were not ignorant of the terrible sacrifices they asked of their men (Sherman claimed, "I value their lives as much as my own"), but they were hardened to war's costs, to the point that they did not hesitate to act with malice toward the enemy, and charity for none. Further, these generals shared a supreme egotism that allowed them to send thousands of young men to their deaths with equanimity, confident that they were making the right military decisions. Men who lacked such self-assuredness were bound to fail. When McClellan, for all his bluster, wrote to his wife after the Battle of Antietam, "Those in whose judgment I rely tell me that I fought the battle splendidly & that it was a masterpiece of art," he revealed as pathetic a lack of self-confidence as one can imagine coming from the pen of a person in his position. The great generals believed in themselves and did not rely on the judgment of others to validate their actions.[14]

Lincoln had no lack of confidence in his ability to make political and moral decisions, but in military matters he frankly sought to rely on the judgment of others. In the war's first year he met frequently with his generals in chief, first Scott and then McClellan, and when he lost faith in McClellan he traveled to West Point to consult again with the retired Scott. In July 1862 when he called "Old Brains" Hal-

---

[13] Schuyler Colfax, *Life and Principles of Abraham Lincoln* (Philadelphia: J. B. Rodgers, 1865), 18; Sherman to Ellen Sherman, June 30, 1864, in Mills Lane, ed., *"War Is Hell!": William T. Sherman's Personal Narrative of His March through Georgia* (Savannah, Ga.: Beehive Press, 1974), 59.

[14] Sherman to John Sherman, December 31, 1864, in Rachel Sherman Thorndike, ed., *The Sherman Letters: Correspondence between General and Senator Sherman from 1837 to 1891* (New York: Da Capo Press, 1894), 241–42; McClellan to Mary Ellen McClellan, September 18, [1862], in Stephen W. Sears, ed., *The Civil War Papers of George B. McClellan: Selected Correspondence, 1860–1865* (New York: Ticknor & Fields, 1989), 469.

leck to Washington to become general in chief, he expected Halleck to serve as his personal military adviser. In December 1862, when a number of high-ranking officers in the Army of the Potomac disagreed with the strategy proposed by the army's commander, Burnside, Lincoln shrank from mediating the conflict and referred it to Halleck. "If in such a difficulty as this you do not help," he wrote to his general in chief, "you fail me precisely in the point for which I sought your assistance." That others sensed Lincoln's lack of confidence in his military judgment is suggested by the difficulties he experienced in trying to motivate his generals to act more aggressively. From McDowell at Bull Run, to McClellan on the Peninsula, to Buell in East Tennessee, to Meade after Gettysburg, to Thomas in Nashville, Lincoln sent a stream of orders, suggestions, pleas, and threats to try to spur his generals into action. In every case, as he admitted to Hay in reference to Meade, "nothing I could say or do could make the army move."[15]

As president, Lincoln was able to employ his political skills, especially his gift of persuasion. He was able to strike an exquisite balance between mercy and determination, and to identify and define the complexities and ambiguities of a war in which "[b]oth [sides] read the same Bible, and pray to the same God; and each invokes His aid against the other." The demands of battlefield command would have changed this. To Lincoln's personal and political detriment, he would have had to forego persuasion for command. He would have had been denied the opportunity to express the basic kindness of his nature, suppressing his conciliatory side for long stretches of time, perhaps until it atrophied. His sympathy for the Southern people would have been tested by daily confrontations with them, as enemy soldiers, as sullen prisoners, as implacable guerillas, as bitter refugees.[16]

Worse, he would have found himself in situations where success comes only to those who, by training and temperament, are certain of their actions. Lincoln's humble awareness that "events have controlled me" as much as he controlled events may have made him a better man, but it would not have made him a better general. Lincoln's recognition of the humanity of the enemy, and his sympathy for even the miscreants among his own soldiers, would have been

---

[15] Lincoln to Henry W. Halleck, January 1, 1863, in *Collected Works of Lincoln*, 6:31; Burlingame and Ettlinger, eds., *Inside Lincoln's White House*, 62.

[16] Second Inaugural Address, March 4, 1865, in *Collected Works of Lincoln*, 8:332–33.

no advantage on the battlefield. In short, Lincoln could not have commanded well without betraying the qualities for which he is best remembered.[17]

But what if Lincoln had indulged his fantasy of military command not for months at a time but just once, in July 1863? What if he had taken over at the moment when, as he wrote in the letter addressed to Meade, "Our Army held the war in the hollow of their hand & they would not close it"? Could he have closed it? Could Lincoln have sealed the fate of the Army of Northern Virginia and ended the war in an afternoon? There is no good reason to think so. Historians have debated this hypothetical situation at excruciating length, but the fact remains that no Civil War field army was ever attacked and destroyed on the battlefield. In only one battle, at Nashville in December 1864, was a field army defeated so badly that it could not fight again, and that occurred only after John Bell Hood had used up his depleted, demoralized, ill-fed Army of Tennessee in a series of suicidal attacks against George Thomas's defensive works at Franklin. But Lee was not Hood; one Pickett's Charge had been enough for him, and he would fight all his remaining battles with his men behind breastworks or in trenches, or sheltered by woods from the terrible federal artillery. He would not throw his men away again. Had Meade, or Lincoln, attacked Lee's army after Gettysburg, the results would have differed little from those of the Wilderness, Spottsylvania, or Cold Harbor: thousands more dead and wounded, but both armies still capable of fighting.[18]

Once Lee's men began to rely on prepared defensive positions instead of fighting in the open, they posed a tactical conundrum for the attacking forces that would continue to puzzle military thinkers until the end of the First World War. Lincoln, for all his virtues, did not have the answer to that problem. Fortunately, for his reputation and for the fate of the nation, Lincoln's virtues did include a high degree of self-knowledge. After gaining the therapeutic value of writing his letter criticizing Meade for failing to destroy Lee's army, Lincoln filed it away, unsent. After venting his emotions by telling young Hay that "If I had gone up there, I could have whipped them myself," Lincoln returned to the business of being president, and let the idea remain forever a fantasy.

---

[17] Lincoln to Albert G. Hodges, April 4, 1864, ibid., 7:281–82.

[18] Burlingame and Ettlinger, eds., *Inside Lincoln's White House,* 64–65.

7

"In for Four Years More": The Army of Northern Virginia and the United States Presidential Election of 1864

J. Tracy Power

IN THE SUMMER of 1864 the oppressive heat in the seemingly endless trenches, earthworks, and reserve lines stretching over thirty miles from Petersburg to the Confederate capital at Richmond matched the apprehension of Union and Confederate soldiers—and most Northern and Southern white civilians as well—over the outcome of the presidential election being held in the United States that November. After three years of a bloody civil war the likes of which no one could have predicted, a sitting president was facing the unprecedented challenge of seeking reelection with the fate of the Union still very much in doubt—indeed, in many ways, tied intimately to the result of the election itself.

The Republican Party, less than a decade old, had been founded with the outright abolition of slavery as its ultimate goal. Many white Southerners viewed Abraham Lincoln's election as the sixteenth president of the United States in 1860 as a threat to their "peculiar institution," responding with the secession of the Deep South during the winter of 1860–61, followed by the secession of the Upper South once the war began in April. Lincoln's party, renamed the National Union Party for the duration of the war, faced fierce opposition from the Democratic Party, whose more vocal members were accused of

Portions of this essay are revised from material originally published in the author's *Lee's Miserables: Life in the Army of Northern Virginia from the Wilderness to Appomattox* (Chapel Hill: University of North Carolina Press, 1998). Reprinted by permission of the University of North Carolina Press.

being misguided opponents of the war at best and traitors at worst. Though many "war Democrats" across the North supported the war effort, they did so more out of patriotic motives rather than any real enthusiasm for Lincoln or the Republicans. They were both outnumbered and less influential than the "peace Democrats," who believed that the war was a dismal failure on all fronts. They pointed to the dreadful casualties piling up every day on the battlefields and in the trenches of Virginia and Georgia; to controversies over the Emancipation Proclamation and the enlistment of black troops into the U.S. Army; and to the administration's willingness to trample state rights and individual liberties in order to pursue its policies. They argued, furthermore, that Lincoln and the Republicans had transformed a war to save the United States into a war to abolish slavery, and that nothing, not even the concept of the Union, was worth the wholesale destruction of American lives, property, and wealth that had occurred since the spring of 1861.

As the war dragged on into its fourth summer with no clear resolution in sight, there seemed to be no realistic hope that either of the major Federal armies could win one clear and decisive victory that might end the fighting at one stroke. Countless observers on both sides pointed to the stalemates as conclusive evidence supporting their fears or their hopes that a war for the Union might never be won. In both of the major campaigns so far that year the Confederate armies—the Army of Northern Virginia and the Army of Tennessee, commanded by Robert E. Lee and Joseph E. Johnston, respectively—had frustrated the best-laid plans of the Federal armies facing them–the Army of the Potomac, under the watchful eye of Ulysses S. Grant, newly appointed general in chief of the United States armies, and the armies of the Cumberland, Ohio, and Tennessee, under the overall command of William T. Sherman. The spring and early summer campaigns in Virginia from the Wilderness to Petersburg and in Georgia from Dalton to Atlanta had cost thousands of Yankee and Rebel lives but had accomplished little else of any consequence. Some saw Grant and Sherman as now resorting to—or being forced to accept—campaigns in which maneuver and position would largely take the place of frontal assaults against well-entrenched armies in field fortifications or more formal siege lines.

Many Confederates, whether soldiers, politicians, newspaper editors, or civilians, believed that the outcome of the presidential election in the North represented the South's best chance for ending the war before 1865. There was no hope for foreign intervention by Great Britain or France, and little reason to believe that a smashing battlefield victory in the Napoleonic style might result in the surrender or even destruction of a major Federal army and convince Lincoln's administration to sue for peace. Observers across the South viewed the election as a significant way to gauge the depth and breadth of the North's commitment to the war—and to the Union itself. If Lincoln lost the election to a Democratic candidate, almost certain to run on a platform that claimed the Union war effort had failed and that peace should be pursued aggressively, then the Confederacy might very well win its independence, or at least gain a temporary armistice, by a settlement that might even preserve slavery. If Confederates in Virginia and Georgia could only keep Grant and Sherman at bay through the summer and into early fall, denying Lincoln's administration the political benefit of any battlefield victory, then the Northern people might very well decide that there was no hope of defeating the "so-called Confederate states," as Lincoln consistently referred to Jefferson Davis's nascent nation. Even the twin disasters of Gettysburg and Vicksburg a year earlier were not quite as decisive as they would appear to be later, after Appomattox and the luxury of hindsight allowed participants, observers, and generations of historians to proclaim that the events of the first week in July 1863 had demonstrated the inevitability of Union victory and Confederate defeat.[1]

Numerous officers and men in the Army of Northern Virginia, the Confederacy's most famous and most successful army, were confident that they would hold Petersburg and Richmond against any maneuvers or assaults the Federals might launch against them, no

---

[1] For the election of 1864, see David E. Long, *The Jewel of Liberty: Abraham Lincoln's Re-election and the End of Slavery* (Mechanicsburg, Pa.: Stackpole Books, 1994); John C. Waugh, *Reelecting Lincoln: The Battle for the 1864 Presidency* (New York: Crown Publishers, 1997); and Albert Castel, "The Atlanta Campaign and the Presidential Election of 1864: How the South Almost Won by Not Losing," in his *Winning and Losing in the Civil War: Essays and Stories* (Columbia: University of South Carolina Press, 1996), 15–32. For the election as viewed through Confederate eyes, see Larry E. Nelson, *Bullets, Ballots, and Rhetoric: Confederate Policy for the United States Presidential Contest of 1864* (Tuscaloosa: University of Alabama Press, 1980); and William C. Davis, "The Turning Point That Wasn't: The Confederates and the Election of 1864," in his *The Cause Lost: Myths and Realities of the Confederacy* (Lawrence: University Press of Kansas, 1996), 127–47.

matter what other reverses occurred elsewhere. They often referred to General Lee—and themselves as well—as the only hope of the South in 1864, and described their army in such terms as "the mainstay of the Confederacy," or "of extraordinary quality, tho' we say it ourselves."[2] Some of them, frustrated at the constant bad news from other theaters, made a point of unfavorable comparisons between their army and other Confederate armies, claiming, "the Army of Northern Virginia alone is the last hope of the South, to say nothing of what may be done elsewhere," or that "unless our troops *fight* and our generals do better, Georgia and South Carolina will be lost, the army of northern Virginia cannot do every thing."[3] Captain Watson D. Williams wrote his fiancée from Richmond on July 4, hoping to cheer up her discouraged father at home in Texas. "The Confederacy is all right," he reassured her. "Safe; perfectly so. It is almost the universal opinion here that this campaign will virtually end the war."[4] Officers and men such as Williams, though somewhat disappointed at their inability to win a decisive victory over Grant and the Army of the Potomac after two months of fighting, believed that General Lee still might find a way to do so.

Some members of Lee's army believed that the campaign from the Wilderness through Cold Harbor, in a ghastly month in which they inflicted more than fifty thousand casualties on their foes in the Army of the Potomac and lost about thirty thousand casualties themselves, demonstrated that they could withstand anything, even carnage that made the battles of 1861, 1862, and 1863 pale in comparison. Many Confederates viewed Grant's perseverance in spite of such staggering losses as based on Lincoln's need for a clear-cut battlefield vic-

---

[2] John Bratton to his wife, September 5, 1864, John Bratton Papers, South Carolina Department of Archives and History, Columbia, S.C. (hereafter cited to as ScCoAH); John Hampden Chamberlayne to Mrs. Sally Grattan, August 19, 1864, in C. G. Chamberlayne, ed., *Ham Chamberlayne–Virginian: Letters and Papers of an Artillery Officer in the War for Southern Independence 1861–1865* (Richmond, Va.: Press of the Dietz Printing Company, 1932), 259.

[3] Ezekiel D. Graham to Miss Laura Mann, September 14, 1864, United Daughters of the Confederacy, Georgia Division, Typescripts, Volume 2, Georgia Department of Archives and History, Atlanta, Ga.; Charles Kerrison to his uncle, September 19, 1864, Kerrison Family Papers, South Caroliniana Library, University of South Carolina, Columbia (hereafter cited as ScU).

[4] Watson D. Williams to his fiancée, July 4, 1864, Watson Dugat Williams Papers, Confederate Research Center, Hill Junior College, Hillsboro, Tex. (hereafter cited as TxHiC).

tory—no matter how modest—before the fall election, as much as on any long-range Federal hopes of defeating Lee or taking Richmond. "God grant that his failure this time may be complete," a South Carolinian hoped, "& that with it we may have an end of this horrible tragedy."[5] A few soldiers went so far as to accuse the United States and the Northern people in general, and Lincoln in particular, of an almost pathological hatred of the Confederacy and its people. Captain Andrew Jackson McBride of the 10th Georgia believed that the dead of both armies had been "slaughtered at the bidding of Abraham Lincoln," exclaiming, "Alas! yes almost before the shriek of his wounded who perished in the flames of the burning wood in the Wilderness and at Spotsylvania have died upon our ears, almost before their blood has dried upon the earth, he is ready with an unparalleled cruelty to offer new victims."[6] One common theme of Confederate correspondents and diarists throughout the summer and into fall was that Southern soldiers and civilians alike should persevere on to victory and independence rather than submit to such a cruel enemy. The ghosts of thousands of dead officers and men would certainly haunt those left behind if their sacrifices proved to have been made in vain. "I am sick at heart," Sergeant John F. Sale of the

---

[5] John W. McLure to his wife, July 28, 1864, McLure Family Papers, ScU; see also, for other examples from the summer, Watson D. Williams to his fiancée, June 16, 1864, Williams Papers, TxHiC; and Stephen Elliott to his wife, June 25, 1864, Elliott Family Papers, ScU. For examples from the period just before the election on November 8, see Wade Hampton to his sister, October 11, 1864, in Charles E. Cauthen, ed., *Family Letters of the Three Wade Hamptons 1782–1901* (Columbia: University of South Carolina Press, 1953), 109–10; William J. Pegram to his sister, October 24, 1864, Pegram-Johnson-McIntosh Family Papers, Virginia Historical Society, Richmond, Va. (hereafter cited as ViHi); William T. Poague to his mother, in Monroe F. Cockrell, ed., *Gunner with Stonewall: Reminiscences of William Thomas Poague, Lieutenant, Captain, Major and Lieutenant Colonel of Artillery, Army of Northern Virginia, CSA, 1861–65: A Memoir Written for His Children in 1903* (Jackson, Tenn.: McCowat-Mercer Press, 1957), 141; and Edward Laight Wells to his mother, November 9, 1864, in Daniel E. Huger Smith et al., eds., *Mason Smith Family Letters 1860–1868* (Columbia: University of South Carolina Press, 1950), 146–47.

[6] Andrew J. McBride to his wife, May 29, 1864, Andrew J. McBride Papers, Duke University, Durham, N.C. (hereafter cited as NcD). See also, for example, Robert C. Mabry to his wife, August 27, 1864, Robert C. Mabry Papers, North Carolina State Archives, Raleigh (hereafter cited as Nc-Ar); Charles Kerrison to his sister, September 27, 1864, Kerrison Family Papers, ScU; William T. Poague to his mother, November 4, 1864, in Cockrell, ed., *Gunner with Stonewall*, 143; and Henry Calvin Conner to his wife, November 4, 1864, Henry Calvin Conner Papers, ScU.

12th Virginia wrote in his diary, "when I look over the past and reflect over the many valued ones we brought from home and have left on every field and portion of this vast burial ground and think can all this brave blood and these vacant homes be of no avail."[7] Charles Kerrison, an aide to the colonel of the 2nd South Carolina, wrote even more pointedly, "War to the knife or death, alone can save us. . . . We have lost too much, our dead lie too thick upon the many battle fields to pause now without gaining liberty. Twould be madness and murder."[8] A member of Pickett's Division cautioned that those in the army and at home should not rely on the almost constant rumors of peace that summer, arguing, "It is certain that our generals and the armies under them are the only peace-makers just now."[9]

Other soldiers, still willing to do their part, were considerably less enthusiastic in support of continued fighting—or less willing to express such opinions in writing. They seemed more interested in widespread indications that their Federal counterparts, and the Northern people as well, were becoming as war-weary as they were, perhaps even more so. Conversations with Yankees across the Petersburg-Richmond lines who traded Northern newspapers and coffee for Southern newspapers and tobacco, editorials and news articles from New York and other Northern papers, and second- or third-hand reports of comrades' conversations with enemy prisoners or deserters all led many Confederates to believe, as one Georgian wrote his sister, "this may be the last year of the war. . . . I think most of the fighting is already over."[10]

[7] John F. Sale, Diary, September 6, 1864, John F. Sale Papers, Library of Virginia, Richmond (hereafter cited as Vi); see also, for example, Joseph F. Maides to his mother, September 23, 1864, J. Francis Maides Papers, NcD; Stephen D. Ramseur to his wife, October 2, 1864, Stephen Dodson Ramseur Papers, Southern Historical Collection, University of North Carolina, Chapel Hill (hereafter cited as NcU); and Alfred M. Scales to his wife, October 9, 1864, Alfred M. Scales Papers, Nc-Ar.

[8] Charles Kerrison to his sister, September 27, 1864, Kerrison Family Papers, ScU.

[9] "Soldier," Pickett's Division, August 2, 1864, in *Richmond Sentinel*, August 6, 1864.

[10] Arthur B. Simms to his sister, July 3, 1864, in Jane Bonner Peacock, ed., "A Georgian's View of War in Virginia: The Civil War Letters of A. B. Simms," *Atlanta Historical Journal* 23, no. 2 (January 1979): 113; see also, for example, Watson D. Williams to his fiancée, June 16, 1864, Watson Dugat Williams Papers, TxHiC; John W. McLure to his wife, July 28, 1864, McLure Family Papers, ScU; William A. Kelly, Diary, August 31, 1864, William Aiken Kelly Papers, College of Charleston, Charleston, S.C. (hereafter cited as ScCC); Abner E. McGarity to his wife, Septem-

It was indeed over for many reluctant Federal soldiers. As numerous Union regiments completed their three-year terms of enlistment and mustered out of service, entirely new units replaced them along the lines. Many, if not most, of these were made up of conscripts, either native-born men who had either somehow managed to stay out of the army up to that point or foreign-born men who were induced to enlist in the hope of a cash bounty or sometimes nothing more than a drink or two. Those who found it impossible to adjust to a soldier's life, whether after an initial trial by fire or simply after a short while under siege, often decided that desertion, even to the Confederate lines, was their best way out of their predicament. The cumulative effects of almost constant combat from the Wilderness to Cold Harbor and the day-to-day tension of life in the trenches on the Petersburg-Richmond front convinced some gloomy Federals that this was a war that could not be won, and persuaded a few of them that it was also a war that they wanted no part of. Some of them, whether all-too-willing prisoners or outright deserters, said as much to Confederates they encountered. "[M]any declare that their men won't fight much longer," Colonel David Lang of the 8th Florida reported after interviewing a group of demoralized enemy prisoners in the aftermath of Cold Harbor.[11] Southerners believed, with some reason, that numbers of their foes across the way were so ready for peace that they would accept something less than victory if it would only end, and soon. One Federal among many who held that view was described by a private in the 2nd Vermont, in the Sixth Corps of the Army of the Potomac. "I have been out here long enough," he said (during a discussion of the upcoming presidential election), "and now I want to go home and so do you." As Wilbur Fisk explained in a letter to a newspaper back home, his fellow Yankee's opinion was that "The war had lasted long enough and it was time to have the trouble settled."[12] For every Federal soldier ready to give up and go

ber 1, 1864, in Edmund Cody Burnett, ed., "Letters of a Confederate Surgeon: Dr. Abner Embry McGarity, 1862–1865, Part IV," *Georgia Historical Quarterly* 30, no. 1 (March 1946): 37; and Jacob Shook to Julia Deane, September 4, 1864, Julia Deane Papers, NcD.

[11] David Lang to his cousin, June 7, 1864, in Bertram H. Groene, ed., "Civil War Letters of Colonel David Lang," *Florida Historical Quarterly* 54, no. 3 (January 1976): 364.

[12] Wilbur Fisk to the *Green Mountain Freeman* (Montpelier, Vt.), October 12, 1864, in Emil and Ruth Rosenblatt, eds., *Hard Marching Every Day: The Civil War*

home, however, there were many more still willing, even determined, to see the war through to the end, an end that for them meant nothing less than Union victory and Confederate defeat.

Public opinion in the North was in many ways largely dependent on the progress—or lack of it—being made by Grant and Sherman. Many observers thought that the upcoming presidential election would be a referendum not only on Lincoln and his administration but also on the war itself and whether the Union and emancipation had been, or would ever be, worth the sacrifices made so far or likely to be made in the foreseeable future. The major Northern newspapers, such as Horace Greeley's *New York Tribune,* James Gordon Bennett's *New York Herald,* both often remarkably critical of Lincoln, or Henry J. Raymond's *New York Times,* a staunch supporter of the president, spilled gallons of opinionated ink on the stalemate and on the election throughout the grim months of July and August. Greeley, who believed that emancipation was every bit as holy a cause as the Union, was impatient for results and thought that Lincoln was unequal to the task before him, stating flatly, "Mr. Lincoln is already beaten. He cannot be elected."[13] Bennett, on the other hand, believed that the preservation of the Union was the only legitimate reason for the war and thought that the radical members of the Republican Party who had forced emancipation on Lincoln risked the destruction of the United States. "What has President Lincoln done to entitle him to a re-election?" a Bennett editorial had asked even before the spring campaigns opened, arguing that "his deplorable mismanagement of our most important armies, with . . . disastrous and alarming consequences," disqualified him for a second term and that Grant would make a better candidate and better president.[14] Raymond, in contrast to both Greeley and Bennett, believed that Lincoln was the right man at the right time, and worked tirelessly behind the scenes to galvanize support among Northern soldiers and civilians alike, claiming that Lincoln's reelection would "do more to demoralize the rebellion, than twenty National victories in the field" and that it would bring about the "quick and final collapse" of the

---

Letters of Private Wilbur Fisk, 1861–1865 (Lawrence: University Press of Kansas, 1992), 264.

[13] Quoted in Waugh, *Reelecting Lincoln,* 270.

[14] *New York Herald,* January 29, 1864, quoted ibid., 101.

Confederacy.[15] Confederate soldiers who read editorials criticizing Lincoln and predicting his defeat at the polls, whether in the original Northern papers or as reprinted in the Southern press, sometimes mentioned them approvingly in their letters home that summer and fall. "If we can only be successful here & at Atlanta," one of Lee's staff officers wrote from Petersburg in late July, "even in maintaining our present positions, I imagine we might look forward to peace with well grounded hopes. The discussions of the subject at the North, show that they are getting very tired of the fruitless prosecution of the War, & a few more successes on our part would make them willing to give it up altogether, at least I trust it may be so."[16]

It seemed to some Confederates as if they had ample opportunities to win such successes before the end of July. What began at the beginning of the summer as a campaign to clear Federal forces from the Shenandoah Valley, for which Lee detached a significant portion of his army under Jubal A. Early, had by mid-July reached the very outskirts of Washington itself. Though Early's raid into Maryland, the District of Columbia, and Pennsylvania accomplished nothing of lasting significance, it did provide a momentary boost to Southern morale and a corresponding, if short-lived, blow to Northern morale by playing on fears for the safety of the capital. In Georgia, meanwhile, Davis's patience with Johnston was worn past any reasonable limits. Frustrated by Johnston's inability to prevent Sherman from advancing to the gates of Atlanta and his unwillingness to share his plans with any Confederate civil or military authorities, Davis removed him from command of the Army of Tennessee on July 18. He replaced Johnston with John B. Hood, a veteran division commander in the Army of Northern Virginia who had risen to corps command in the western theater and who would not abandon Atlanta without a fight. Hood's assaults against Sherman in the battles of Peachtree Creek, Atlanta, and Ezra Church on July 20, 22, and 28 blocked the Federal advance and gave renewed hope, if only temporarily, to those Southerners who believed that fighting Yankees was preferable to retreating from them, but cost the Army of Tennessee officers and men it could not afford to lose. Near Petersburg, meanwhile, Confederates who looked daily for the one great fight that might decide

---

[15] *New York Times*, October 1, 5, and 7, 1864, quoted ibid., 323.
[16] John W. McLure to his wife, July 28, 1864, McLure Family Papers, ScU.

the fate of that city—and perhaps Richmond as well—were astonished by the Battle of the Crater on July 30, in which Grant detonated
four tons of gunpowder under Lee's lines in an attempt to force a
breakthrough but was unable to take advantage of the opportunity.
Operations in the Shenandoah, around Atlanta, and along the Petersburg-Richmond front seemed, at least for the moment, to lend credence to the belief that the South could hold out for the rest of the
summer and well into the fall.

A few members of the Army of Northern Virginia, just as gloomy
and demoralized as some of their counterparts in the Army of the
Potomac, were less enthusiastic at the prospect of fighting for
months, perhaps years, to come. Some of them feared that the war
might last indefinitely unless something—whether a major Confederate victory on the battlefield or the outcome of the election in the
North—forced the issue. Private Benjamin Mason of the 60th Alabama wrote sadly to his wife and children, "This cruel war is going
on and I am in it and cant help my self."[17] A Virginian cautioned
about the same time, "If some strong, very strong signs of peace
do not soon make their appearance I fear for the fortitude of our
soldiers."[18]

Other Confederates, more optimistic for the time being, hoped
that the Democratic convention held in Chicago at the end of August
might produce just those "very strong signs of peace" in the form of a
presidential candidate who might defeat Lincoln's bid for reelection.
General George B. McClellan, former commander of the Army of
the Potomac, was nominated on August 31, with George H. Pendle-
ton, a prominent "peace Democrat," for his running mate. The second plank of the platform claimed that the war was an utter failure
and that "Justice, humanity, liberty and the public welfare demand
that immediate efforts be made for a cessation of hostilities."[19]
Though the Democrats insisted on the preservation of the Union,
their position that four years of war had been for nothing left them—
and McClellan, as their candidate—vulnerable to charges that they
were Copperheads, outright traitors, or even conspirators in league

---

[17] Benjamin Mason to his wife and children, September 1, 1864, Benjamin Mason
Papers, Auburn University, Auburn, Ala.
[18] John F. Sale, Diary, September 6, 1864, Sale Papers, Vi.
[19] Quoted in Phillip Shaw Paludan, *The Presidency of Abraham Lincoln,* American
Presidency Series (Lawrence: University Press of Kansas, 1994), 283.

with the Confederates. Within the week McClellan accepted the Democratic nomination in a letter that made it plain that he repudiated the peace plank, explaining that he "could not look in the face of my gallant comrades of the army and navy who have survived so many bloody battles, and tell them that their labors and the sacrifices of so many of our slain and wounded brethren had been in vain."[20] It soon became obvious to most thoughtful observers in the North, though not to many in the South who wanted desperately to believe otherwise, that McClellan would never give up the Union for the sake of peace.

Rumors circulated through Lee's army about this time that the end of the war might be at hand after all. "I heare a heap of talk heare about the army mistress not to fight no more for a surten length of time," a North Carolinian wrote his sister the day the Democratic convention opened. "It is hope[d] they will come to some conclusion for an honorable peace. I am tired of this war."[21] A South Carolinian echoed those sentiments, observing, "I do hope an honourable peace may be brought about this fall for I am Sick and tired of camp and the teriable Slaughter of human Life which is going on from day to day."[22] Captain Frank Coker, a Georgian serving as adjutant of an artillery battalion in the Third Corps, wrote an impassioned letter home in mid-August, exclaiming,

> The war seems to drag terribly slow to those who are suffering its hardships, separated from all that can give them happiness here below. Hundreds of thousands, yes, *millions* of hearts are praying today in silent agony for it to close. . . . Three months *must* make a terrible change in matters some way, yes, *60 days* will do it, for in that time we shall know pretty nearly who will be the next Yankee President:— whether he is to be a *war* man or a *peace* man. . . .But it is idle to speculate—worse than idle:—it is all in the hands of God, if there is a God; and if none, then it is all chance, and the future will be just *as it happens.* So let us be as *easy* as possible and wait for a better day.[23]

---

[20] Quoted in Waugh, *Reelecting Lincoln,* 301.

[21] James King Wilkerson to his sister, August 29, 1864, James King Wilkerson Papers, NcD.

[22] Henry Calvin Conner to his wife, September 3, 1864, Henry Calvin Conner Papers, ScU.

[23] Francis Marion Coker to his wife, August 13, 1864, Florence Hodgson Heidler Collection, University of Georgia, Athens, Ga. (hereafter cited as GU).

Captain William Aiken Kelly of the 1st South Carolina believed that Confederate hopes for peace based on McClellan or the Democratic Party were "fatal ones, & if entertained by us, will lead us astray; weaken our efforts; & do our cause much harm." Kelly's opinion that "The only peace party upon whom we can rely for any good to ourselves, are our Armies in the field" seemed to be confirmed within a few days when word reached the Army of Northern Virginia that Atlanta had at last fallen to Sherman on September 2.[24] The loss of that vital city dashed many soldiers' hopes that the Confederacy might be able to sue for peace in the near future and stunned those who had believed that the Federal armies and the Northern people might be losing the will to continue the war. One officer remarked that the news from Georgia "cast a sort of grim gloom over this whole army which is, I dare to say, a pretty good idea of its reception by the country at large."[25] Almost every soldier in Lee's army who mentioned the fall of Atlanta also predicted that the peace movement in the North would lose a great deal of its momentum and that Lincoln's chances of winning a second term had improved dramatically as a result of Sherman's victory in Georgia. Sergeant Calvin Conner of the Palmetto Sharpshooters called it "indeed mortifying to us to Loose Atlanta at this time when the peace party ware gaining ground So rapidly at the North and I feare it will have a tendancy to prolong the war but it is gone and we must make the most of it."[26] The gloom over the fall of Atlanta was even more profound among the many Georgians serving in the army, who naturally feared for the safety of their families and homes. "It falls on my mind like the doom of the Almighty," one officer wrote his wife on September 5 from Petersburg. This Georgian, resigning himself to the fact that the Confederacy might not survive, continued, "If we are to be crushed & slavery destroyed, so be it. It (the fall of Atlanta) don't take me by surprise at all . . . but let it come, we must bear the end whether it be shame and suffering, or glory and independence."[27] A few days later he ob-

---

[24] W. A. Kelly, Diary, August 31, 1864, Kelly Papers, ScCC.

[25] John Bratton to his wife, September 5, 1864, Bratton Papers, ScCoAH.

[26] H. C. Conner to his wife, September 9, 1864, Conner Papers, ScU. See also Henry Duplessis Wells to his sister, September 5, 1864, Henry D. Wells Papers, Petersburg National Battlefield, Petersburg, Va.; Henry M. Talley to his mother, September 5, 1864, Henry C. Brown Papers, Nc-Ar; and Thomas Claybrook Elder to his wife, September 11, 1864, Thomas Claybrook Elder Papers, ViHi.

[27] F. M. Coker to his wife, September 5, 1864, Heidler Collection, GU.

served, "The peace element at the North, seems for the moment obscured & darkened by the great victory of the Capture of Atlanta. I have speculated on the future till I grow tired & sick of uncertainties, & feel sometimes disposed to *let it rip.*"[28]

Other members of the army, who freely admitted that the loss of Atlanta was a Confederate disaster, did not think that it would materially affect their own performance on the Petersburg-Richmond front. The observations of a young Virginian emphasized one reason for such thinking among Lee's soldiers, who were proud of their association with "Marse Robert" and confident that he would lead them to victory. Lieutenant Frederick Fleet of the 26th Virginia quoted Northern claims that Richmond would fall next, but commented in a letter to his father, "I don't think it can be done as easily as they can talk about it, however, as . . . [Grant] hasn't the Western army to fight here."[29]

A new phase of the Shenandoah Valley campaign took place soon after the fall of Atlanta, one in which a reinforced Federal army commanded by Philip H. Sheridan swept Early's force from its positions at Winchester, Fisher's Hill, and Cedar Creek on September 19 and 22 and October 19. Three crushing battlefield disasters in succession, coming hard on the heels of Hood's defeat in Georgia, convinced many observers that the Confederacy might not be able to withstand a concerted and coordinated Northern strategy focusing on its weary and rapidly dwindling armies.

Throughout the fall numerous members of the Army of Northern Virginia looked forward to the presidential election with great anticipation. "There is a good deal of Speculation here in regards to who will be elected Lincoln or McClellen and which of them would be most Likely to be beneficiel to the South," a South Carolina sergeant wrote his wife a few days before the election. "Some perfer Lincoln and others McClellen but for my own part I do not have much choice but if I had any I would perfer McClellen as he seems to be the

[28] F. M. Coker to his wife, September 10, 1864, Heidler Collection, GU.

[29] Alexander Frederick Fleet to his father, September 13, 1864, in Betsy Fleet and John D. P. Fuller, eds., *Green Mount: A Virginia Plantation Family during the Civil War: Being the Journal of Benjamin Robert Fleet and Letters of His Family* (Lexington: University of Kentucky Press, 1962), 338–39. See also Theodore Gaillard Trimmier to his wife, September 7, 1864, Trimmier Collection, Tennessee State Library and Archives, Nashville, Tenn.; and T. C. Elder to his wife, September 11, 1864, Elder Papers, ViHi.

most honourable and would perhaps conduct the war uppon a more
civilized principal than the other."[30] Some soldiers had high expectations for a Democratic victory, followed by an early peace settlement.
A Virginia captain reported that "Yankee deserters all say the yankees
are tired of fighting and that a Peace President will be elected," while
one of Lee's division commanders wrote his sister-in-law, "I earnestly
hope that this may be the end of the war, should Lincoln be elected
it may continue for years, but I cant believe it will. Should McClellan
be elected I hope it will be brought to a speedy close & by our independence."[31] Other Confederates thought Lincoln would be reelected but commented that they would rather continue the war
against an administration that was a known quantity than try to make
terms with an administration they knew nothing about. "In my opinion Old Abraham will come in again, and I believe it would be best
for us," a surgeon commented to his wife. "McClellan might have the
Union restored, if elected. I should prefer to remain at war the rest
of my life rather than to have any connection with the Yankees
again."[32] One Georgia staff officer, who usually wrote his wife several
times a week and whose letters had been generally cheerful until the
fall of Atlanta, expressed a renewed optimism over the impending
election in the North. "If Lincoln is elected," he wrote on November
4, "I believe the dissatisfaction in the North at the idea of carrying
on the war will be so great that he will be forced to abandon his war
policies and change his plans. If McC. is elected I think other plans
for restoring peace will be resorted to besides fighting which of
course is independence to us. All we require is to get the fighting
once stop'd. and our independence is certain."[33] The hopes and fears
of many in the Confederacy, soldiers and civilians alike, seemed to

[30] H. C. Conner to his wife, November 4, 1864, Conner Papers, ScU.

[31] Henry Thweat Owen to his wife [undated, but October/November 1864], Henry
T. Owen Papers, Vi; Cadmus M. Wilcox to his sister-in-law, October 18, 1864, Wilcox Papers, Library of Congress, Washington, D.C.

[32] Spencer Glasgow Welch to his wife, November 3, 1864, in Spencer Glasgow
Welch, *A Confederate Surgeon's Letters to His Wife: By Spencer Glasgow Welch,
Surgeon, Thirteenth South Carolina Volunteers, McGowan's Brigade* (New York:
Neale, 1911), 114. See also Crenshaw Hall to his father, October 24, 1864, Hall
Family Papers, Alabama Department of Archives and History, Montgomery (hereaf-
ter cited as A-Ar).

[33] F. M. Coker to his wife, November 4, 1864, Heidler Collection, GU.

hinge on the election. They believed that once Lincoln was reelected, or McClellan elected, the Federal strategy for the remainder of the war would reveal itself and they could then respond accordingly.

"This is the day that our enemies are to elect their next President for 4 years," a South Carolinian observed in his diary on November 8, "with every indication of Lincoln's reelection, which will have the appearance that they are determined to carry on the war for 4 more years."[34] Other soldiers, in the interval between the election and the confirmation of its results in the newspapers, commented on its implications for the Confederacy. One Georgian, for example, wrote his wife, "The Yankee election has come and gone:—whether for weal or woe of the people of this Continent, the thing is settled and done. With that, and in that election may have been decided the fate of the Southern Confederacy, and of thousands of brave and noble men."[35]

After the news reached the army that Lincoln was indeed reelected, many correspondents and diarists expressed the opinion that another four years of war was inevitable and that the Confederacy should resign itself to that fact. "I indulged the hope all fall that the election for president would bring about a change in [the] war but now I feel no prospect of it," one noncommissioned officer wrote his wife in late November, "and I Suppose that we may as well make up our minds [to] fight untill our enemys Get tired of the war."[36] John Esten Cooke, the popular Virginia novelist and poet who was serving as a staff officer in the Cavalry Corps, recorded bluntly in his diary, "Lincoln elected: all right. More war—tedious but necessary."[37] One of Lee's generals, who had long commanded a veteran North Carolina brigade, declared simply, "Lincoln is certainly elected & there is no telling when the war will end. We must just determine to fight it out & look for the end when it comes."[38] Several members of the army, perhaps as much to reassure themselves as to convince their families and friends, viewed a prolonged war as a necessity they could bear for the sake of independence. "Lincoln's Reelection is consid-

---

[34] John A. F. Coleman, Diary, November 8, 1864, John Alfred Feister Coleman Papers, Confederate Miscellany I, Emory University, Atlanta (hereafter cited as GEU).

[35] F. M. Coker to his wife, November 10, 1864, Heidler Collection, GU.

[36] H. C. Conner to his wife, November 24, 1864, Conner Papers, ScU.

[37] John Esten Cooke, Diary, November 15, 1864, John Esten Cooke Papers, NcD.

[38] A. M. Scales to his wife, November 12, 1864, Scales Papers, Nc-Ar.

ered by most thinking men, as the best thing that could happen for the Confederate States," a young South Carolinian declared to his parents. Captain Edward Wells, who commanded the "Charleston Light Dragoons" of the 4th South Carolina Cavalry, continued, "We know him, & his party, & are ready, & willing to fight them, as long, as it may continue agreeable to them."[39] Such assessments of the election's significance, while by no means universal, reflected the predominant views of correspondents and diarists who commented on the subject. "We are in for four years more," Captain John Elmore Hall of the 59th Alabama wrote his father. "Well, I can stand it, & on my own account dont dread it at all, but I do feel for the many in our country who will suffer from it," he commented, acknowledging the effect Lincoln's reelection was likely to have on many soldiers and civilians.[40]

Other Confederates, just as Hall had predicted, were discouraged when they realized that there would be no quick peace settlement and that the war was going to continue for the foreseeable future. "We are doomed to another four years war[.] God forbid," two sergeants of the 1st North Carolina Cavalry exclaimed in a letter home.[41] Still others took Lincoln's reelection and the prospect of an even longer war as their cue to desert, or as some wags commented, "voting with their feet." Some of them even admitted as much to their comrades before leaving the lines or to their former enemies after going over to the Federal lines. A captain in General William H. Wallace's South Carolina brigade reported in his diary that a private in the 23rd South Carolina deserted, as he explained it, because "A. Lincoln is elected for four more years. He could not stand the idea of hardship of four more long years of war."[42] Another deserter from Wallace's Brigade who went over to the Federals was interviewed along with nineteen other Confederates from various units who deserted the same day. According to one Federal officer, the deserters'

---

[39] Edward Laight Wells to his parents, November 17, 1864, in Smith et al., eds., *Mason Smith Family Letters*, 148. See also J. Mark Smither to his sister, November 12, 1864, J. Mark Smither Papers, TxHiC; and A. F. Fleet to his sister, November 26, 1864, in Fleet and Fuller, eds., *Green Mount*, 348.

[40] J. E. Hall to his father, November 10, 1864, Hall Family Papers, A-Ar.

[41] George F. Adams and Barzella C. McBride to Adams's parents, November 16, 1864, Alfred Adams Papers, NcD.

[42] J. A. F. Coleman, Diary, November 16, 1864, Confederate Miscellany I, GEU.

"principal reason for coming over [was] the fact of Mr. Lincoln's re-election and no prospect of the war ending."[43]

While numerous soldiers who were already inclined to give up found ample justification to do so after the election, many who had never before despaired of an ultimate Confederate victory now began to doubt that it was possible. Private John A. Everett of the 11th Georgia, who feared that Sherman might "distroy Every thing" in his home state, wrote his mother, "if I had the yanks all in my Power I would have an Earth quake and Kill the last one of them at once," explaining, "It looks like that we have got to fight them 4 years longer and I tell you the truth I dont think that we will bee able to Stand up to the War 4 years more for we have got our last army in the field and they can keep recruiting thair army all the time."[44]

Many observers claimed that they were more discouraged by signs of despondency among the Confederate people—from the politicians, to the newspaper editors, to their families and friends at home—than by conditions in the army, and that they would prevail if the citizens would only rally to their support. While many members of the army thought that its officers and men were in reasonably good spirits, most of them were also realistic enough to recognize that their chances for victory and independence were waning with every day. A Virginia lieutenant wrote his brother, "I think it is the desire of the Army at large to fight it out to the bitter end if we can remain united as we have been, if not let us give it up at once."[45]

There was a growing sense among Lee's soldiers, even those who wrote hopefully of the future, that the army's morale was considerably lower than it had ever been before and that it would be difficult, if not impossible, to recapture some of the old spirit of 1862 and 1863. Many members of the army, who had previously been willing to suffer some shortages in clothing and rations for the sake of the

---

[43] Capt. John McEntee, Provost Marshal Gen.'s Dept., Army of the Potomac, to Maj. Gen. A. A. Humphreys, Chief of Staff, Army of the Potomac, November 22, 1864, in *The War of the Rebellion: A Compilation of the Official Records of the Union and Confederate Armies*, 128 vols. (Washington, D.C.: Government Printing Office, 1880–1901), ser. I, 42, pt. 3:680–81.

[44] John A. Everett to his mother, November 27, 1864, John A. Everett Papers, GEU.

[45] Luther Rice Mills to his brother, December 5, 1864, in George D. Harmon, ed., "Letters of Luther Rice Mills—A Confederate Soldier," *North Carolina Historical Review* 4, no. 3 (July 1927): 305.

country, now questioned continued deficiencies that seemed to serve no purpose. They also entertained serious doubts that the Confederacy would even survive the opening of the 1865 campaign. Such doubts, among veterans and conscripts alike, were certainly fueled by the downward spiral in Confederate fortunes that began with Sherman's capture of Atlanta and Sheridan's victories in the Valley, then accelerated through November and December with Lincoln's reelection, Sherman's march through Georgia, and the virtual destruction of the Army of Tennessee at Franklin and Nashville. "I believe there is at this time more dissatisfaction in our army than I ever saw in it before," Private William Horace Phillips of the 14th Virginia commented in late November. "I raly believe there will be a general bash up in our army before next March."[46] Conscripts who complained of the hardships of military life were often joined by veterans weary of several years' service, such as those described by a South Carolina cavalryman who wrote in early December, "The spirit of the army is ever fluctuating, as the tide of the ocean."[47] Private John Johnson of the 19th Georgia wrote candidly a few days later in a letter to his fiancée, "The 'morale' of the army is not as good as it was 2 years ago. I look for a good many to desert next spring for they are tired and can see no signs of a prospect of peace and neither can I."[48]

By the end of the year many members of the army now began to question the wisdom, or even the necessity, of continuing to oppose the vast Federal armies facing them. As one North Carolina veteran put it, "a good many say the Confederacy has 'gone up' . . . and that we are whipped. I have never seen the men so discouraged before."[49] While numerous Confederates expressed such fears in their letters and diaries, hundreds of others discussed them in conversations in camp or on the march. Still others kept to themselves, saying little or

[46] William Horace Phillips to his father, November 26, 1864, William Horace Phillips Papers, NcD.

[47] W. T. [or W. G.] Field, to J. E. Hagood, December 3, 1864, James Earle Hagood Papers, ScU.

[48] John A. Johnson to his fiancée, December 15, 1864, John A. Johnson Papers, NcU.

[49] Walter Raleigh Battle to his mother, January 15, 1865, in Laura Elizabeth Lee, ed., *Forget-Me-Nots of the Civil War: A Romance, Containing Reminiscences and Original Letters of Two Confederate Soldiers* (St. Louis: Press A. R. Fleming, 1909), 125.

nothing about the war and its possible outcome. Most soldiers were simply weary of fighting Yankees. It became more and more difficult for many of Lee's officers and men, whatever their mode of expression, to endure personal sacrifices or accept enormous losses in Southern lives and property when they had no confidence that anything good would ever come of it. One young Georgian spoke for many of his comrades when he admitted gloomily, "I Wish this War would come to a Close and I dont care how all I want is Peace."[50] Lincoln's reelection, one of the last great blows to the collective will of the Southern people and the Confederate soldiers who defended them, gave an already-creeping hopelessness added momentum through the end of 1864 and into 1865, and made the end result only a matter of time.

---

[50] J. A. Everett to his mother, December 29, 1864, Everett Papers, GEU.

8

"A Matter of Profound Wonder": The Women in Lincoln's Life

Frank J. Williams

FIRST LET ME STATE what this paper is not.

It is not a series of biographical sketches about the women in Lincoln's life, nor is it a treatise on whether he was referring to his natural mother or his stepmother when he called one of them "my angel mother."[1] And it does not examine whether it is, as Lincoln himself put it, a "matter of profound wonder"[2] that he finally married Mary Todd.

But I hope to suggest an interpretation of the personality of Abraham Lincoln through relationships he had with women and how that influenced his style of leadership. Although some of the relationships are sparsely documented, a pattern emerges that strongly suggests the development of a normal, healthy personality. The record shows he valued women as individuals, treated them with respect and equality, and learned from them. He would apply these traits in his public policies. Lincoln advocated a major advancement in equality because women had taught him the values of human dignity.

EARLY BONDING WITH WOMEN

The first three women in Abraham Lincoln's life were his mother, Nancy Hanks Lincoln, his stepmother, Sarah Bush Johnston Lincoln, and his sister Sarah Lincoln. Although the information is limited, the

---

[1] Joshua F. Speed, *Reminiscences of Abraham Lincoln and Notes of a Visit to California: Two Lectures* (Louisville, Ky.: J. P. Morton, 1884), 19.

[2] Roy P. Basler et al., eds., *The Collected Works of Abraham Lincoln,* 9 vols. (New Brunswick, N.J.: Rutgers University Press, 1953–55), 1:305.

picture is clear. He valued his mothers as "angels." When he lost his mother, he was deeply shaken, such a loss perhaps triggering later episodes of depression. And it is also clear that he maintained his relationship with his stepmother, showing concern for her welfare. Though very little is known about his sister, her early death seems to have contributed further to his tendency to melancholy. In each of these relationships, Lincoln emerges as a deeply caring man able to empathize with others who lost loved ones. We see this in the letter he wrote in the 1860s, with the nation embroiled in the Civil War, to young Fanny McCullough, the daughter of an old Illinois friend who died in battle:

Dear Fanny

It is with deep grief that I learn of the death of your kind and brave Father; and, especially, that it is affecting your young heart beyond what is common in such cases. In this sad world of ours, sorrow comes to all; and, to the young, it comes with bitterest agony, because it takes them unawares. The older have learned to ever expect it. I am anxious to afford some alleviation of your present distress. Perfect relief is not possible, except with time. You can not now realize that you will ever feel better. Is not this so? And yet it is a mistake. You are sure to be happy again. To know this, which is certainly true, will make you some less miserable now. I have had experience enough to know what I say; and you need only to believe it, to feel better at once. The memory of your dear Father, instead of an agony, will yet be a sad sweet feeling in your heart, of a purer, and holier sort than you have known before.

Please present my kind regards to your afflicted mother.

Your sincere friend

A. Lincoln[3]

His letters to Fanny McCullough as well as to Mrs. Bixby, who, the president believed, lost five sons in the Civil War, emanate compassion and empathy: "I feel how weak and fruitless must be any words of mine which should attempt to beguile you from the grief of a loss so overwhelming."[4] Lincoln emerges as profound and sensitive, expressing his empathy and tenderness, despite the demands of war on the president.

---

[3] Ibid., 6:16–17.

[4] Ibid., 8:116–17. It takes nothing away from Mrs. Bixby's loss that only two of her sons were killed in battle. One other was honorably discharged, one deserted, and one may have deserted or died in a Confederate prison camp.

SEARCHING FOR A SIGNIFICANT OTHER

Between his leaving home and his eventual marriage, Lincoln sought the company of women. The pattern in this stage of his life seems to range from tragedy to humor. His short relationship with Ann Rutledge may have been his first true love, but unfortunately, it ended tragically. Yet the mere existence of this relationship suggests a Lincoln searching for a significant other. His subsequent awkward and bumbling relationship with Mary Owens imparts the same motivation. He was still searching. Married women who knew him also showed their concern by trying to find him a wife.

MARRIAGE AND MATURITY: EQUALITY

The best-documented woman in Lincoln's life is Mary Todd. Lincoln's motivation to marry is clear. He married up, and she polished him as much as she could. Mary, too, was an "engine that knew no rest"[5] in promoting and encouraging his political advancement. Theirs may have been a turbulent marriage, but they learned to deal with one another's deficits to forge an enduring relationship that was enriched by the love they had for their children. Less well documented is how Lincoln treated his wife and Mariah Vance, their Springfield housekeeper. The picture that emerges is that he treated women, whether a well-born Southern belle or a lowly African American laundress (and her family),[6] with respect, concern, and even affection. The Emancipation Proclamation was not an aberration in Lincoln's life, nor was his willingness to support women's rights.

LEADERSHIP: MASCULINE OR FEMININE

Lincoln exemplifies democratic leadership and gives it an unexpected dimension. Contrary to the traditional association of masculinity and

---

[5] William H. Herndon's description of Lincoln's ambition, quoted in Richard Nelson Current, *The Lincoln Nobody Knows* (New York: Hill and Wang, 1958), 188.

[6] See Lloyd Ostendorf and Walter Olesky, eds., *Lincoln's Unknown Private Life: An Oral History by His Black Housekeeper Mariah Vance, 1850–1860* (Mamaroneck, N.Y.: Hastings House, 1995).

detached objectivity, the most haunting images of Lincoln often are unmistakably feminine.

"Lincoln is a man of heart—as gentle as a woman's and as tender," William Herndon said of his law partner, then president-elect.[7] Yet not all observers considered Lincoln's feminine qualities as an attribute. Historian Francis Parkman ranked Lincoln well below Washington as a president because Lincoln "failed to meet his standard that men should be masculine and women feminine."[8] But the more typical view of Lincoln was expressed by Robert Ingersoll, Republican politician and celebrated agnostic, in a line that evokes nineteenth-century sentimentality but is still touching: "He is the gentlest memory of our world."[9]

Yet Lincoln's tender heart was tempered by a staunch will and resolute disposition. After citing Lincoln's tender feelings, Herndon immediately emphasized that "he has a will strong as iron."[10] Charles Dana, Lincoln's assistant secretary of war, recalled that "one always felt the presence of a will and an intellectual power which maintained the ascendancy of the President."[11]

Lincoln's control of his temper and virility demanded considerable self-discipline. As a young man active in partisan politics, Lincoln had become embroiled in a number of personal contentions where his combative personality would surface. In 1842 he almost found himself in a duel with James Shields, who was outraged over a satirical attack that Lincoln had published under a pseudonym. Lincoln responded indignantly to a political handbill that distorted his own legislative record, vowing to the voters of Sangamon County, "All I have to say is that the author is a *liar* and a *scoundrel,* and that if he will avow the authorship to me, I promise to give his proboscis a good wringing."[12]

Lincoln displayed qualities that should have satisfied the most strident advocates of manliness in his flexible determination to carry

---

[7] Paul Angle, ed., *Herndon's Life of Lincoln* (Greenwich, Conn.: Fawcett Publications, 1961), 374.

[8] Henry Dwight Sedgwick, *Francis Parkman* (Boston: Riverside Press, 1904), 310–11.

[9] Allen Thorndike Rice, ed., *Reminiscences of Abraham Lincoln by Distinguished Men of His Times* (1885; reprint, New York: Harper and Brothers, 1909), 428.

[10] Angle, ed., *Herndon's Life of Lincoln,* 374.

[11] Rice, ed., *Reminiscences of Abraham Lincoln,* 271.

[12] *Collected Works of Lincoln,* 8:429.

the Civil War through to a successful conclusion, as in his sarcastic complaint about those who fought the war with "elder-stalk squirts, charged with rose water,"[13] and in his willingness to endorse such brutal methods of warfare as those used by William Tecumseh Sherman. Conventional definitions of masculinity were not foreign to his own thought and were apparent in his response to those who appealed to him to let the South secede: "There is no Washington in that—no Jackson in that—no manhood nor honor in that."[14]

Yet it can also be said that Lincoln's keen sense of timing and his ability to assess a difficult situation were based on a more feminine component of intuition. Lincoln can thus be seen as a leader who was unusual in his ability to reconcile the masculine and feminine dimensions of his personality. Such a conclusion is a metaphorical statement about his character rather than a psychological statement about his sexual identity. Possessing and utilizing qualities that American culture has normally labeled as masculine and feminine, he had little in common with more exclusively masculine political leaders, such as Andrew Jackson and Ulysses S. Grant. Nonetheless, Lincoln's merging of his masculine/feminine character was central to his practice of great leadership. In fact, the Lincoln example suggests that a great leader should synchronize the traditional masculine and feminine aspects of behavior. A leader should have the strength of purpose and tenacity of will that American culture has generally designated as masculine, as well as the sensitivity, openness, and willingness to nurture others, traits that American culture has typically viewed—and often disparaged—as women's ways.

ETHICS OF CARE AND ETHICS OF RIGHTS

In order to understand Lincoln as a leader, it is necessary to look not only at his success in leading the nation, but also at his dealings with individuals. He treated leadership as a *relationship* involving individuals as well as large groups. His compassionate and nurturing practices, his resistance to quarreling and his freedom from malice, most fully revealed his integrated masculine/feminine nature of leadership.

[13] Ibid., 5:346.
[14] Ibid., 4:341.

Without mentioning Lincoln by name, Carol Gilligan shows how a person with Lincoln's character combines both masculine and feminine qualities. Gilligan suggests that the moral development of males usually entails the learning of an "ethic of rights" geared to "arriving at an objectively fair or just resolution to moral dilemmas." In contrast, women develop an "ethic of care" with its focus not on the application of abstract justice but on "sensitivity to the needs of others and consideration of other points of view."[15] Lincoln has long been understood as one of America's greatest proponents of an "ethic of rights," for he is often quoted for his rigorous opposition to those who advocated the spread of slavery. However, Lincoln can also be understood as epitomizing an "ethic of care."

Despite the burdens and responsibilities of the Civil War presidency—major military strategy, recruitment of hundreds of thousands of troops, conflicts with Congress over emancipation and reconstruction—Lincoln insisted upon remaining accessible to individuals who wanted to see him personally. Although the time spent with all these visitors intensified Lincoln's exhaustion, he could not shut them out. He felt empathy with many of them. He told Senator Henry Wilson, "They don't want much; they get but little, and I must see them."[16] He described his hours spent with ordinary people in the White House as "public opinion baths."[17] Just as he learned from the women in his life, he remained open to other people and learned from them as well.

Of all the personal requests he received, Lincoln was most concerned with pleas for pardons. He did not always agree to grant pardons, and he ordered executions to be carried out in what he considered to be "very flagrant cases." Yet he granted so many pardons that stories of his clemency toward the condemned became a major part of his contemporary reputation and subsequent legend. The stories are largely true and genuinely moving and reveal not only a kind man but also a leader who knew political uses of kindness. As Richard Nelson Current observed, Lincoln "had to deal with an army consisting mainly of citizen soldiers. . . . With such men as these,

---

[15] Carol Gilligan, *In a Different Voice: Psychological Theory and Women's Development* (Cambridge, Mass.: Harvard University Press, 1982), 16, 21–22, 30, 164.

[16] Angle, ed., *Herndon's Life of Lincoln*, 374.

[17] Stephen B. Oates, *With Malice toward None: The Life of Abraham Lincoln* (New York: Harper & Row, 1977), 246.

frequent pardons may have been bad for discipline, but the regimen of the regular army, if unrelieved, might have been even worse for morale. The service needed to be made as popular and attractive as it could be, and Lincoln's clemency made it less unattractive than it otherwise would have been."[18] One does not, however, have to choose between an interpretation of Lincoln's pardons as saintly forgiveness or as canny politics, for Lincoln knew that what was kind was often political as well. This tenet he learned from the women in his life.

Lincoln's balanced temperament also allowed him to work with the Radicals amid storms of abuse. Lincoln opened himself fully to their arguments, meeting frequently with delegations, even attending antislavery lectures. And he was careful not to speak ill of the Radicals in public, no matter what they said publicly about him.

The man who would avoid quarrels would also avoid resentment and grudges. Lincoln taught himself to resist antagonistic feelings toward those who had caused him grief. Having lost his mother as a child, Lincoln understood that anger was futile. The final passage of his Second Inaugural Address amplified a personal code of conduct expressed earlier in the war: "I shall do nothing in malice. What I deal with is too vast for malicious dealing."[19] Lincoln was outraged by the South's initial arguments for secession and assaults on free government, but he reminded himself to "judge not that we be not judged,"[20] and he planned to treat the miscreant section with magnanimity, if they would allow him. Although he was troubled by Secretary of the Treasury Chase's scheming to eliminate him for the 1864 Republican nomination, Lincoln treated Chase with patience and forgiveness, later nominating him as chief justice of the United States.

As Lincoln matured personally and politically, he began to construct the amiable and gentle self with whom we are familiar. In his eulogy for President Zachary Taylor in 1850, there are several passages that reveal Lincoln's efforts to learn from Taylor a democratic leadership style free from contentiousness. Lincoln wrote of Taylor, "[H]e was alike averse to *sudden,* and to *startling* quarrels; and he

---

[18] Current, *The Lincoln Nobody Knows,* 175.

[19] *Collected Works of Lincoln,* 5:346.

[20] Ibid., 8:333.

pursued no man with *revenge.*" Lincoln went on to praise Taylor's relationships with his troops: "Of the many who served with him through the long course of forty years, all testify to the uniform kindness, and his constant care for, and hearty sympathy with, their every want and every suffering; while none can be found to declare, that he was ever a tyrant anywhere, in anything."[21] These same words could be used to describe Lincoln as president.

Lincoln did not avoid quarrels and resentments from a stance of superiority or indifference to his subordinates but from a genuine concern for the feelings of others. He did not treat subordinates as instruments of his masterful will but rather followed the dictates of an ethic of care and paid heed to their individual needs and feelings. For example, he wrote to Secretary of War Edwin M. Stanton that the change of command at New Orleans General "X" to General "Y" "must be so managed as to not wrong, or wound the feelings of Gen. Banks."[22]

This sincerity was rare in an American political leader but had been rooted in empathy and linked to the early women in his life. Having endured his share of wounded feelings, Lincoln wrote to James Hackett, "I have endured a great deal of ridicule without much malice; and have received a great deal of kindness, not quite free from ridicule."[23] But sensitivity was also an obligation for the kind of democratic leader that Lincoln sought to be. By avoiding quarrels, by shunning resentments, by paying attention to feelings, Lincoln could approach others with respect for their talents, their services, and their dignity, and thereby lessen the inherent distance between leader and subordinates. This sensitivity made possible a successful dialogue between leader and subordinates.

Lincoln's gentleness and kindness were not the marks of an effusive character. He could be aloof, brooding, and mysterious. But out of the depths of his multifaceted personality and in response to his experiences with women he developed a masculine/feminine temperament that governed his personal relationships. His fusion of an ethic of rights and an ethic of care was a matter of political conviction as well as personal nature. As a democratic leader, Lincoln believed he

---

[21] Ibid., 2:87–88.
[22] Ibid., 6:76.
[23] Ibid., 6:559.

must not only represent and educate the people collectively but also care for the dignity and needs of the individual.

Defending the humanity of the slave in the 1850s against the assaults of proslavery apologists, Lincoln had considered African Americans as passive victims of injustice. But during the Civil War he came to recognize African Americans as active and vital participants in the cause of democracy. He was particularly impressed by the contributions of African American soldiers. To detractors of the Emancipation Proclamation, he pointed out that when peace came and the Union was restored, "there will be some black men who can remember that, with silent tongue, and clenched teeth, and steady eye, and well-poised bayonet, they have helped mankind on to this great consummation; while, I fear, there will be some white ones, unable to forget that, with malignant heart, and deceitful speech, they have strove to hinder it."[24]

DEMOCRATIC PURPOSES

Abraham Lincoln demonstrated how powerful ambition could be reconciled with—and serve—democratic purposes. Lincoln was history's most striking confirmation of John Adams's assertions about the political importance of the "passion for distinction." Lincoln had plenty of passion as well as being an advocate of reason, "cool, unimpassioned reason."

By moderating the masculine view of leadership, Lincoln achieved a masculine and feminine fusion that has been too little understood. He recognized that the democratic dignity of citizens requires nurture and that the democratic perspective of leaders requires an openness to the views of others and a sensitivity to their needs. His approach avoided paternalism—except perhaps in the case of African Americans—about which he continued to learn, because he began from the premise of mutuality, always regarding ordinary citizens as capable of everything he himself had achieved. Lincoln's self-assertion was balanced with his regard for others. He overcame much of the distance between leaders and followers by identifying himself with those followers. In his final years, he demonstrated how demo-

---

[24] Ibid., 6:410.

cratic leadership could combine an abstract set of principles—an ethic of rights—with a concrete and empathetic ethic of care.

Lincoln also demonstrated how an ethic of care could be practical politics. The side of him that is characterized as feminine neither undercut his masculine political skills nor weakened him as a leader. Lincoln's career reveals the inadequacy of the hard-boiled perspective that equates leadership with power, dominance, and manipulation. He gained political support through his kindness and political insight through the mutuality of relationships. He was able to evolve into a strong democratic leader because he had reconciled his masculine and feminine sides.

CONCLUSION

In a broad sense, one can surmise that it was the positive impact women had on Lincoln that helped form him. Through those relationships involving hardship, loss, rejection, and compromise, the women in Lincoln's life provided a necessary balance. We do better not to revere him but to understand him and to consider his relevance as an image and as a model. Perhaps because of his ability to recognize and utilize both masculine and feminine qualities in his character and conduct, Lincoln became and remains the role model for American leadership.

The full extent of the complicated relationships that Lincoln experienced with the women in his life can never be fully understood. Too little documentary evidence survives, and Lincoln, a notoriously "shut-mouthed" man about all personal matters, seldom confided his feelings to even his closest friends.

But something in his character and his relationships molded Lincoln into a human being little like other males of his time. His sensitivity set him apart as distinctly as his eloquence and intellect.

Surely, the women in his life helped create that personality. The answer can never be definitely known, but the question remains worth asking.

9

Mary Lincoln: Symbol, Historical Target, and Human Being

Jean H. Baker

I COME BEFORE YOU as a principal defender of Mary Todd Lincoln, that complex, controversial woman who has exerted such a fascination not just for historians but also for the American public. Americans who have no idea what Lincoln's Reconstruction policies were or who his cabinet officers were have precise information about Mary Todd—from her apocryphal predictions as a child to Henry Clay that she would someday live in the White House to information about the expensive, stylish boas and shawls that she wrapped around her shoulders.[1] Why are we so enduringly interested in her?—and believe me, my mail suggests that we are. It is an interest, by the way, that rubs off onto discussions of the Lincoln marriage and onto the character and personality of her son Robert Todd Lincoln.

One reason for our fascination is quite simply that Mary Todd Lincoln is an easy target, and vilification is a pleasurable, satisfying category of nonanalysis. It warms the cockles—literally the deepest parts of our emotions—to castigate those whom we label villains. Moreover we live in an age of what Joyce Carol Oates once called "pathobiography"—that is, a reductive emphasis on dysfunction that not only overshadows the subject's achievements but also makes them virtually inconceivable. Although she has fared better in recent years, Mary Todd Lincoln ranks among the most detested public women in American history, surpassing as our worst First Lady Florence Harding, Ida McKinley, and Nancy Reagan.[2] Invariably she is placed at

---

[1] Katherine Helm, *The True Story of Mary, Wife of Lincoln* (New York: Harper, 1928), 1–4.

[2] Betty Boyd Caroli, *First Ladies* (New York: Oxford University Press, 1987), 385–86.

the bottom of those polls ranking first ladies, although some say that she is about to move up—a benefit of the Woman's Movement and recent scholarship.

As evidence of the Mary-Lincoln-is-beyond-contempt school, I submit the recent work of Michael Burlingame, who seems to have collected almost every bad thing that anyone ever said about Mary Lincoln.[3] And there was plenty of hearsay evidence about her failings. But Burlingame and Mary Todd's other critics have made little effort to consider the perspectives of these contemporary critics, nor evidently have they considered any positive comments about Mary or any of her contributions, in terms of what she did, for her family and friends and later for the White House.

Surely some of the negative comments about Mary Todd Lincoln reflect the degree to which she represented a disorderly woman— and I do not mean by disorderly woman an out-of-control drunk. Rather, I mean a woman who moved out of the traditional typecast roles expected of nineteenth-century women whose lives were supposed to be enclosed by domesticity, piety, purity, submissiveness, and passivity in what is now labeled by historians as "the cult of true domesticity."[4] She was interested in politics; she made judgments about her husband's cabinet; she had a temper that she did not bother to hide, but that was almost never exercised against her children; she spent a lot of money fixing up the White House. Like many Americans today, she was a magnificent shopper and consumer. Indeed, she began the practice of showcasing elegant and expensive gowns for designers, and in return for her advertisement she expected, like Nancy Reagan, to receive these clothes free. In a significant miscalculation after her husband's assassination when she needed money, like Princess Eugénie of France, she tried to sell her clothes in 1868 and gained from this sad venture only more humiliation and vilification.

There is much about Mary Lincoln's life that resembles that of modern Americans as she assumed roles that most of us take for granted for today's women. But in her day such radical behavior drew a string of negative assessments that have long corrupted our view of

---

[3] Michael Burlingame, *The Inner World of Abraham Lincoln* (Urbana: University of Illinois Press, 1994), 268.

[4] Carroll Smith-Rosenberg, *Disorderly Conduct: Visions of Gender in Victorian America* (New York: Alfred A. Knopf, 1985).

her. And so with some exceptions she is condemned and demonized. Sometimes the historians' vilification of Mary Lincoln is reminiscent of Captain Ahab's pursuit of the White Whale in *Moby Dick,* as she becomes "all that most maddens and torments / All that stirs up the lees of things / all demonisms of life and thought."

Another reason we are enduringly interested in Mary Lincoln is that she demonstrates, for her critics, her husband's humanity. The president who dealt so generously with the afflicted—the deserters, the traitors, the former Confederates, even his half sister-in-law, the eternally rabid Confederate Emilie Helm—and so flexibly with his cabinet, generals, and patronage seekers learned, in this understanding, to do so through his private life with a shrew. It is, of course, not a solely American idea that men of great sensibility, like Socrates, often endure wives of abominable temper, like Xanthippe.

In our national version of this myth Lincoln, the most venerated of American heroes, daily practiced tolerance in his home with a cantankerous female who was neither his first nor greatest love—nor if we are to believe some of the critics, his love at all. If the great Abraham ensures his wife's tainted immortality, the maligned Mary guarantees her husband's nobility. And in turn, the supposedly insane Mary Lincoln ensures her son Robert's ambivalent reputation.[5] For how many sons would organize an insanity trial, gather witnesses and legal council, and not even bother to discuss what they intended with the victim—in this case their mother?

But if Mary Lincoln is interesting to us, we need to consider her on her own terms—not as the woman Abraham Lincoln had to marry. This brings me to the interpretations of their courtship, which one recent historian has characterized as superficial. In the speculation of her critics, Abraham Lincoln married Mary Todd out of an exaggerated sense of duty—not even because she was pregnant or not because he loved her, but because he felt he had to on the grounds of some verbal commitment.[6]

He was really, so goes this interpretation, either still in love with

---

[5] On the supposed insanity, see Mark E. Neely, Jr., and R. Gerald McMurtry, *The Insanity File: The Case of Mary Todd Lincoln* (Carbondale: Southern Illinois University Press, 1986); also Jean H. Baker, *Mary Todd Lincoln: A Biography* (New York: W. W. Norton, 1987), 315–50.

[6] Douglas L. Wilson, *Honor's Voice: The Transformation of Abraham Lincoln* (New York: Alfred A. Knopf, 1998).

Anne Rutledge, who had died seven years before his marriage, or he was in love with Mary's cousin-by-marriage, Matilda Edwards. He felt duty-bound to honor a previous commitment and so entered a loveless relationship. But surely it is more dishonorable to enter a lifelong relationship with a woman whom you do not love.

This interpretation is a classic instance of male-centered history, for courtship is a two-sided arrangement. Specifically, courting is a time when women have far more power than they will after their marriage, when in this generation they lose all their legal and civic rights.[7] To speculate that Lincoln married for honor is simply too heroic and sacrificial even for an American icon, and it leaves Mary Todd—the woman whom her brother-in-law once said could make a bishop forget his prayers—entirely out of the romance. It also makes Lincoln into a hypocrite. And it removes his courtship from its context at a time when the older tradition of arranged marriages is giving way to romantic attachments, when love meant going beyond routine existence to find fulfillment in another.[8]

If we consider Mary Lincoln on her own terms, and from the perspective of women's history, what is her importance? Why, as some foolish soul once asked of Eleanor Roosevelt, study her when she had no power? Surely we know better now. Certainly Mary Lincoln left no published work except for her letters, which are intelligent and perceptive and give some indication of what she saw in her husband and in her.[9] Mary Lincoln joined none of the reform movements, although she was active, like other Union women, raising money for the wounded soldiers and the newly freed former slaves who fled into Washington during the Civil War. She said nothing about the women's movement during a period of incipient feminism initiated by women like Elizabeth Cady Stanton and Susan B. Anthony and very little about slavery. She did not influence public policy or secretly author Lincoln's speeches. Moreover her status as a wealthy, well-educated Todd of Lexington and her marriage to a lawyer who became president of the United States remove her from any authentic

---

[7] Ellen K. Rothman, *Hands and Hearts: A History of Courtship in America* (New York: Basic Books, 1984), 57.

[8] Peter Gay, *The Bourgeois Experience: Victoria to Freud*, vol. II, *The Tender Passion* (New York: Oxford University Press, 1986), 51–60.

[9] Justin G. Turner and Linda Levitt Turner, *Mary Todd Lincoln: Her Life and Letters* (New York: Alfred A. Knopf, 1972).

representation of nineteenth-century womanhood. So why should we study her?

Exceptional in many ways, Mary Lincoln nevertheless accepted conventional views about women and held as her ideal "a nice home, a loving husband and precious child."[10] Wives, she believed, should be what she never was: quiet, submissive, and out of the public's eye. To be sure, she was in actuality just about as submissive as today's Southern Baptist wives are to their husbands. But there is in her life a persistent tension between the ideal and the real, between actuality and principles, and between her ambitions and their terrible inadvertent price. After her husband's assassination, she explained to a friend the irony of her circumstances. "My own life, has been so chequered," she wrote, "naturally so gay & hopeful—my *prominent desires,* all granted me—My noble husband, who was my 'light and life,' and my highest—ambition gratified—and *that* was, the great weakness of my life. My husband—became distinguished above all. And yet, owing to *that fact,* I firmly believe he lost his life & I am bowed to the earth with Sorrow."[11]

Thus we are interested in Mary Lincoln because of the range of her experience, her remarkable independence and survival instincts, and her courage. She tells us a lot about other more invisible women in the nineteenth century, especially as widows. Like a flawed marble statue, the cracks of which leave it susceptible to daily hammering by the elements, Mary Lincoln was a unique victim battered by personal adversity and terrible luck, and trapped by destructive pervasive conventions of Victorian domesticity. But she was also an agent of her life.

Hers, then, is an existence that illuminates the human conditions of family love and loss, of conventions and nonconformity, of pride and humiliation, and of determination and destiny. Mary Lincoln is exceptional not because she married Abraham Lincoln, although that is one of the reasons we remember her, but because of the range of her experience, the persistence of her tragedies, and the means of her survival. Her life was amplified, and her endurance immense. But within these particulars, she suffered universal experiences and was, dangerously, ourselves—you and I as we journey the paths of

---

[10] Baker, *Mary Todd Lincoln,* 101.
[11] Turner and Turner, *Mary Todd Lincoln,* 302–3.

our fortune with much that shapes our lives beyond our control. And so here are three reasons for our interest in this Lincoln woman: she is easy to criticize, she establishes her husband's humanity, and in historical terms she leads an interesting life.

Let me turn now to some of the specific aspects of this life. Of course, it is well known that Mary Lincoln was a spiritualist, and always whenever I am about to talk about her, it seems that she returns—hovers, as those who believe in the return of the spirits would say. I am never sure where she is—perhaps hovering in the chandelier or in the podium. "Tell them the good things about me." And so, intimidated by this spectral presence, I will tell you some of the good things about her—as a mother, a wife, and a widow. And I will rely on what she did for the most part, rather than the hearsay evidence that has encrusted her reputation.

From her perspective—and the evidence for this exists in her letters and her behavior—child raising was one of the critical aspects of her life. I believe she did it well. She was, I submit, an engaged, interested mother concerned with her children's welfare, health, and education. Even the domestic helpers who did not like Mary Lincoln testified to this. In the White House, when she could afford to, she declined to have any nanny or governess serve as a surrogate mother to raise her children.

Like many upwardly mobile American white middle-class parents, the Lincolns controlled their fertility in a time when other middle-class Americans were doing so and when the American birth rate for married white women who survived to menopause was dropping to under four from the eight it had been at the beginning of the nineteenth century.[12] There were never more than three Lincoln children, in keeping with this mid-nineteenth-century understanding that children were no longer miniature farm workers used for increasing productivity, as Abraham had been on his father Thomas Lincoln's hardscrabble farms in Kentucky, Indiana, and Illinois. In towns like Springfield where you got ahead with your brain rather than your brawn, children were human investments—expensive projects demanding financial and emotional venture capital. Nor could

[12] Janet Farrell Brodie, *Contraception and Abortion in Nineteenth-Century America* (Ithaca, N.Y.: Cornell University Press, 1994); Ansley J. Coale and Melvin Zelnik, *New Estimates of Fertility and Population in the United States* (Princeton: Princeton University Press, 1963).

you invest as much love and affection—not to mention resources—in them if you had fifteen children—as Mary Todd's father Robert Todd had.

But after Eddie died of tuberculosis in 1850, Mary was almost immediately pregnant with Willie, and because this third Lincoln son needed a playmate, Thomas—universally called Tad—was born in 1853. Only one of these four sons—Robert—survived his mother. In assessing her maternity, it is worth noting that contrary to some interpretations of her selfishness, she was a generous neighbor who loved children—once serving, in an age without infant formulas or rubber nipples, as a wet nurse for a neighbor.[13] Another Springfield mother admired Mary Lincoln so much that she named a daughter after her.[14]

Mary Lincoln, like her husband, was a permissive parent. "We never controlled our children much," Lincoln acknowledged as he worried that the unschooled Tad would get "pokey"—by which the president meant that his son would lose his exuberant sense of freedom. How to raise a child was one of several significant areas about which husband and wife agreed, and it is, by the way, according to today's marriage counselors, an area of significant disagreement between spouses. In the case of the Lincolns the children brought the parents closer together.

To a great extent the Lincoln household revolved around these children, as do many households in our enormously child-centered twenty-first-century world, but this was not the case in most nineteenth-century households. With her husband out of town three or four months a year, riding the circuits not because he did not want to be home with her, but because the 8th Illinois Judicial Circuit was 930 miles long and 100 miles wide and he couldn't get home, she did most of the parenting.

Ahead of her time, Mary Lincoln organized birthday parties for large groups of Robert's, Willie's, and Tad's friends, and she was one of the first women in Springfield to undertake what she called "a children's gala." She dressed up in costume for her eldest son's roles in plays based on Sir Walter Scott's novels, and did the same for the

---

[13] Louis Dusinberre to Ruth Randall, n.d., Ruth Randall Papers, Library of Congress.
[14] Turner and Turner, *Mary Todd Lincoln*, 85–86.

elaborate theatricals her younger sons organized in the White House. She read constantly to and with the boys. She took pride in their academic progress—once boasting to a friend that "our eldest at ten is studying Latin and Greek."[15] She encouraged the boys to come downstairs when there were guests and, to the irritation of these friends who naturally believed their children just as smart, to recite Browning and Shakespeare.

She permitted an impossible menagerie of animals in her house, and in the White House the Lincoln zoo expanded to include turkeys, goats, ponies, and cats. On a trip to Lexington she was furious when her stepmother would not let Eddie keep a kitten. "Let the boys have a good time," visitors to the White House often heard her say, and this included no parental intervention even when the irrepressible Tad led his goat Nanko attached to a cart through the Gold Room during a reception. Only when Tad placed a Confederate flag on a balustrade of the White House roof did his parents intervene.

According to her husband, it was Mary Lincoln who named these children—first after her father, then after the prominent, popular political star of the town Edward Dickinson Baker in a testament to this couple's ambitions; then after her brother-in-law William Wallace, who had been so sympathetic during the illness and death of Eddie; and finally Tad after her husband's father, Thomas. She also gave them the affectionate terms of endearment that suggest her attachment to them. They were "precious," "dear darlings," and "angel boys." It was one of the ironies of her sad life that a woman who might have been consoled by a daughter in her later years instead bore four sons. For she knew the proverb as well as any nineteenth-century American—"A son is a son until he marries; a daughter is a daughter is a daughter forever."

Mary Lincoln, herself one of the most educated women in the United States with twelve years of formal schooling in private academies and boarding schools, also collaborated with her husband about the boys' schooling. They agreed to leave Tad out of school; they agreed in a very unusual choice to send Robert to Harvard. There is only tantalizing evidence about how this idea of sending sixteen-year-old Robert across the plains in the 1850s to the most famous university in America emerged. Certainly only a handful of families in the

---

[15] Baker, *Mary Todd Lincoln*, 121–23.

entire state of Illinois sent their sons east to college before the Civil War. At the very least this decision suggests parental consensus about the ambitions they held for their sons and their common understanding that education was an important tool for success in a modernizing America.

A warm, loving mother, Mary Lincoln was also a warm, loving wife. One of the things that attracted Abraham Lincoln to his wife was her sensuality. Said Lincoln to a Union officer during a reception at the White House after twenty years of marriage, "There is the little woman I fell in love with and once more never fell out of love with." And there are several recollections of the president's observations about the low-cut dresses ("our cat has a long tail tonight") that many thought inappropriate when worn by a forty-year-old-plus matron.[16] Evidently Lincoln did not agree, once joking to his wife that she might consider taking the long train of her satin dress and filling in the front of her plunging neckline. These two, despite his taciturn periods of depression and her high temper, were devoted to each other.

This is not to say that theirs was a placid marriage. Lincoln was a difficult man. He seems to have saved his warmth for his magnificent public messages, and one of his friends once commented that he "was deficient in those little links which make up the great chain of womans happiness."[17] But Mary Lincoln did not think so, writing that her husband's heart was as large as his arms were long. Certainly some of her outbursts were efforts to catch the attention of this very distracted man.

And Mary Lincoln was a difficult woman, who had a tremendous adjustment to make when she married, an adjustment that is often overlooked by her male critics. Alexis de Tocqueville in his journey to the United States in 1831 noted the contrast between the nation's independent, active, vibrant unmarried women and its submissive, sequestered matrons. For Mary Lincoln the change in her status to a sequestered matron was especially difficult. Accustomed to ten slaves

---

[16] Elizabeth Keckley, *Behind the Scenes or Thirty Years a Slave and Four Years in the White House* (New York: G. W. Carleton, 1868), 101; Baker, *Mary Todd Lincoln*, 195–96.

[17] Douglas L. Wilson and Rodney O. Davis, eds., *Herndon's Informants: Letters, Interviews, & Statements about Abraham Lincoln* (Urbana: University of Illinois Press, 1998), 256.

who did the housework for her family in Lexington, she took on novel domestic roles energetically and uncomplainingly in Springfield.[18]

When the Lincolns took up housekeeping after a short stint in a boarding house, she criticized her husband's absences. Yet she faithfully cooked, cleaned, scrubbed, beat the rugs in those biannual climaxes of housecleaning in the spring and fall, changed the linens that served as diapers, and sewed and organized the family clothing in the domestic rounds that became the principal enterprises of her life. Worried about her working too hard, Lincoln once wrote, "get another [girl] as soon as you can to take charge of the dear codgers."[19] As a result, Lincoln, a homebody according to one of his relatives, was, in the words of his definitive biographer, David Herbert Donald, "happy in his home," and that was primarily because of his relationship with his wife.

Besides running the house, Mary Lincoln educated Abraham Lincoln into the middle-class ways that he had not learned on his father's rough farms in the frontier Midwest. As Americans we like to pretend that we want our elected officials to be men and women of the people. But, in fact, we nominate and elect not the poor or nearly poor or even lower middle class, but the middle class and the rich. Mary Lincoln made substantial contributions to her husband's political career when she turned energetically to the task of gentrifying her husband.

It is not surprising that the most substantial purchase of the Lincolns' first year of marriage was a new suit of "superior black cloth." Ever after she battled to make his pants longer, his socks match, and his waistband conform to his natural contours. According to Mary Lincoln's principal antagonist, William Herndon, who stamped her reputation, "She played merry war when he persisted in using his knife in the butter rather than instead the special silver-handled one."[20] Yet these were the manners important for any aspiring politician.

[18] Alexis de Tocqueville, *Democracy in America* (New York: Alfred A. Knopf, 1993), 592; Turner and Turner, *Mary Todd Lincoln*, 30.

[19] Roy P. Basler et al., eds., *The Collected Works of Abraham Lincoln*, 9 vols. (New Brunswick, N.J.: Rutgers University Press, 1953–55), 1:496.

[20] Henry Rankin, *Personal Recollections of Abraham Lincoln* (New York: G. P. Putnam's Sons, 1916); Harry E. Pratt, "The Lincolns Go Shopping," *Journal of the Illinois State Historical Society* 48 (spring 1955): 66; William H. Herndon and Jesse W. Weik, *Herndon's Life of Lincoln* (New York: A. & C. Boni, 1930), 344–45.

This, then, was a marriage of opposites, with Mary and Abraham complementing each other physically and emotionally. He was tall and thin; she, short and always tending to, if not, fat. On his bad days he was depressed and melancholic; on hers she became excited and hot tempered. He was scruffy in dress, she fashionable. He was plebeian and unschooled, she aristocratic and snobbish. He was humble in the manner of the self-confident, she egotistical in the manner of self-doubters. He was on good terms with everyone, she on bad terms with many.

For those who describe the Lincolns' marriage as a constant hell, there is plenty of counter-evidence. "How much, I wish instead of writing, *we* were together," she wrote in May of 1848 when Lincoln was a congressman in Washington and she was visiting her family in Lexington. And he responded, "In this troublesome world, we are never quite satisfied. When you were here, I thought you hindered me some in attending to business; but now, having nothing but business—no variety—it has grown exceedingly tasteless to me. . . . I shall be impatient till I see you. . . . [C]ome when you please."[21]

And in another display of spousal affection when Mary Lincoln had gone to New York in early 1861 to buy some eastern clothes so that the Lincolns would not be thought western rubes in sophisticated Washington, the train from the East was delayed for three days in a snowstorm. And each night a devoted husband went to the station to meet his wife. These are deeds, not words or the opinions of others.

In 1865 as the Civil War drew to a close, there is poignant testimony of their affection as Mary and Abraham Lincoln took several carriage rides during which they talked about what they would do after his second term was ended. And then, on that sad April night in 1865, they meant to enjoy another of the things that they shared—a love of the theater. But the comedy *Our American Cousin,* intended to be a diversion for an exhausted president, turned out to be a tragedy for all Americans—but especially for Mary Lincoln, who saw her husband murdered before her eyes.

Now began the final phase of Mary Lincoln's life—a period of seventeen years from 1865 until her death in 1882 as a widow. It is in this period that Mary Lincoln demonstrates an impressive and, I

---

[21] Turner and Turner, *Mary Todd Lincoln,* 38; *Collected Works of Lincoln,* 1:465, 477, 496.

believe, unacknowledged courage. True, she was certainly an agent provocateur in some of the tragedy that overtook her. But she was also a victim of some bad judgments on the part of her only surviving son, Robert Lincoln.

After her youngest son Tad died in 1871—again, as with her sons Eddie and Willie and her husband, she watched him die—Mary Lincoln became a confirmed spiritualist, traveling from spa to faith healer, buying too many things, though it was her money after Lincoln's estate was divided, bothering her son Robert, who in 1875 began the legal proceedings that ended in his mother's confinement in an insane asylum.

What is admirable about this episode as it reveals the character of Mary Lincoln is her solitary struggle to get out of the Bellevue asylum in Batavia, Illinois. Alone, deserted by her closest relative, who no doubt thought that he was doing the right thing insofar as his mother was concerned, Mary Lincoln waged a solitary struggle. She had been sentenced to an indeterminate sentence with her confinement necessary until, in the words of the Illinois statute, "her reason was restored" or at least until Dr. Robert Patterson, who ran the asylum, and her son allowed that it was. Discharge through a writ of habeas corpus was easier than it had been in the past, but especially for women whose relatives disapproved of their being discharged, obtaining releases was still a difficult matter.

Suffice it to say that she was successful; suffice it to say that she somehow got a letter past the two men who censored her mail—that is, the superintendent and Robert; suffice it to say that she was successful because she enlisted the support of one of the only female lawyers in the United States—Myra Bradwell, who in turn orchestrated a public campaign that focused on the theme "Why is Mary Lincoln in an Insane Asylum? She is as sane as any woman."[22]

Indeed, Mary Lincoln was sane, no matter how neurotic in today's terms we might judge her. For if she were insane, how is it that she lived alone in France for the next four years? And why is it that she spent such a short time in an asylum without any treatment? Certainly Mary Lincoln had one of the shortest incarcerations in Bata-

---

[22] Jean H. Baker, "Myra Colby Bradwell: Champion of Women's Legal Rights," in Susan Ware, ed., *Forgotten Heroes: Inspiring American Portraits from Our Leading Historians* (New York: Free Press, 1998), 103–10.

via's history. She was in the asylum exactly three months and three weeks, during which she was in prudent advertisement of her sanity a model patient. Unlike most of her fellow patients, she received no chloral hydrate (the Prozac of its time), which she had been taking for her insomnia, no *cannabis indica*, no morphine or laudanum, and no physical restraint. Yet in those days mental illness was often considered a moral failing, and so she did receive a great deal of rest and a lot of irrelevant moral instruction from the superintendent.

Released from her incarceration but with her money still under Robert's control, Mary Lincoln waited a year in Springfield until the period of his conservatorship ended. And then she fled to Europe because she believed that her son's need to justify his actions would always make him suspicious and ready to send forth his detectives and doctors to imprison her again.

So Mary Lincoln lived among strangers in Pau, a city in southern France near the Pyrenees, a place much heralded for its medicinal powers. The air was fresh, the barometric pressure constant, and warm mineral springs were available in the nearby mountains. Here for four years she stayed, until in 1880 at the age of sixty-two her health deteriorated. Blind and arthritic, she returned to Springfield to live with her sister Elizabeth.

"I wish I could forget myself," Mary Lincoln once lamented. It was a lifelong battle that she often lost, though in the process of remembering herself, she made certain that we would too. Let us make sure we do so with fairness and balance.

Undoubtedly the most famous autographed photo of Lincoln, this magnificent 1861 print by an unknown photographer was inscribed to "Mrs. Lucy G. Speed, from whose pious hand I accepted the present of an Oxford Bible twenty years ago." It was signed "Washington, D.C., October 3, 1861" by "A. Lincoln." The photograph itself has faded badly, though the inscription remains crisp. Lincoln never wrote a longer or more personal inscription. (*Collection of the J. B. Speed Art Museum, Louisville, Kentucky*)

How the Civil War aged Abraham Lincoln: left, the youthful-looking, robust fifty-one-year-old as he appeared in June 1860 in Springfield, Illinois, a few weeks after winning the Republican nomination for the presidency, in a photograph by Alexander Hesler; right, looking haggard and careworn less than five years later as he sat for his last studio photograph at the gallery of Alexander Gardner in Washington on February 5, 1865. The president's private secretary, John M. Hay, wrote, "As time wore on and the war held its terrible course, upon no one of all those who lived through it was its effect more apparent than upon the President. . . . [T]he eye grew veiled by constant meditation on momentous subjects; the air of reserve and detachment from his surroundings increased. He aged with great rapidity." (*Library of Congress*)

Lincoln and his early military captains confer in the White House, in a fanciful but handsome 1861 engraving by an unknown printmaker. From left to right: Lincoln, Secretary of State William H. Seward, General Winfield Scott, Secretary of War Simon Cameron, General George B. McClellan, General Benjamin F. Butler, General John E. Wool, Major Robert Anderson, and General John C. Frémont. It is highly unlikely that such a large group of key military officers ever gathered together at the executive mansion at the same time, but such pictures gave Northern picture buyers assurance that the war was being managed by professional soldiers. (*Library of Congress*)

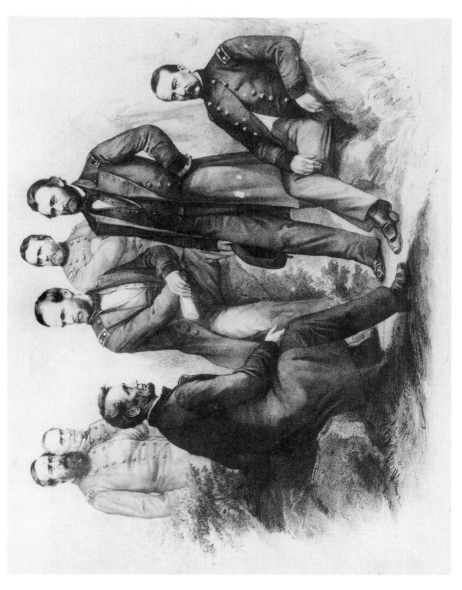

Lincoln and His Generals, an 1865 lithograph by Jones & Clark of New York, showed the commander in chief with the later navy and army heroes who helped win the war: Admiral David D. Porter, Admiral David G. Farragut, Lincoln, General William T. Sherman, General George H. Thomas, General Ulysses S. Grant, and General Philip H. Sheridan. This imaginary council of war appears to take place on the battlefield and, unlike the 1861 print of the president with his original military family, focuses viewer attention squarely on Lincoln, on whom all eyes here are focused. (*Library of Congress*)

Two important generals who served under Lincoln during the Civil War: left, the flamboyant George B. McClellan, whose reluctance to launch offensive campaigns frustrated Lincoln in the early years of the conflict (*Library of Congress*); and right, Ulysses S. Grant, whose tenacity fatally eroded Confederate strength in Virginia in 1864 and 1865 (*The Frank and Virginia Williams Collection of Lincolniana*). Ironically, both generals figured in Lincoln's campaign for reelection in 1864: Grant rejected overtures that he consider challenging his commander in chief, and McClellan accepted the Democratic nomination to oppose him—and lost decisively.

The Battle of Gettysburg, a chromolithograph issued by Kurz & Allison of Chicago in 1884, showed the fiery climax of the third and final day of the most famous military encounter of the Civil War. Confederate General Lewis Armistead is shown falling dead from his horse on July 1, 1863, as Pickett's Charge fails and the Union prevails at the so-called "high water mark of the Confederacy." The victory—and the sacrifice of the battle dead—inspired Lincoln's most famous oration four months later. (*Collection of Harold Holzer*)

By 1861, an outpouring of pro-Union graphics by Northern artists and printmakers helped revive Lincoln's postinaugural reputation. This lithograph, *After a Little While* by Charles Magnus of New York, contrasted a heroic Lincoln, marching to victory amid the cheers of working people, to the slouching figure of his Confederate counterpart, Jefferson Davis, confronting a gallows built for "southern fanatics." In truth, the military veteran Davis was an exceptional rider, while the long-limbed, quintessentially civilian Lincoln often looked ridiculous on horseback. (*Collection of Harold Holzer*)

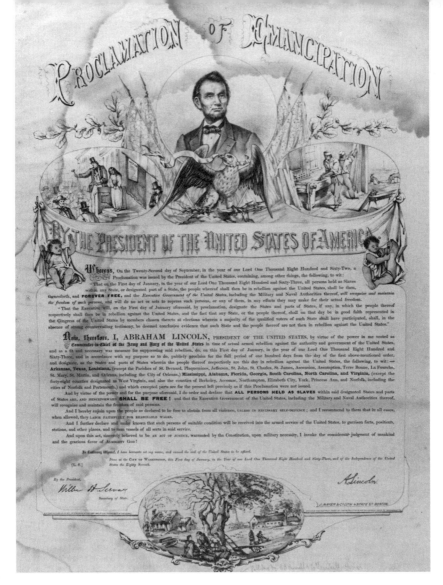

Lincoln's 1863 Emancipation Proclamation forever changed the sixteenth president's reputation. "If my name ever goes down in history," Lincoln confided as he prepared to sign the document, "it will be for this act." Publishers issued a number of pamphlet and broadside reproductions of the document as early as 1863. Though its legalistic prose was not particularly inspiring, these decorative pieces were often displayed in pro-Republican households. This lithographed example, complete with a portrait of Lincoln surmounting the words of the proclamation, was published by J. Mayer of Boston in 1864. The vignette scenes flanking the Lincoln image are meant to represent the proclamation's impact on the status of African Americans: at left, a woman is sold at a degrading slave auction; at right, freed blacks become paid laborers. (*The Lincoln Museum, Fort Wayne, Indiana, Neg. No. 2501A*)

Lincoln's early presidential reputation suffered a severe blow when he agreed to pass through the hostile city of Baltimore incognito en route to his inauguration. Cartoonists exaggerated his "disguise" that day, suggesting that he traveled in a Scotch tam and a military greatcoat. Copperhead Baltimore artist Adalbert Volck so depicted him in this 1862 etching, portraying a frightened president-elect emerging from a freight car and cowering before the sight of a harmless cat. (*Collection of Harold Holzer*)

UNION AND LIBERTY!   AND   UNION AND SLAVERY!

Two pro-Lincoln cartoons from the 1864 presidential campaign. At top, Lincoln's platform of "Union and Liberty" is contrasted to Democratic candidate George B. McClellan's platform of "Union and Slavery." In fact, McClellan rebuked his party's call for immediate armistice, but that did not stop some artists from assailing him. Here he is shown greeting Confederate President Jefferson Davis at a slave auction. The lithograph was issued by M. E. Siebert of New York. (*Library of Congress*) Bottom: New York printmakers Currier & Ives issued *The Old Bull Dog on the Right Track,* which suggested that Ulysses S. Grant's fierce determination would soon conquer the Confederacy—a result that Lincoln's Democratic foe, McClellan, had failed to achieve while he was commanding the Army of the Potomac. (*The Lincoln Museum, Fort Wayne, Indiana, Neg. No. 2598*)

THE OLD BULL DOG ON THE RIGHT TRACK.

Not all of the graphic art produced for the 1864 presidential campaign presented Lincoln in a positive light. Some cartoons assailed him mercilessly, none more so than *The Commander-in-Chief Conciliating the Soldier's* [sic] *Votes on the Battle Field.* Sold by the anti-Lincoln *New York World*, the lithograph suggested that Lincoln had insensitively requested comic songs while walking among the Union dead and wounded at the Antietam battlefield. The charge reportedly outraged Lincoln, who contemplated writing a refutation of the allegation. Note that Lincoln is shown holding a Scotch tam, the disguise he had allegedly worn to evade assassins in Baltimore three years earlier—a symbol frequently employed thereafter to symbolize Lincoln's supposed cowardice. (*Library of Congress*)

Lincoln in City Point by German printmaker Gustave Bartsch was probably intended to portray the commander in chief riding triumphantly through the conquered and devastated Confederate capital of Richmond (not City Point, which was the Union army's headquarters). Notwithstanding this crucial error, the print evocatively suggests that the president had been an active participant in the subjugation of the Confederacy and the liberation of the slaves, who are shown here kneeling in gratitude as Lincoln rides by in triumph. General Grant and Secretary of War Edwin M. Stanton are relegated to the background. (*Library of Congress*)

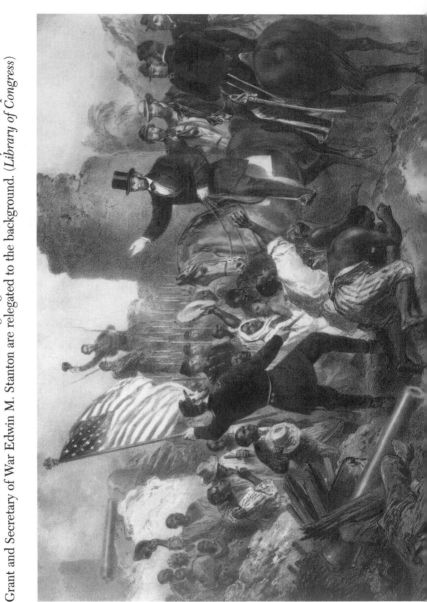

The only photograph of Lincoln making a speech was taken by Alexander Gardner at the inaugural ceremonies of March 4, 1865. Standing on the portico of the U.S. Capitol, behind a lectern that is much too low for the tall president, Lincoln holds his inaugural address in his hands; he is about to ask for a peace "with malice toward none, with charity for all." Justices of the Supreme Court sit in the front row at right, and cabinet secretaries and the outgoing and incoming vice presidents sit at left. Note that an observer at top right is holding the tip of the American flag. The weather was blustery that day, and listeners probably found it difficult to hear the inaugural address; the helpful gentleman was probably clutching the flag to prevent it from flapping loudly in the breeze and drowning out Lincoln's extraordinary words. (*Library of Congress*)

Lincoln's martyrdom inspired a huge outpouring of graphic and musical tributes to the fallen hero. The medium that combined both artistic impulses was illustrated sheet music. For this handsome example, a New York lithographer provided a portrait based loosely on an 1864 Mathew Brady Studio photograph, and publisher Horace Waters provided a funeral march dedicated to Lincoln's memory. (*The Frank and Virginia Williams Collection of Lincolniana*)

Mary Todd Lincoln (1818–82), who sometimes called herself "Mrs. President Lincoln," aroused much controversy during her husband's term of office—and ever since. During her first year in the White House, she often modeled her newest, most lavish gowns for Washington's leading photographers. Here she poses (left) in a particularly becoming frock, adorned with fresh flowers, for Mathew Brady's camera in 1861. (*The Frank and Virginia Williams Collection of Lincolniana*)

Wearing black in mourning for her son Willie, Mary Todd Lincoln posed for
a Brady Studio portrait issued around 1863. She would never again be
photographed, except in mourning regalia. Note that in the later portrait,
she even wears specially made mourning jewelry.

After Lincoln's death, image makers concocted composite scenes of the Lincoln family, who had never posed together in life. They sold the results to a public eager to believe that the martyred president had enjoyed the solace of domestic life during the anguishing days of the Civil War. In the romanticized print at left, the Lincolns' sons Robert (in uniform) and Willie listen with their mother as the president reads before the family hearth. In fact, Willie had died in 1862, all but wrecking his mother's fragile mental health. Robert spent much of the war at college, and his younger brother, Tad, who is not portrayed in this curious print, became the only child living in the Lincoln White House. (*The Lincoln Museum, Fort Wayne, Neg. No. 2263*) Below, W. H. Robertson of New York issued this far grander scene, showing the entire family together. (*The Frank and Virginia Williams Collection of Lincolniana*)

The first serious Lincoln collector was the president's own first-born son, Robert Todd Lincoln (1843–1926), the only one of the Lincolns' children to survive to maturity. Robert became a lawyer and wealthy business tycoon, and kept close—some believe obsessive—personal watch over his father's papers for the rest of his long life. Under the terms of Robert's will, the material was kept from the public until 1947. (*The Lincoln Museum, Fort Wayne, Indiana, Neg. No. 3803*)

One of the greatest recent Lincoln acquisitions was this letter from Lincoln to General Grant, asking him to take Robert Lincoln into his "military family" if it could be accomplished "without embarrassment to you, or detriment to the service." Lincoln offered to pay for Robert's salary himself, but Grant obligingly placed him on his official staff to accommodate his commander in chief. (*The Forbes Museum, New York*)

Executive Mansion,

Washington, Jan. 19 . 1865

Lieut. General Grant:

        Please read and answer this letter as though I was not President, but only a friend. My son, now in his twentysecond year, having graduated at Harvard, wishes to see something of the war before it ends. I do not wish to put him in the ranks, nor yet to give him a Commission, to which those who have already served long, are better entitled, and better qualified to hold. Could he, without embarrassment to you, or detriment to the service, go into your Military family with some nominal rank, I, and not the public, furnishing his necessary means? If no, say so without the least hesitation, because I am as anxious, and as deeply interested, that you shall not be encumbered as you can be yourself.

        Yours truly,

        A. Lincoln

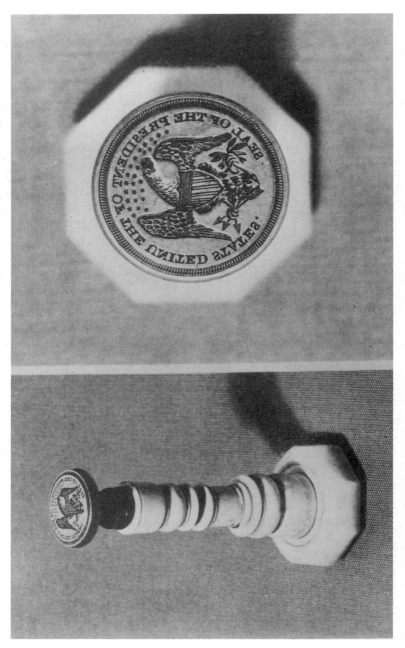

Lincoln's ivory-handled, brass presidential seal was one of the great personal mementos owned by pioneer Lincoln collector Oliver R. Barrett, and sold at the auction of his fabulous trove in 1952. The relic fetched only $650. (*From a Parke Bernet Catalog, 1952*)

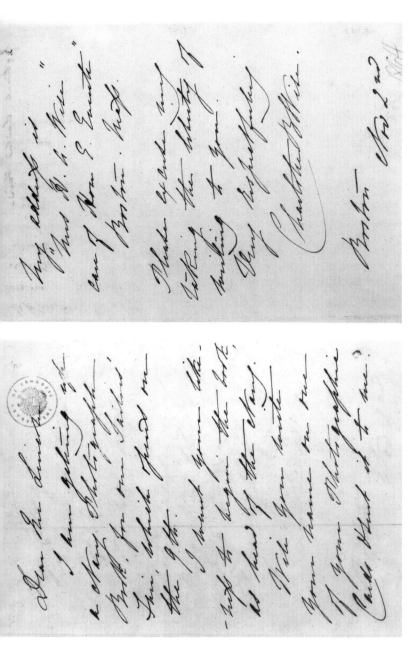

An early request for an autographed Lincoln photograph, sent by Charlotte Wise of Boston in 1864. Mrs. Wise took "the liberty of writing" in order to secure a keepsake that could be sold at a sailors' charity fair. Lincoln no doubt obliged—especially since Mrs. Wise asked that the photo be sent care of Edward Everett, the distinguished orator who had shared the speakers' platform with the president the previous November at Gettysburg. (*Library of Congress*)

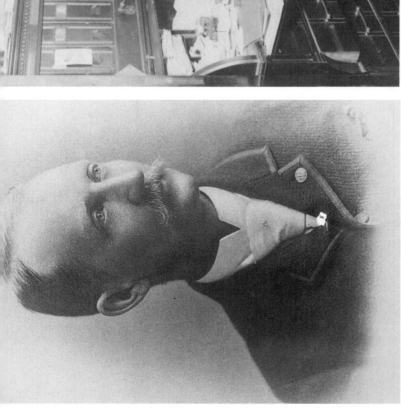

Two of the greatest of the early Lincoln collectors: left, Osborn H. Oldroyd, who lived in both Lincoln's Springfield home and, later, the Washington boarding house where Lincoln died; and right, Daniel Fish, whose massive book collection became the nucleus of the library of the Lincoln Museum. (*The Lincoln Museum, Fort Wayne, Indiana, Neg. Nos. 2497, 2575*)

Many of the great private Lincolniana collections ultimately became the core holdings of great public Lincolniana collections. The extraordinary collection of Daniel Fish, for example, was sold to the Lincoln National Life Foundation (now the Lincoln Museum) in Fort Wayne, Indiana. Many of his books and collectibles are visible in this photograph of the foundation's former headquarters. *(The Lincoln Museum, Fort Wayne, Indiana)*

I CERTIFY, That *George Warburton* volunteered and served *as a private* in the Company of Mounted Volunteers under my command, in the Regiment commanded by Col. SAMUEL M. THOMPSON, in the Brigade under the command of Generals S. WHITESIDE and H. ATKINSON, called into the service of the United States by the Commander-in-Chief of the Militia of the State, for the protection of the North Western Frontier against an Invasion of the British Band of Sac and other tribes of Indians,—that he was enrolled on the *21st* day of *April* 1832, and was HONORABLY DISCHARGED on the *7th* day of *June* thereafter, having served *4 F days*

Given under my hand, this *11th* day of *September* 1832.

A Lincoln
Cpt.

Abraham Lincoln once confided that his election as captain of volunteers in the Black Hawk War in 1832 "gave me more pleasure than any I have had since." In this rare surviving document from that era, Captain Lincoln signs a discharge for Private George Warburton. Such mementos of Lincoln's early life are extremely rare—and remain avidly pursued by collectors. (*The Frank and Virginia Williams Collection of Lincolniana*)

10

Abraham Lincoln's Body and Body Politic: Two Puzzles in Mid-Nineteenth-Century American Political Language and Culture

Iver Bernstein

DURING A VISIT to the Soldier's Home in Washington, D.C., one summer evening in 1862, President Abraham Lincoln walked over to a companion, clapped his hand on the back of the man's head, and said,

> Here is a tumor, drawing upon the vitality of your body. You must be rid of it or it will destroy your life. Now we bring in three physicians to have a consultation over this tumor. All agree that it must be removed, but each one has his own opinion of the proper course to be pursued. One wants to poultice it and sweat it and so evaporate it. Another is positive that it should be taken out at once, that it should be cut around and pulled out, even at the risk of the patient's life. But the third doctor says, "Gentlemen, I differ from you both as to the treatment proposed. My advice is to prepare the patient for the operation before venturing upon it. He must be depleted and the amount of his blood diminished." Now, my opinion is that the third doctor is about right.[1]

Lincoln was, of course, speaking of slavery, and his story about the doctors and the tumor came as a parenthetical and illustrative com-

I thank Harold Holzer, John Y. Simon, and the participants at the November 2000 Lincoln Forum at Gettysburg, and colleagues at the October 2000 Washington University History Department Colloquium, for their commentary.
[1] Don E. Fehrenbacher and Virginia Fehrenbacher, eds., *Recollected Words of Abraham Lincoln* (Stanford: Stanford University Press, 1996), 367–68. Lincoln's words were recalled years later by Elbert S. Porter, clergyman and editor of a religious newspaper.

ment in a set of remarks about slavery as "no small affair" and as something that could not "be done away with at once." Slavery, he elaborated, had grown up with and now permeated the Union. Like a cancer, it had insinuated itself into politics, commerce, industry, and religion, North and South. Attacking so pervasive an evil might annihilate the Union and destroy what he called "our national life"— the promise of the world's freest and most successful democratic government. Here was the thorniest of dilemmas: the spread of slavery destroyed the freedom of blacks, fatally compromised the freedom of whites, and had to be stopped. But if the Union did not live, *no one* would or could be free.[2]

Lincoln returned to the metaphor of slavery as a cancer repeatedly. Significantly, he came to it, perhaps for the first time, in the wake of the furor over the Kansas-Nebraska Act of 1854. That bill repealed the Missouri Compromise, which had restricted the sphere of slavery in the territories of the Louisiana Purchase and was regarded by many, along with the Constitution, as part of the legal basis for American nationality. At Peoria, in October 1854, Lincoln said, "I particularly object to the NEW position which the avowed principle of this Nebraska law gives to slavery in the body politic." Referring to the absence of the words "slave" or "slavery" in the Federal Constitution and to the clause putting off the prohibition of the African slave trade for twenty years, he observed, "the thing is hid away, . . . just as an afflicted man hides away a wen or a cancer, which he dares not cut out at once, lest he bleed to death; with the promise, nevertheless, that the cutting may begin at the end of a given time."[3] In the debate between Lincoln and Stephen A. Douglas at Alton in 1858, Lincoln said of the danger of the expansion of slavery, "How do you propose to improve the condition of things by enlarging slavery—by spreading it out and making it bigger? You may have a wen or cancer upon your person and not be able to cut it out lest you bleed to death; but surely it is no way to cure it, to engraft it and spread it over your whole body. That is no proper way of treating what you regard a wrong."[4]

Lincoln could vary the image and, as he did in 1864, compare

[2] Ibid.

[3] Roy P. Basler et al., eds., *The Collected Works of Abraham Lincoln,* 9 vols. (New Brunswick, N.J.: Rutgers University Press, 1953–55), 2:274.

[4] Robert W. Johannsen, ed., *The Lincoln-Douglas Debates of 1858* (New York: Oxford University Press, 1965), 317.

slavery to a gangrenous limb, an analogy that a nation in the midst of a bloody war could well appreciate. He told the British antislavery orator George Thompson and a group of Thompson's friends, "The moment came when I felt that slavery must die that the nation might live. I have sometimes used the illustration, in this connection, of a man with a diseased limb and his surgeon. So long as there is a chance of the patient's restoration, the surgeon is solemnly bound to try to save both life *and* limb; but when the crisis comes, and the limb must be sacrificed as the only chance of saving the life, no honest man will hesitate."[5] In part, Lincoln was explaining to this group of abolitionists why he issued the Emancipation Proclamation when he did, and not earlier. It is also worth noting that, by 1864, the context had shifted. Now, at the height of the war and after the proclamation, Northerners hardly had to be reminded, as they had to be a decade earlier, that slavery was a festering wound that would not heal itself and would keep disrupting the lives of those reckless enough to ignore it.[6] Now, in 1864, Lincoln could look back on what he called a "great revolution in public sentiment," which made it possible to save the life of the nation and take final action against slavery.[7]

Lincoln, as historian James M. McPherson has aptly observed, was especially adept at using metaphors to make the issues of the war era vivid and relevant to the concerns of his audience of ordinary Americans.[8] And certainly his analogies to disease and the human

[5] Fehrenbacher and Fehrenbacher, eds., *Recollected Words of Abraham Lincoln,* 83.

[6] See Wayne D. Fields, "The Making of An Issue: A Rhetorical Analysis of the Lincoln-Douglas Debates" (Ph.D. dissertation, University of Chicago, 1972), 161–62.

[7] It is also worth noting that Lincoln could find corporeal metaphors pertinent when describing political and constitutional problems *other* than those posed by slavery. I have in mind the well-known letter of June 1863 to Erastus Corning and others, in which Lincoln says that suspending habeas corpus was a strong remedy appropriate for a sick wartime body politic afflicted with "a clear, flagrant, and gigantic case of Rebellion." Such a treatment was like an emetic—and you could no more apply the therapeutic rules for a healthy peacetime body politic to the wartime version, than you could expect a person to continue to have an appetite for emetics after he or she was well again. See *Collected Works of Lincoln,* 6:264, 267.

[8] James M. McPherson, "How Lincoln Won the War with Metaphors," in *Abraham Lincoln and the Second American Revolution* (New York: Oxford University Press, 1991), 93–112.

body were among his most inventive and effective.[9] For our purposes, it is worth noting Lincoln's highly self-conscious and persistent use of the metaphor of the body politic: "I have *sometimes used the illustration,* in this connection, of a man with a diseased limb and his surgeon," he told abolitionist Thompson and company, regarding the relation between the death of slavery and the life of the nation.[10] It is also important to point out that the diseased limb metaphor, like the cancer metaphor, allowed Lincoln to pinpoint a specific and physically identifiable evil that was part of the body politic and a deadly threat to its existence. The question of why Lincoln found such analogies between the Union and its Constitution, on the one hand, and the "constitution" of the human body, on the other, so compelling, and further, what they meant to him and his audiences, is one that historians have generally overlooked, and one that represents, I hope to suggest, a historical problem of the first order.

This question can be fruitfully paired with another. Why did Lincoln continually refer in his political speech to *his own specific body*—his inevitably self-deprecating references to his physical height, face, and so forth? His comment made on the stump in 1858—"Nobody ever expected me to be President. In my poor, lean, lank face, nobody has ever seen that any cabbages were sprouting out"—comes to mind, as does his satirizing of his own physical height but modest standing in national politics as an antislavery outsider, in contrast to the status of his diminutive opponent Senator Stephen A. Douglas, known as the "Little Giant," as one of the U.S. Senate's so-called "great men."[11] In the post-Revolutionary era, and indeed, well into the antebellum years, no political figure of proper character would have been caught dead referring to their body in public discourse. Why, for Lincoln, in what appears to be a striking departure, did such references become standard oratorical fare?

To link these questions and answer them, we will have to make a

---

[9] On the subject of the use of inflammatory language to depict slavery by antislavery activists of the 1850s, see Charles Sumner to Theodore Tilton, July 21, [18]60, Charles Sumner Papers, Houghton Library, Harvard University. In response to what appears to have been Tilton's observation that certain language might be off-putting, Sumner wrote, "But can I find anything which drives the subject home more?"

[10] Italics are mine.

[11] *Collected Works of Lincoln,* 2:467 ("They remind us that *he* is a very *great man,* and that the largest of *us* are very small ones").

foray into the history of political speech in the nineteenth century. But it will first be necessary to offer some observations about the histories of the two kinds of "constitutions"—that is to say, changing understandings of the U.S. Constitution and medical conceptions of the human body (and particularly views of disease and remedy) in the mid–nineteenth century. Then we can return to the subject of Lincoln's rhetoric of the body politic and his own physical body, able to appreciate how in the 1850s Lincoln and some of his Northern contemporaries were experimenting with new forms of political and constitutional thinking that would become widespread in the North by the end of the Civil War.

One of the most notable of the innovations of the framers of the new government of the United States in 1787 was embodied in the principle of constitutional amendment. By this means, historian Gordon S. Wood has written, "Americans had in fact institutionalized and legitimized revolution."[12] The metaphor of the "body politic" and the legal fiction of the "king's two bodies" had endowed the British monarchy with stability and permanence: even with the death of the king in his physical body he survived in his "mystical body," in which capacity "the king is esteemed to be immortal, invisible, not subject to death, infirmity, nonage, etc."[13] In response to the question "Where. . . is the King of America?" Thomas Paine's 1776 manifesto of the American Revolution *Common Sense* proclaimed that "in America THE LAW IS KING."[14] And so it is not surprising that the Founders turned to metaphors of bodily disease and cure to explain what was so pathbreaking about their new conception of law, that is, constitutional rule by the people. Thomas Pownall saw "*a healing principle*" in Americans' constitutional ability to alter their governments, and James Wilson called the principle of amendment "the

---

[12] Gordon S. Wood, *The Creation of the American Republic, 1776–1787* (Chapel Hill: University of North Carolina Press, 1969), 614.

[13] Sir Edward Coke, *Calvin's Case*, 7 Co. Rep. 18 (1608), quoted in David T. Konig, "Legal Fictions and the Rule(s) of Law: The Jeffersonian Critique of Common-Law Adjudication," in Christopher L. Tomlins and Bruce H. Mann, eds., *The Many Legalities of Early America* (Chapel Hill: University of North Carolina Press, 2001), 100. The starting point for all discussion of the body politic is Ernst H. Kantorowicz, *The King's Two Bodies: A Study in Mediaeval Political Theology* (Princeton: Princeton University Press, 1957).

[14] Thomas Paine, *Common Sense* (1776; reprinted, London: Penguin Books, 1976), 98.

great panacea of human politics," delivering the new American republic from the age-old tendency of governments, and especially, of
republics, to dissolve into violence and tyranny.[15] The idea of a self-
healing republic whose ingeniously constructed fundamental law allowed it to weather the transience and instability historically associated with popular rule was a compelling one for the Founding
generation.

Historians are beginning to ponder the significance of the fact that
after the flurry of the first twelve amendments between 1791 and
1804, the Constitution was not again amended until the passage of
the Thirteenth Amendment abolishing black chattel slavery in 1865
(and that, only at the conclusion of a titanic civil war).[16] By the 1840s,
the founding document had not been altered for decades, and the
text's preservation, "as it was," was considered by most Americans
to be necessary for the preservation of popular liberties.[17] How this
antebellum commitment to a static constitution, so different from the
Founding generation's pride in the document's "healing principle,"
came to be is an important historical question whose answer would
take us beyond the confines of this essay. But some of what was at
stake becomes evident in the rhetorical efforts of Senator Henry Clay
of Kentucky to adjust the nation's founding political contract in the
heyday of this era of constitutional stasis, during the congressional
debates over what was to become the Compromise of 1850. The differences between Clay's use of the metaphor of the body politic, in
1850, and Lincoln's, in 1854, are instructive.

As the national political crisis deepened in late spring 1850, Henry
Clay argued on the Senate floor for the need for a comprehensive
approach to all of the controversies that divided North and South:

> Now, what is the plan of the President? I will describe it by a simile,
> in a manner which cannot be misunderstood. Here are five wounds—
> one, two, three, four, five—bleeding and threatening the well being, if
> not the existence of the body politic. What is the plan of the President?
> Is it to heal all these wounds? No such thing. It is only to heal one of
> the five, and to leave the other four to bleed more profusely than ever,

---

[15] Quoted in Wood, *Creation of the American Republic*, 613–14.

[16] See Michael Vorenberg, *Final Freedom: The Civil War, the Abolition of Slavery,
and the Thirteenth Amendment* (Cambridge, Mass.: Cambridge University Press,
2001), 11–18.

[17] Ibid., 15.

Honest old Abe on the Stump. Springfield 1858. Honest old Abe on the Stump, at the ratification Meeting of Presidential nominations. Springfield 1860. Printmaker unknown. This campaign caricature contrasted a two-faced Lincoln's onetime, self-professed lack of ambition as a Senate candidate, to his growing appetite for attention as the presidential race began two years later. The print features Lincoln's famous 1858 declaration "In my poor, lean, lank face, nobody has ever seen that any cabbages were sprouting out" reprinted within the lithograph in what appears to be not merely a voice balloon, but a deflating trial balloon as well. *(Photo: Library of Congress)*

by the sole admission of California, even if it should produce death itself. I have said that five wounds are open and bleeding. What are they?

"First," Clay went on,

> there is California; there are the territories second; there is the question of the boundary of Texas the third; there is the fugitive slave bill the fourth; and there is the question of the slave trade in the District of Columbia fifth. The President, instead of proposing a plan comprehending all the diseases of the country, looks only at one. . . . After the observations which I addressed to the Senate a week ago, I did hope and trust there would have been a reciprocation from the other end of the avenue, as to the desire to heal, not one wound only, which being healed alone would exasperate and aggravate instead of harmonizing the country, but to heal them all.

"Unless," Clay would conclude, "some such measure will prevail, instead of healing and closing the wounds of the country, instead of stopping the effusion of blood, it will flow in still greater quantities, with still greater danger to the Republic."[18]

It is hard not to be struck by the confidence of Clay's pronouncement, and not only because he is facing down a sitting president, Zachary Taylor. Clay was offering himself, in rhetorical terms, as a kind of physician of the body politic, whose analogy of "five wounds" could frame how Americans understood the tangle of issues roiling the Congress and lead them to a safe political and constitutional solution that would keep the Union and Americans' project of popular self-government intact. It is also crucial to recall that the "gag rule" sponsored by the South Carolinian John C. Calhoun and his allies—a ban against any discussion of the subject of slavery on the floor of Congress—had been lifted only five-and-a-half years before.[19] There remained among many congressmen (and not only those from the South) a strong sentiment that slavery was a "private" matter, within the white slaveholder's purview and dominion as property owner and *paterfamilias*, and thus an inappropriate matter for public and political debate.[20]

---

[18] *Cong. Globe,* 31st Cong., 1st sess., Appendix pt. I, 614–15 (May 21, 1850).

[19] See William Lee Miller, *Arguing about Slavery: The Great Battle in the United States Congress* (New York: Alfred A. Knopf, 1996), for a full discussion of the history of the gag rule in the U.S. Congress.

[20] It should be stressed that many of those who took this position also argued passionately that slavery was explicitly protected by the Constitution and, on the eve of the Civil War, would lobby for a congressionally enacted federal slave code.

This overlapped with another concern of many mid-nineteenth-century Americans: that the "independent" male public that participated in voting and other forms of political decision making maintain a commitment to "reason"—both to ensure that the private domain of the family not be overrun or corrupted by the turmoil of electoral politics and to protect the "rationality" of the male-dominated political sphere from the passions of "dependent" women, children, and slaves who could not rule themselves (and hence, could not govern others) and were accordingly defined solely by their status within the household and denied a role in political life. In this context Clay's use of the image of the body politic was like the surgeon's elaborate routine of donning mask, gown, and gloves and scrubbing in before proceeding with a delicate and dangerous operation. The metaphor allowed Clay to handle the potentially septic "private" matter of slavery without unduly invading the dominion of the slave-owning *paterfamilias* and the "protected" status of slaves and other dependents therein, and to do so without compromising the rationality of the public, political sphere for which he spoke in his capacity as U.S. senator.[21] Further, Clay shared with many other adherents of the Whig Party a neoclassical faith in the prophetic orator who could apply the fruits of a comprehensive knowledge to the practical conditions of American society.[22] He was confident that he could mobilize his oratorical gifts to play a dramatic but highly sensitive role: that is, contain within the domain of *talk* the controversies over the status of fugitive slaves, the refractory demands of the state of Texas, and the admission of California as a free state, which all had the potential to spark revolutionary *action*.

Clay's use of the metaphor of the body politic, then, was part of a bold effort to open up, examine, and renegotiate the constitutional contract, but to do so within tightly scripted constraints, under the political trusteeship of select leaders, without unleashing the destabilizing and more fully democratic possibilities of mobilizing those who

---

[21] Of course, it was the contention of many of slavery's defenders—fiercely contested by northern antislavery critics—that the slave-owning family did protect slaves as cared-for "dependents" and not degrade and exploit them as chattel property.

[22] On the neoclassical conception of oratory, see Robert A. Ferguson, *Law and Letters in American Culture* (Cambridge, Mass.: Harvard University Press, 1984); for the importance of oratory within Whig political culture, see Daniel Walker Howe, *The Political Culture of the American Whigs* (Chicago: University of Chicago Press, 1979).

were not considered to be full parties to that contract. It represented a form of surrogate amendment—a rhetorical remaking of the Constitution. Langdon Cheves, Charleston lawyer and president of the Bank of the United States, wrote Clay regarding his 1820 Compromise:

> The Missouri question has done, irremediably, much evil, and the disease can never be Completely eradicated. But you have accomplished all that was Practicable & so much as leaves the Patient a whole Constitution—I Perceive while Writing that the metaphor is not Solemn enough for the Occasion & that to speak literally is best to express its importance & difficulty—The Constitution of the Union was in danger & has been Saved.[23]

The elderly former president James Madison congratulated Clay after his 1833 speech on the tariff that helped seal that year's historic compromise: "I need not repeat what is said by all, on the ability and advantages with which the Subject was handled. It has certainly had the effect of an Anodyne on the feverish excitement under which the public mind was laboring; & a relapse may happily not ensue."[24] Clay's biographer Calvin Colton did not, like Cheves and Madison, use bodily imagery, but he similarly saw Clay's intervention as a one-time-only event that promised permanent constitutional remedy without significant change:

> In every instance in which he employed it, he sprung it on the nation, . . . as a beneficent agent sent down from heaven, to quiet a great social and political agitation, by means which nothing but a creative genius could have devised. When no one else could see how a constitutional and legal remedy could be found, he touches a secret spring, which puts the whole fabric of the Constitution in motion, for the accomplishment of the desired end; and all is peace again. It is Constitution and law operating in a new form; but the parties to it are charged to remember, that this is not only law, but a covenant that is never to be disturbed within the bounds of its limitation, if limited; and never to be invaded, if unlimited. All accept it on these conditions; and the questions in dispute are considered as forever settled.[25]

---

[23] Langdon Cheves to Henry Clay, March 3, 1821, in James F. Hopkins, ed., *The Papers of Henry Clay,* 10 vols. (Lexington: University of Kentucky Press, 1959–91), 3:58.

[24] James Madison to Henry Clay, April 2, 1833, ibid., 8:635.

[25] Calvin Colton, ed., *Works of Henry Clay Comprising His Life, Correspondence and Speeches,* 10 vols. (New York: Henry Clay, 1896), 3:192.

It was this realm of constitutional "anodyne," as Madison put it, soothing action that promised political stability and fell short of actual amendment or radical transformation, that Clay's version of the body politic captured so convincingly for many antebellum Americans.

It is also worth noting how Clay's audience seized on his metaphor of the "five wounds"—how the metaphor served as a "framing device" not only for Clay's comments and perspective, but for an ongoing conversation. In his "Anti-compromise Speech" delivered several weeks later, Thomas Hart Benton knew of

> no distress in the country, no misery, no strife, no distraction, none of those five gaping wounds of which the senator from Kentucky made enumeration on the five fingers of his left hand, and for the healing of which, all together, and all at once, and not one at a time, like the little Doctor Taylor, he has provided this capacious plaster in the shape of five old bills tacked together. I believe that the Senator and myself are alike, in this, that each of us has but five fingers on the left hand; and that may account for the limitation of the wounds. . . . I know nothing of these "gaping wounds," nor of any distress in the country since we got rid of the bank of the United States, and since we got possession of the gold currency.[26]

A New York newspaper editor compared Clay's Compromise with Benton's position: "While the one naturally leads to a rational, friendly, and just compromise of the great questions of the day, . . . the other has no tendency but to prolong the agitation, to keep the wounds of the body politic still bleeding, and to jeopardize the integrity of this great confederacy."[27] Henry Bennett of New York saw the Compromise measures as "concessions. . . made to slavery, to cure the bleeding wounds it has inflicted upon the country": "It is said that these are the five wounds the country is suffering under, and we are to take a large dose, or rather five doses at once, to cure them all. The only connection these matters have is, that whether the evils we complain of are five or five hundred, they arise out of the institution of slavery."[28]

The following summer, Samuel A. Cartwright, the Louisiana physician and proslavery ideologue, contested Clay's notion of the Com-

---

[26] *Cong. Globe*, 31st Cong., 1st sess., Appendix pt. I, 676–77 (June 10, 1850).
[27] *New York Herald*, April 19, 1850.
[28] *Cong. Globe*, 31st Cong., 1st sess., Appendix pt. I, 645–46 (May 27, 1850).

promise as a cure for the nation's "five wounds": instead, claimed Cartwright, "two bleeding wounds" persisted, the denial of the South's "equality" and the forcing of the South into submission, resulting from the perversion of the "political compact" by an "unbridled majority." Clay could not stanch those wounds, nor could the "sovereign people," who lacked the "requisite knowledge of the anatomy of the body politic." Slavery, Cartwright explained, was "not a blot or excrescence" on the body politic. Rather, destroying it would kill off "the organism uniting all the parts of this confederacy into a grand, wonderful and progressive whole": the reason was that "the African is *not* constituted in mind or body, in the skin or under the skin, like the white man."[29] A year later, the black nationalist Martin Robison Delany, who may not have been replying directly to either Clay or Cartwright but may well have seen himself joining a conversation about the body politic, contended in his treatise on "the destiny of the colored people of the United States" that Northern free blacks, like Southern slaves, "are ruled and governed without representation, existing as mere nonentities among the citizens, and excrescences on the body politic."[30] Finally, when Harriet Martineau was explaining to her British audience the significance of the events of 1850 in her 1856 *A History of the American Compromises,* she was drawn directly to Clay's metaphor: "There was sufficient evidence by this time that Mr. Clay's method was mere quackery; but in the stress of difficulty, when the south was declining and discontented, in spite of her predominance at Washington, and her aggressions on neighbouring territories, the great Western leader was applied to once more for his nostrum." Clay, Martineau seemed to say, had violated the physician's duty to do no harm: "The causes of trouble," she observed, "were, in fact, all in existence; and the attempt to compromise them simply made them more manifest."[31]

Lincoln's entry into this conversation about the body politic, that is, his use of the metaphor of slavery as a cancer beginning in 1854,

---

[29] Samuel A. Cartwright, M.D., "How to Save the Republic, and the Position of the South in the Union," *De Bow's Review,* 11 (August 1851): 188.

[30] Martin Robison Delany, *The Condition, Elevation, Emigration, and Destiny of the Colored People of the United States, Politically Considered* (Philadelphia: The Author, 1852), 14.

[31] Harriet Martineau, *A History of the American Compromises* (London: J. Chapman, 1856), 22.

represented an important divergence from Clay's conception. Lincoln's reverence for Clay is well known and was, of course, powerfully conveyed in his "Eulogy on Henry Clay" of July 1852. Lincoln scholar Roy P. Basler's comment that "[o]ne can hardly read any paragraph in [the eulogy] without feeling that Lincoln was, unconsciously or consciously, inviting comparison and contrast of himself with his 'beau ideal of a statesman'" encourages us to wonder whether Lincoln's use of the cancer metaphor at Peoria and thereafter was at least implicitly part of a conversation with Clay and his outlook on the body politic discussed above.[32] In the eulogy Lincoln described Clay's action during the crisis of 1850: "He exorcised the demon which possessed the body politic, and gave peace to a distracted land. Alas! the achievement cost him his life!"[33] For Lincoln and so many other Northern Whigs (and Democrats) of antislavery inclinations, the passage of the Kansas-Nebraska Act of 1854 was a crucial political and ideological turning point. In the 1852 eulogy Lincoln could refer, rather vaguely and abstractly, to a demon taking hold of the body politic. Was that demon slavery? Sectionalism? Party spirit? This sort of generalized and abstract explanation for the crisis mirrored Clay's own understanding, in 1850: "And now let us discard all resentment, all passions, all petty jealousies, all personal desires, all love of place, all hoaning after the gilded crumbs which fall from the table of power. Let us forget popular fears, from whatever quarter they may spring. Let us go to the limpid fountain of unadulterated patriotism."[34] By the time of the Peoria speech, in October 1854, to adherents of the new Republican Party such as Lincoln, the specific responsibility of the expanding system of black chattel slavery for the national crisis of that year was incontrovertibly clear. Vague and loosely conceived enumerations of social and political ills and generalized references to lack of patriotic spirit were still heard, but were growing less frequent, at least among Republicans such as Lincoln. Part of the significance of Lincoln's use of the cancer metaphor in late 1854, then, concerned the way it conceived of slavery as a dangerous and expanding *specific material presence*, directly responsible for the crisis of Union.

---

[32] Roy P. Basler, *Abraham Lincoln: His Speeches and Writings* (Cleveland: World Publishing, 1946), 18.

[33] *Collected Works of Lincoln*, 2:123.

[34] *Cong. Globe*, 31st Cong., 1st sess. Appendix pt. 2, 1413 (July 22, 1850).

Interestingly, the shift in the conception of the ills of the body politic from Clay in 1850 to Lincoln in 1854 (and from Lincoln of the Clay eulogy to Lincoln of the Peoria speech) bore a rough similarity to changes evident in nineteenth-century Americans' understandings of disease and remedy. The middle nineteenth century was a period of transformation and flux in understandings of the causes of and appropriate cures for bodily illness, with older and newer conceptions coexisting side by side and, consequently, profound disagreement and uncertainty evident among practitioners and the public. But for our purposes, it is crucially relevant that the 1840s and 1850s were a period during which American physicians and Americans more widely thought of disease increasingly in terms of specific physical entities. Before that time (and no doubt such generalizations about the chronology of the change are approximate), disease was more often understood in general philosophical terms, as a kind of moral imbalance that altered the state of being of the whole person. Because no single disease had a material "ontology" or distinctive logic, particular diseases were examples of disease in general, and, as the thinking went, one disease could "wear the livery" of another, say, cholera merging with dysentery. The bacteriological discoveries of Koch, which made it clear that diseases such as tuberculosis and cholera were caused by specific "germs," were still well in the future (the 1880s), but in the 1850s Americans were coming to think of biological evil—and social and political evil—in more specific terms.[35]

When at Peoria, Illinois, in 1854, Lincoln proposed that slavery was a "cancer," he and the like-minded among the new Republican Party were now insisting that black chattel slavery in the American South was a specific evil, a deadly and uncontrolled physical growth inside and part of the body politic that had to be excised in order for the United States to continue its benign growth and prosperity. The critic Susan Sontag has observed that an older perspective (dating at least back to Machiavelli) that emphasized the statesman's ability to control the spread of "diseases" of the body politic and restore it to healthful rationality gave way during the Age of Revolution to a much more pessimistic focus on illnesses such as cancer that could *destroy*

---

[35] See especially the discussion of changing conceptions of disease (and the timing of those changes) in Charles E. Rosenberg, *The Cholera Years: The United States in 1832, 1849, and 1866* (Chicago: University of Chicago Press, 1962).

the individual and society.[36] This insight is crucially relevant to understanding the shift from what we might refer to as Henry Clay's optimistic "therapeutic statesmanship" of 1850—his confident sense that he could rhetorically bind up the nation's "five wounds"—to Lincoln's more open-ended, if not indeed ominous, uses of the cancer image at Peoria in 1854 and Alton in 1858.[37]

Lincoln did not question all of Clay's assumptions about the body politic. Both men, like all participants in the midcentury conversation about the body politic, shared the premise that all societies, like the human body, must grow in order to live. All contributors to that conversation distinguished between healthy and unhealthy growth—though the boundary between good and bad growth for the body politic (and for the human body, as it was taken up in midcentury medical discussions) was far from clear, and it was very easy in the context of both discourses for the "spirit," "vigor," "vitality," or "vital force" that was associated with robust health to edge into a state of "sthenic" disease characterized by "excessive stimulation" or "excessive action of the vital phenomena."[38] (Indeed, it was possible for what appeared to be robust vitality to disguise and to be, in fact, an advanced state of overstimulation and physical decline.)

Especially important was the agreement of Clay, Lincoln, and others that the fundamental objective of statesmanship, like that of medical therapy, was to restore the "natural balance" of the political and social system. Certainly this was the assumption behind Lincoln's comments at the Soldier's Home in 1862: proper treatment of the

---

[36] Susan Sontag, *Illness as Metaphor* (1978; reprinted with *AIDS and Its Metaphors*, New York: Doubleday, 1990), 76–87. See also R. I. Moore, "Heresy as Disease, in W. Lourdaux and D. Verhelst, eds., *The Concept of Heresy in the Middle Ages (11th–13th C.)* (Leuven, Belgium: Leuven University Press, 1976), 3.

[37] I hardly mean to give the impression that references to "cancer on the body politic" first appeared in the 1850s. John C. Calhoun used the phrase in Congress in the early 1830s. It also surfaced in political commentary in the 1810s and 1820s (if not earlier). With regard to the last of these points, I thank Robert P. Forbes, Gilder Lehrman Center for the Study of Slavery, Resistance, and Abolition, Yale University.

[38] John Harley Warner, "'The Nature-Trusting Heresy': American Physicians and the Concept of the Healing Power of Nature in the 1850s and 1860s," *Perspectives in American History* (1977–1978): 293–94. The quoted phrases are Warner's. Many of these assumptions informed the works of the American political and legal theorist Francis Lieber, a German émigré who taught at South Carolina College and later at Columbia University; see especially the discussion of the danger of "political asthenia" in Francis Lieber, *On Civil Liberty and Self-government* (1853; reprinted, Philadelphia: J. B. Lippincott, 1888), 366.

diseased body politic could be analogized to a "depletion" of a sick human body. By diminishing the blood, one would deny sustenance to the tumor of slavery, loosen its grip, and restore the balance of intake and outflow, thus weakening the tumor *and* strengthening the body before slavery could be surgically cut out. Similarly, Ernestine Rose was guided by the basic premise of the "natural balance" and "harmony" of the bodily system in her speech to the National Women's Rights Convention in 1860. "It is a well known fact," she began,

> that stagnant atmosphere and stagnant waters can only be purified by agitation. This is no more true in the physical world than in the social and moral world. What, then, is to purify the social and moral atmosphere regarding the wrongs and the rights of woman? Agitation! [To gain a law upholding married woman's property rights] we had to adopt the method which physicians sometimes use, when they are called to a patient who is so hopelessly sick that he is unconscious of his pain and suffering. We had to describe to women their own position, to explain to them the burdens that rested so heavily upon them, and through these means, as a wholesome irritant, we roused up public opinion on the subject.[39]

Rose, two years before Lincoln, may have been adopting a more up-to-date emphasis on "elevation" rather than "depletion" as a remedy, but a concept of balance was at the center of each speaker's vision.

In short, Lincoln's use of the metaphor of the body politic at Peoria, Alton, and the Soldier's Home had elements of both continuity and change. He imagined an ideal body politic in a *generalized* state of rationality, vitality, harmony and balance to be achieved once the *particularized* political disease of slavery was cured. But there was a foreboding undercurrent in Lincoln's choice of the image of cancer that threatened to sabotage the possibility that reason, moral harmony, and balance could ever be achieved in the old body politic, the Constitution "as it was." To call slavery a cancer was to say that it could not be neutral. To those who thought slavery benign, Lincoln was saying at Peoria and Alton, in effect, if you are crazy enough to believe that cancer is good, I cannot convince you. To those who hoped that rational talk—the sort of talk that Lincoln was engaged in—might help heal the wounds of the body politic, the metaphor of

---

[39] *Proceedings of the Tenth National Woman's Rights Convention . . . May 10th and 11th, 1860* (Boston: Yerrinton & Garrison, 1860), 7–9.

cancer must have been disconcerting. One could hardly talk one's way out of cancer, or reason with it. Even the user of such an image, the "physician" who would heal the body politic, was hardly exempt from the taint of a disease like cancer that proliferated through every part of the nation. The logic to which his analogy inevitably led was that the cancer of slavery mortally sickens all Americans; no one could stand outside it.

Accordingly, it was not long after Lincoln's remarks at the Soldier's Home in 1862 that he joined Charles Sumner and others who believed that the old body politic had become so corrupted by slavery that it needed to be destroyed and then reborn, purified, with "new life and a new virtue." This, of course, was the message of the Gettysburg Address, but it was also articulated earlier in mass rallies like the one held in New York City on March 6, 1862, whose call to the public was "The Life of Slavery, or the Life of the Nation." In the North, the "life" of the "nation" (a term replacing "union") was increasingly seen as a biological, physical necessity, a point that Lincoln had made forcefully in his First Inaugural Address. That political nation had its own biological need to preserve itself. The existence of the political nation, grounded in what Lincoln called "the vital element of perpetuity," was *not* subject to individual consent or contractual negotiation and good faith. As Liah Greenfeld has written, the new "self-evident" truth confirmed by the war was that the United States "were one nation, . . . a unity, with no longer many, but one head, one tremendous body, and one soul."[40] E. L. Godkin could confidently present a corollary of this view in July 1865: "the 'social compact' was made only in the imagination of philosophers. . . . It is now well established that society grew, and was not made; that the first social bond was kinship, and not contract."[41] In a remarkable metaphorical aside worth quoting at length, Godkin elaborated the implications of the newly ascendant idea of birthright citizenship— being "born" into the "living organic body" of the state—for newly emancipated black men:

---

[40] Liah Greenfeld, *Nationalism: Five Roads to Modernity* (Cambridge, Mass.: Harvard University Press, 1992), 481–82. Also, see Melinda Lawson, "Patriot Fires: Loyalty and National Identity in the Civil War North" (Ph.D. dissertation, Columbia University, 1997), for a discussion of the emergence of organic nationalism in the Civil War North.

[41] E. L. Godkin, "The Democratic View of Democracy," *North American Review* 101 (July 1865): 107.

[E]very man, as a man, born a member of the state, has a natural right to become a voter by the unhindered attainment of the qualifications prescribed, and then the unhindered exercise of the franchise thus conditioned. This is inherent in the idea of political equality. It comes from the simple fact of a living membership in a living organic body. . . . Deprived of it he must be regarded as something cast loose—by itself—out of social harmony—like a foreign substance having no chemical affinities with the system in which he is unnaturally placed. Now, if there be that analogy, which all experience shows there is, between physical and political organisms, such a state of things must produce great mischief. This loose matter must be expelled, or it must be, in some way, incorporated. Human beings thus *in* the state, yet not *of* the state, present a political anomaly. In this uncombined, inorganic condition, they can be, to the body politic, only a source of irritating pain or of dangerous malignant disease. Thus the colored man, in his former servile relation, may be said to have had, politically, an organic place; he had a representation in the state; he voted, too, strange as the assertion may appear; he was a power in Congress. Now that he is cut off from all civil and social relations, he is in danger of becoming a floating pest, having less affinity, and more morbific, than the noxious entozoan that infest the animal system. . . . What *shall* be done with him? To this question there is only one answer: Make a man of him. To drop all metaphor, we must either drive him out to the society of the beasts; or we must elevate him—permit him, rather, to elevate himself—to a true manhood, with the possible attainment of all that belongs to membership in *one* common humanity.[42]

Godkin's discussion was so specifically biological ("the noxious entozoan that infest the animal system") that it became more a substantive statement or analysis and less a metaphor. Godkin had not fully abandoned the older notions of generalized moral balance and what he called "social harmony," but he made them fully accountable to the empirical and physical evidence of the actual "bodies" that composed the body politic. The social and political well-being of the black freedmen contributed to the health and growth of the nation. The soul of that nation could never be made healthy while the body (or bodies) that composed it were denied opportunities for benign

---

[42] *The Nation,* I, 3 (July 20, 1865): 74. For a discussion of the rise of a conception of birthright citizenship, see James H. Kettner, *The Development of American Citizenship, 1608–1870* (Chapel Hill: University of North Carolina Press, 1978), esp. ch. 10 and epilogue.

growth—hence, Godkin concluded, black suffrage was a necessary counterpart to black slave emancipation.

The significance of references to the body politic and the healthy or disordered state of the political constitution, as I have suggested, was as "framing devices." References to the body politic often appeared at the beginning or end of an analysis or as a pregnant aside, offering the reader scientific warrant for the truth claims following or preceding, allowing the author to create a certain "objective" distance between her or himself and the subject matter, as a "physician" of society or polity. My premise is that it was in the domain of such framing devices, to an extent underappreciated by historians, that some of the most important changes in underlying assumptions about political identity, action, responsibility, and truth claims were taking place at midcentury. Indeed, what made Civil War–era political culture so volatile, in part, is that framing metaphors, such as the "body politic" (and, indeed, those of "Constitution" and "Union"), were themselves no longer serving only or even always primarily as ways of containing conflict and winning assent. They were becoming subjects of fierce contest in their own right. There is no better example of this process than the exchange in Congress in the winter of 1858 begun when Northern antislavery politician Francis Blair, Jr., called slavery a "cancer on the face, which, unless removed, would eat into the vitals of the Republic." Blair drew from Jefferson Davis, the future president of the Confederacy, a retort that such rhetoric would not "render the Union perpetual."[43] Revising Blair's metaphor, Davis observed that the true illness of the body politic was sectionalism: "The meanest thing—I do not mean otherwise than the smallest thing—which can arise among us, incidentally, runs into this sectional agitation as though it were an epidemic, and gave its type to every disease."[44]

The acts of framing to which I have referred necessarily closed off some discussions and opened up others, identified one with certain trends and distanced one from others. Certainly to use biological metaphors to describe society and polity in the mid–nineteenth cen-

[43] *Cong. Globe*, 35th Cong., 1st sess. (1857–58), 293–94.
[44] "Remarks of Jefferson Davis in reference to the Kansas Message, Feb. 8, 1858," in Dunbar Rowland, ed., *Jefferson Davis Constitutionalist: His Letters, Papers, and Speeches*, 10 vols. (Jackson: Printed for the Mississippi Department of Archives and History, 1923), 3:174.

tury was to participate in a kind of transatlantic trend that included European writers such as August Comte and Harriet Martineau as well as the American cast of characters already mentioned. Historians are more aware of the biological analyses of society that had become de rigueur by the time that Andrew Carnegie was putting to use the ideas of Herbert Spencer (and indirectly, those of Charles Darwin) in the late 1880s than they are of the earlier analyses and debates of midcentury. The understanding of nature as a norm signaled by the publication of *The Origin of the Species* in 1859 was itself a culmination of a long intellectual process. Though Comte's materialism and use of Roman Catholicism as a religious model in the 1850s precluded his gaining a wide influence in America, it seems that Comte, Martineau, and many American "physicians" of the body politic were engaged with a similar problem: how to cultivate scientific taste and systematic knowledge among the multitudes in an age in which the theological certainties of prior generations were passing away? How, as Martineau put it, to find a "rallying-point of their scattered speculations . . . an immovable basis for their intellectual and moral convictions"?[45] Though historians of medicine have done much to show how controversies between religion and science affected views of disease and medical practice, historians of American political culture have not yet explored the relevance of such disputes for their subject.

In this context, the significance of the metaphor of the body politic for figures as divergent as Henry Clay and Martin Robison Delany was as a means of framing a domain of society and polity subject to scientific, physical laws of growth and decay—at a time when, as Martineau put it, theological certainties were giving way and yet "scientific taste and systematic knowledge among the multitudes" could hardly be taken for granted. In his famous speech on the tariff of 1824, Clay offered his "American System" of increased import duties as a solution for the "general distress which pervades the whole country," but he began with a justification for why such economic woes fell within the domain of statecraft. Alleviating the depression, Clay began, was not something to be left to divine providence. God's bounty continued to shower upon the United States. Americans' covenant with God was in good order, Clay was saying, and was not

---

[45] Harriet Martineau, preface, to Auguste Comte, *The Positive Philosophy of Auguste Comte* (New York: D. Appleton, 1854), viii.

implicated in the financial downturn. Americans' economic problems grew out of their covenant among themselves. And, accordingly, he observed, "it is the duty of the statesman, no less than the physician, to survey, with a penetrating, steady, and undismayed eye, the natural condition of the subject on which he would operate; to probe to the bottom the diseases of the body politic, if he would apply efficacious remedies."[46] Black journalist Martin Delany was engaged in the same sort of rhetorical business in his 1852 brief on black uplift and emigration: we have already noted his framing comment that Northern free blacks, like Southern slaves, "are ruled and governed without representation, existing as mere nonentities among the citizens, and excrescences on the body politic."[47] For Delany, a liberal Protestant, this physical problem required a scientific remedy and not a resort to the religious responses of the past, which blacks carried too far, in ignorance of "the great physical laws." Delany saw his task as correcting black people's mistaken view that they suffered degradation because God was displeased with them (otherwise, why would whites, in all their wickedness, prosper?). Elevation of any race, Delany observed, was a matter of society's material laws of growth and decay. The metaphor of the body politic, in Clay's and Delany's renderings, signaled to their audiences that ending economic distress and uplifting the condition of the black race operated within the domain of "second causes" and not God's immediate or miraculous intervention.

I have tried to suggest that the use by Lincoln and others of such framing metaphors gives us a vantage point on a historical problem of the first order—the transformation of conceptions of the body politic in the mid–nineteenth century. Americans used the image of the healthy or diseased body politic to make sense of a range of issues that are usually characterized under the rubrics of "constitutionalism" or "citizenship" and, as we have seen, involved profound concerns about the spread of moral and social evil, the growth and decay of nations, the meaning of belonging to a nation, and the relation between a thriving national community and a healthy individual self.

---

[46] Henry Clay, "Speech . . . on A Bill Proposing to Increase the Duties on Various Articles Imported from Foreign Countries, Delivered in the House of Representatives of the United States, March 30, and 31, 1824," in E. B. Williston, *Eloquence of the United States* (Middletown, Conn.: E. & H. Clark, 1827), 3:419–20.

[47] Delany, *Condition, Elevation, Emigration, and Destiny*, 38–40.

Moreover, it is worth underscoring a certain parallelism between the histories of political language and conceptions of the body politic, on the one hand, and medical understanding of the human body that obtained in the mid–nineteenth century, on the other. It was no accident that a reviewer of a medical treatise on cholera complained in 1849 that the treatise's author was "in much the same position as the prospective author of a Fourth of July oration or a eulogy of General Washington. There was nothing new to say."[48]

I do not mean to suggest that there was a lockstep agreement between changes in the domain of political language and those in the area of conceptions of the body, but rather a rough parallelism and, at times, creative cross-fertilization. Both domains were shaped by notions of "constitution"—a kind of generalized characterization of the temperament of the national body politic or the organization of the human bodily frame. Both areas were undergoing a transformation from a dominant emphasis on the truth value of generality (evident in the writer or speaker's ability to identify himself and his audience with a vision of America's history and destiny or in the practitioner's ability to take control of the general equilibrium of the body) to a growing concern for the truth value of specificity (to be found in the writer or speaker's use of specific rhetorical strategies for different audiences and the practitioner's effort to divide the body into more "discrete" systems to be addressed individually as "specific physiological processes" subject to specific physiological disorders).[49] In what might be called the epistemological ancien régime of both domains, moral character was a crucial, defining element. In the world of the antebellum orator, "ethical argument"—the speaker's own moral credentials as a visionary prophet of America's destiny, and ability to give voice to the moral aspirations of the audience and work an emotional change in the audience through sublime rhetoric—was the ultimate cause to be espoused and effect to be achieved. In the sphere of medicine, the faith of the physician in his or her own moral and religious efficacy and the ability of the physician to gauge the moral status of the patient were crucial to his or her goal of

---

[48] Rosenberg, *Cholera Years,* 164 (the words quoted are Rosenberg's paraphrase).
[49] Fields, "Making of An Issue"; John Harley Warner, *The Therapeutic Perspective: Medical Practice, Knowledge and Identity in America, 1820–1885* (Cambridge, Mass.: Harvard University Press, 1986).

restoring a "natural" moral balance or harmony.[50] Finally, by 1850, both the domains of political oratory and medical practice seemed to many Americans to have become crippled in their self-referential quality, their assumption of a correspondence between verbal or physiological effects and a wholly manifest and essential constitutional well-being, and their inability to produce imaginative responses to the crises of their day (cholera epidemic or slavery controversy) and address the everyday concerns of ordinary Americans. In both spheres there seems to have been an imaginative impasse at about roughly the same time—"nothing new to say," as that medical reviewer put it in 1849.

We are now ready to return to Lincoln's body and body politic. Not only was Lincoln's use of corporeal metaphors that referred to specific, material deadly disease new in American political culture, but so, too, was his continuing reference to *his own specific body* in political speech—his inevitably self-deprecating references to his physical height, face, and so on. For Lincoln, in what appears to be a departure from the practice of politicians in the early years of the Republic, such references had become standard fare. Why?

First, the dominant tradition of political rhetoric of the antebellum period was the belletristic, orotund style brought to high refinement by Senate orators such as Edward Everett and Daniel Webster. Although Lincoln certainly could and did employ elements of that style, his references to his own body drew from a distinct western tradition of stump speaking, political satire, and humorous fiction, which posed the speaker's body and references to sex and scatology as a kind of truth test for the grandiloquent and hyper-literate phrasemaking of the senatorial orators. Bodily references were a western mode of puncturing the pretensions of self-important easterners who were removed from the concrete daily concerns of ordinary people. In the hands of the writer of *Davy Crockett's Almanack, of Wild Sports of the West, and Life in the Backwoods*, Crockett's imagined debate with the erudite Senator Everett began with animal barks and hoots.[51] Certainly Lincoln cleaned up and tailored the use of bodily

---

[50] Regarding "ethical argument," see Fields, "Making of An Issue"; Hugh Blair, *Lectures on Rhetoric and Belles Lettres*, 2 vols. (Carbondale: Southern Illinois University Press, 1965); also see Richard M. Weaver, *The Ethics of Rhetoric* (Chicago: H. Regnery, 1953); Warner, *Therapeutic Perspective*, 17.

[51] *Davy Crockett's Almanack, of Wild Sports of the West, and Life in the Backwoods* (Nashville: Snag and Sawyer, 1835), 106–7.

analogies and metaphors for his aspiring middle-class audience of the 1850s, but the same purpose of using the concrete language of bodily analogy and everyday experience as a counterpoint to inflated eastern rhetoric remained.

And yet Lincoln's self-deprecating references to cancer and self-deprecating references to his own body were hardly a simple capitulation to a dichotomy of East equals mind and spirit and West body and matter. Rather, they were highly self-conscious and even ironic moves in a conversation about self-representation and an artist's or orator's ability to orchestrate the determinate and indeterminate truths that comprised his or her narrative of self-making.[52] Lincoln was setting forth the character of the "bodily Lincoln" before his audience and inviting them to peer beyond it to see the Lincoln of carefully constructed rational and logical argument and practical common sense—engaging the audience's imagination and treating it as an intellectual equal, not as an inferior in the manner of the belletristic orators of the Senate tradition. The point is that Lincoln's references to slavery as a bodily cancer and to the defects of his own body opened up multiple imaginative possibilities that were discouraged by the prevailing assumption in antebellum rhetoric, that political language was a manifest expression of a speaker's "character" and "virtue" and an affirmation of the essential public truths of the polity.[53]

Lincoln's comment that no one had seen cabbages growing out of his lean, lank face and ironic references to his tall body but small reputation (compared to Douglas, "The Little Giant") did not directly invoke the cause of the slave, but that cause could never be far off-stage in any of the antislavery Lincoln's public representations. Indeed, in a sense, the black chattel slave in the late antebellum South existed *only* in the specificity of her or his body. It was the goal of the slave market and an often-adjunct scientific racism to attempt to dictate a process by which the black body of the slave was converted into only one form of value, a commodity in "white" society.[54]

---

[52] I make this point with regard to changing conceptions of the body politic; see Fields, "The Making of An Issue," for an analogous point with regard to changing rhetorical styles.

[53] See Fields, "The Making of An Issue," on this point; see also the discussion in Robert Montgomery Bird, M.D., *Nick of the Woods, or the Jibbenainosay. A Tale of Kentucky* (Chicago: W. B. Conkey, 1853), 55–56.

[54] On the antebellum slave market, see Walter Johnson, *Soul by Soul: Life inside the Antebellum Slave Market* (Cambridge, Mass.: Harvard University Press, 1999).

Implicit, I would argue, in Lincoln's humorous references to his own body was a more serious democratic assumption that bodies labeled defective were capable of good growth. Lincoln had been discredited for much of his mature political career with the label "Black Republican"; Douglas had referred to Lincoln's political appeal in Illinois's northern tier as "jet black"; and even if Lincoln probably never saw the Democratic campaign pamphlet in 1864 that called him "Abraham Africanus the First," it hardly would have surprised him.[55] He appreciated what it was like to be identified with—and *perhaps,* may have even sensed what it was like to inhabit—a maligned black body. Lincoln was saying, covertly but by clear implication, in his comments about his own body, that the outcast slave body could generate benign growth. That maligned body, Lincoln implied, could serve as a framing device, a determinate truth that would allow slaves, and, by extension, all citizens of the antislavery nation, access to the indeterminate, mystical truths of the spirit. The insight was not fundamentally different from that of Nathaniel Hawthorne in the framing introductory essay of the 1850 novel *The Scarlet Letter,* that the author, "decapitated" and "a politically dead man" now that he had been removed from his Custom House post through political maneuvering, had the opportunity, as an artist, to become "a citizen of somewhere else."[56] It was the imaginative license of an outsider to manipulate and orchestrate both the determinate truths of the body and the indeterminate truths of the spirit that, Lincoln recognized, may have represented the most deeply meaningful freedom that a democratic society could offer. To the extent that Lincoln's references to his own maligned body did invoke the cause of the slave, we might say, they represented a symbolic and subversive form of "constitutional" amendment in the era of Constitutional stasis before slave emancipation.

---

[55] David Herbert Donald, *Lincoln* (New York: Simon & Schuster, 1995), 537.

[56] Nathaniel Hawthorne, *The Complete Novels and Selected Tales of Nathaniel Hawthorne* (New York: Random House, 1937), 110–11.

11

The New Gettysburg Address: A Study in Illusion

Barry Schwartz

THAT AMERICANS CONSTANTLY REINVENT their past to fit the present is a tedious proposition, but no one can deny it—nor can one deny that some historians take as many liberties with the past as laymen, perhaps more because of the depth of their ideological commitments. Events of ambiguous meaning and consequence, however, are more susceptible to ideological interpretations than others. The blurring of the line between thinking *about* history and thinking *with* history, between describing or explaining reality and modifying the past to fit reality, is a major problem of contemporary scholarship, and no document brings this out better than the Gettysburg Address.

The Gettysburg Address's abstractness suits it to the reconstructive machinery of collective memory.[1] Since each generation endows its members with "a common location in the social and historical pro-

---

[1] "The reconstructive machinery of collective memory" works best in eras of declining authority. Roland Barthes has observed that in egalitarian environments like ours, authors (and authorities in general) can no longer define absolutely the meaning of anything—not even the meaning of their own words. Texts are thus "read without the father's signature . . . [or] guarantee"; "From Work to Text," in Josué V. Harari, ed., *Textual Strategies: Perspectives in Post-structuralist Criticism* (Ithaca, N.Y.: Cornell University Press, 1979), 78. See also "Death of the Author," in *Images, Music, Text* (New York: Hill and Wang, 1977), 148. One need not accept literally Barthes's pronouncement of the "Death of the Author" to appreciate his logic, which requires author-reader relations to change as traditional authority structures erode, and this change must affect the way we interpret all historical documents. Thus, in considering the American Revolution, Pauline Rosenau explains, "[n]o claim can be made that the exact intentions of the founding fathers who drafted the United States constitution need be considered or respected"; *Post-modernism and the Social Sciences: Insights, Inroads, and Intrusions* (Princeton: Princeton University Press, 1992), 32. Texts break loose from their authors as the latter's authority recedes and meaning becomes more dependent on readers' viewpoints.

cess" and predisposes them "for a certain characteristic mode of thought and experience,"[2] new generations are naturally inclined to draw new meanings out of the Gettysburg Address and to find new ways of contemplating what Lincoln meant to say when he wrote it. No matter how fixed its formal and stylistic features, the significance of the Gettysburg Address changes with the concerns of the day; yet it remains a sacred text because it is enigmatical enough, that is to say, profound enough, for successive generations to see themselves in.

To know what Lincoln meant when he wrote the Gettysburg Address, what his audience and later readers took its meaning to be, and what its consequences were is important not only for what it tells us about a matchless funeral eulogy but also because it helps to clarify a vexing problem about collective memory, namely, the difference between emphasizing and distorting history in order to make present situations meaningful. Knowing that such a difference must be discerned is essential to distinguishing current interpretations of the Gettysburg Address, which focus on emancipation and racial equality, from earlier interpretations, which emphasized democracy and patriotic sacrifice. Current interpretations, emerging during the heat of the civil rights movement and 1961–65 Civil War Centennial are, to say the least, problematic. The new historians write as if the content of the Gettysburg Address were a hindrance to getting at its true meaning. Discrepancy between the text's content and the needs of its readers resolves itself through a prodigious expansion of sensitivity and, in some influential circles, including higher education and the media, a carefully crafted deference to all minorities. Because so much contemporary experience has become race-sensitive—or, more broadly, ideological—in some half-understood sense, the old Gettysburg Address, lacking reference to slavery or racial injustice, makes us nervous. The discovery of a new Gettysburg Address calms by making the old one manageable, bringing it into closer conformity with our values. The new Gettysburg Address speaks so directly to the present ideal of equality and minority justice, is so relevant to the issues of race, diversity, and inclusiveness, appears so "politically

---

[2] Karl Mannheim, "The Problem of Generations," in Paul Kecskemeti, ed., *Essays on the Sociology of Knowledge* (1928; reprinted, London: Routledge and Kegan Paul, 1952), 291.

correct," in short, is so *contemporary,* as to require the closest examination.

No one can say for certain what went through Lincoln's mind as he wrote the Gettysburg Address, but we can reconstruct the setting that made his words meaningful. David Wills, the Gettysburg ceremony organizer, invited Lincoln to the cemetery dedication for definite reasons: to honor the dead, comfort their survivors, and inspire the men who would fight and die in future battles:

> It is the desire that . . . you, as Chief Executive of the nation, formally set apart these grounds to their sacred use by a few appropriate remarks. It will be a source of great gratification to the many widows and orphans that have been made almost friendless by the great battle here, to have you here personally; and it will kindle anew in the breasts of the comrades of these brave dead, who are now in the tented field or nobly meeting the foe in the front, a confidence that they who sleep in death on the battlefield are not forgotten by those highest in authority; and they will feel that, should their fate be the same, their remains will not be uncared-for. We hope you will be able to perform this last solemn act to the soldier dead on this battlefield.[3]

Wills's letter is an unambiguous charge for a statement that is understandable, memorable, emotionally moving, and reverential.

Dedication Day was unforgettable: "The demonstration of the military, of high officials, Secretaries and citizens in the procession, was superior to anything of the kind ever witnessed in this country."[4] The grand procession to the cemetery, the spine-tingling invocation, inspiring musical interludes, the slow but moving dirge, the final benediction—the people had never seen or heard anything like it before. As Reverend Stockton read his prayer, blessing the souls of the dead, "[t]he vast assembly stood uncovered in breathless attention during the invocation and few indeed were the hearts, however obdurate, that did not unite with him in prayer for the great American nation." The reverend's words set a powerful tone, moving people and representatives alike: "The President evidently felt deeply, and, with the venerable statesman and patriot, Hon. Edward Everett,

---

[3] John G. Nicolay and John Hay, *Abraham Lincoln: A History,* 10 vols. (New York: Century, 1886–90), 8:190.

[4] *Detroit Advertiser and Tribune,* November 21, 1863: 4.

who was by his side, seemed not ashamed to let their sympathetic tears be seen."[5]

The day's major performance was Everett's. During his first forty minutes, the former Massachusetts governor, U.S. representative, and president of Harvard University summarized the battles that "conducted the armed hosts of rebellion to your doors on the terrible and glorious days of July" and led to the deaths that so many had gathered to commemorate; in the middle of the speech he discussed the origin and character of the war; at the end, its meaning. Gettysburg's dead saved America: "You now feel it a new bond of union, that they shall lie side by side, till the clarion, louder than that which marshaled them to the combat, shall awake their slumbers. God bless the Union; it is dearer to us for the blood of brave men which has been shed in its defense."[6] Few of the many people present heard Everett's every word, but those who did learned what the fighting was about—if they did not know already.

Some contemporary historians, including David Herbert Donald, believe that Lincoln wrote his address fearing that Everett might call for a return to "the Union as it was," with all its constitutional guarantees of state sovereignty, including slavery. Everett had, in fact, never wavered in his support of Lincoln's antislavery policy, and his speech never hinted at compromise. After he finished, Lincoln grasped his hand "with great fervor" and said, "I am more than gratified, I am grateful to you."[7]

When Lincoln himself rose to speak, an eyewitness observed that he seemed "impressed with the sanctity of the occasion."[8] How could he fail to be impressed? The battles had left almost 3,000 Union men dead, 6,643 missing, 13,709 wounded. To make sense of such carnage, Lincoln had to know not only what the war meant to its survivors but also what they were prepared—and not prepared—to die for. Lincoln's knowledge informed the content of his eulogy:

> four score and seven years ago our fathers brought forth on this continent, a new nation, conceived in Liberty, and dedicated to the proposition that all men are created equal.

---

[5] Ibid.

[6] *Address of Hon. Edward Everett at the Consecration of the National Cemetery at Gettysburg, 19th November, 1863, with the Dedicatory Speech of President Lincoln and the Other Exercises of the Occasion* (Boston: Little, Brown, 1864), 69, 81.

[7] David Herbert Donald, *Lincoln* (New York: Simon & Schuster, 1995), 464.

[8] Stakel to Markens, June 29, 1911, Library of Congress, Manuscript Division.

Now we are engaged in a great civil war, testing whether that nation, or any nation so conceived and so dedicated, can long endure. We are met on a great battle-field of that war. We have come to dedicate a portion of that field, as a final resting place for those who here gave their lives that that nation might live. It is altogether fitting and proper that we should do this.

But, in a larger sense, we can not dedicate—we can not conse-crate—we can not hallow—this ground. The brave men, living and dead, who struggled here, have consecrated it, far above our poor power to add or detract. The world will little note, nor long remember what we say here, but it can never forget what they did here. It is for us the living, rather, to be dedicated here to the unfinished work which they who fought here have thus far so nobly advanced. It is rather for us to be here dedicated to the great task remaining before us—that from these honored dead we take increased devotion to that cause for which they gave the last full measure of devotion—that we here highly resolve that these dead shall not have died in vain—that this nation, under God, shall have a new birth of freedom—and that government of the people, by the people, for the people, shall not perish from the earth.[9]

Many who came to Gettysburg on November 19 wanted to see where their relatives and friends had died and been buried. The Ar-rangements Committee anticipated as much. Graves mattered most, and the committee expended every effort to find and reinter as many of the dead as possible before November 19. Even as Everett and Lincoln spoke, people wandered among the graves and surrounding fields, searching for markers, signs, and relics of the dead.

Lincoln's words affected those who heard them or later read them, but most literate Americans in 1863 never knew what he had said at Gettysburg, let alone how to interpret what he had said. Among thirty-five newspapers tracked, including Democratic and Republi-can, Southern and Northern, eastern and western papers, eleven, or about 31 percent of the total, made no mention of the Gettysburg Address. Seventeen newspapers, a little less than half, reprinted the Address, many along with Everett's, without comment. The six news-papers that did assess Lincoln's words split along party lines. Demo-cratic newspapers attacked either him or Everett; Republicans

---

[9] Roy P. Basler et al., eds., *The Collected Works of Abraham Lincoln,* 9 vols. (New Brunswick, N.J.: Rutgers University Press, 1953–55), 7:23.

complimented both. The Democratic *Harrisburg Patriot and Nation* condemned the entire proceeding as a "panorama that was gotten up more for the benefit of [Lincoln's] party than for the glory of the nation and the honor of the dead."[10] A more influential opposition newspaper, the *Chicago Times,* found in Lincoln's speech clear evidence of a desire to make blacks and whites equal. How dare he deny the true cause for which they died! The fallen of Gettysburg "were men possessing too much self-respect to declare that negroes were their equals, or were entitled to equal privileges."[11] But the *Times,* like most of the Democratic press, had found this evidence in all Lincoln's previous speeches and would also find it in his later speeches. As the *Harrisburg Telegraph's* abolitionist editor put it, "[I]n the utter distraction and bitterness of the copperheads, every proceeding of the American people is now denounced as the acts of Abolitionism."[12]

Republican editors remarked on the appropriateness and beauty of Lincoln's words; few found in them any implication of abolition, let alone racial equality. The Gettysburg Address seemed instead to stir feelings of militancy: "More than any other single event," the *Gettysburg Times* reported, "will this glorious dedication nerve the heroes to a deeper resolution of the living to conquer at all costs."[13] The *Boston Transcript's* editor, likewise, noted: "The ideas of duty are almost stammered out . . . as the inspiration not only of public opinion, but of public action also. One sentence should shine in golden letters throughout the land as an exhortation to wake up apathetic and indolent patriotism. 'It is for us the living rather to be dedicated here to the unfinished work that they have thus far so nobly carried on.'"[14] *Harper's Weekly* also recognized the militancy of Lincoln's words: "The few words of the President were from the heart to the heart. They cannot be read, even, without kindling emotion. 'The world will little note nor long remember what we say here, but it can never forget what they did here.'"[15] These lines seemed to capture

---

[10] (Harrisburg) *Patriot and Nation,* November 24, 1863, Library of Congress, L. C. Martin Papers, Box 4.

[11] *Chicago Times,* November 23, 1863, 1–2.

[12] *Harrisburg Telegraph,* November 24, 1863, 2.

[13] Cited in *Gettysburg Times,* November 19, 1863, 6.

[14] Library of Congress, compiled by Emily B. Mitchell, Portfolio AC 4561, November 20, 1863, 3.

[15] *Harper's Weekly,* November, 1863.

the tone of the dedication itself: "A powerful impression was made this day upon the nation. More than any other single event will this glorious dedication move the patriotism and deepen the resolution of the living to conquer at all hazards. More than anything else will this day's work contribute to the nationality of this great republic."[16]

Lincoln's contemporaries had no reason to remember, let alone contemplate, his Gettysburg speech. Not one lithograph or statue of Lincoln at Gettysburg appeared during or after the Civil War.[17] Neither the press nor the public regarded it as a great production; few intellectuals described it as such.[18] Not until the early twentieth century, when an industrial democracy replaced an obsolete rural republic and Lincoln's reputation soared, did his speech become part of the "New Testament" of America's civil religion.[19] "The true applause" for the Address "comes from this generation," Charles E. Thompson wrote in 1913.[20] In the same year Major William H. Lambert told the Pennsylvania Historical Society that none of Lincoln's contemporaries saw unusual merit in his Gettysburg Address: "[I]t is difficult to realize that [the Address] ever had less appreciation than [it does] now."[21]

The Gettysburg Address became prominent in the early twentieth century because it was more resonant with the life of the Progressive Era than with Lincoln's own generation. Lincoln's references to the

---

[16] Ibid.

[17] Albion Harris Bicknell's *Lincoln at Gettysburg*, a life-size painting commissioned in Philadelphia for the Centennial, was the first significant commemoration of the Gettysburg Address.

[18] See Ward Lamon's assessment of the Gettysburg Address's prominence in William E. Barton, *Lincoln at Gettysburg* (Indianapolis: Bobbs-Merrill, 1930), 201. Lamon declared that Lincoln "was wiser than his audience, wiser than the great scholars and orators who were associated with him in the events of that solemn day. He had unconsciously risen to a height above the level of even the 'cultured thought' of that period." Harold Holzer, in an otherwise insightful essay, suggested that Lamon was mistaken about the Gettysburg Address's impact because he was influenced by the criticism of Democratic newspapers; "Lincoln's 'Flat Failure,'" in *Lincoln Seen and Heard* (Lawrence: University Press of Kansas, 2000), 195–96. That the politically informed Lamon would base his judgment on Democratic papers alone is doubtful.

[19] Robert N. Bellah, "Civil Religion in America," in *Beyond Belief: Essays on Religion in a Post-traditional World* (New York: Harper and Row, 1966), 177–78.

[20] *New York Times*, sec. V, June 6, 1913, 3.

[21] William H. Lambert, "The Gettysburg Address: When Written, How Received, Its True Form," *Pennsylvania Magazine of History and Biography* 33, no. 4 (1909): 391–92. See also 399.

equality of all men and the government belonging to the people seemed so right to a twentieth-century society concerned to regulate growing inequities of political power and wealth. Theodore Roosevelt's assertion that "Lincoln and Lincoln's supporters were emphatically the progressives of their day," and that "the Progressive platform of to-day is but an amplification of Lincoln's,"[22] did not convince everyone, but in 1913 it seemed reasonable. American progressives, whether friends or enemies of Roosevelt, defined Lincoln's presidency as the first phase of their movement; the Gettysburg Address, its manifesto. In 1913 a *Nation* commentator complained: "Nobody knows, and there is nothing in Lincoln's acts or words to tell, whether or not he would have been for the initiative and referendum, or for endowment of motherhood, or for single tax; yet enthusiastic advocates of almost any 'advanced' proposal of our day find little difficulty in persuading themselves that it is a corollary of the Gettysburg address."[23]

Racial justice was definitely not a corollary of the Gettysburg Address—at least not in the early twentieth century. David Blight, arguing that efforts to unify white Northerners and Southerners occurred at the expense of the African American, could not have been more right, and he could not have chosen a better occasion than the Gettysburg Reunion of 1913—one year before the eruption of World War I and four years before America's entry—to illustrate why white Americans considered the settlement of deep-seated regional resentments more imperative than racial conciliation.[24] Nathaniel Stephenson, too, had it right: refracted by the resurgent nationalism of World War I, the Gettysburg Address "gave utterance, in yet another form, to [Lincoln's] faith that the national idea was the one constant issue for which he had asked his countrymen, and would continue to ask them, to die."[25] Clearly, regional relations were as problematic in the early twentieth century as are race relations today.

---

[22] Theodore Roosevelt, *Lincoln Day Speech* (Progressive National Committee: Progressive Service Documents, 1913), 1, 3. For rebuttal see Judd Stewart, *Abraham Lincoln on Present-Day Problems and Abraham Lincoln as Presented by Theodore Roosevelt* (Columbus, Ohio: State Constitutional Convention, 1912).

[23] *The Nation*, July 10, 1913, 27.

[24] David W. Blight, *Race and Reunion: The Civil War in American Memory* (Cambridge, Mass.: Harvard University Press, 2001).

[25] Nathaniel Wright Stephenson, *Lincoln: An Account of His Personal Life, Especially of Its Springs of Action as Revealed and Deepened by the Ordeal of War* (Indianapolis: Bobbs-Merrill, 1922), 329.

Lincoln's speech, filtered through Progressivism's rhetorical prism, evolved into an "Americanist" interpretation of democracy. In November 1863, reactions to the Gettysburg Address made infrequent reference to democratic government;[26] by 1918 that theme assumed central importance. Junius B. Remensnyder, present at the Gettysburg dedication, recalled in 1918 how Lincoln had eased the burden of the people by revealing "the generic truths of democracy."[27] By then the last line of that revelation, concerning government of, for, and by the people, would become a war cry and appear frequently on war bond announcements. With the war over, Representative Wells Goodykoontz called the Address "the most perfect definition ever given of the word democracy,"[28] while Albert Griffith found in it "the mighty reality, the fundamental essential," of "people's government."[29] In a sense, the word "democracy" played the same part in the public vocabulary of the Progressive decades as the word "Union" played in the years leading up to the Civil War. That Union faded from the public vocabulary after the Civil War suggests why it was so pervasive before. During the antebellum decades, Union meant "disunion" or at best "not quite a union," "not quite a nation."[30] During the first quarter of the twentieth century, democracy meant "freer and more equal, but not fully so." Nevertheless, the democracy that Remensnyder, Goodykoontz, and Griffith found in their Gettysburg Address was more encompassing than the democracy Lincoln put into his. During Lincoln's lifetime, political participation was the privilege of white men—less than half the population—and the fruit of democracy was vast inequality resulting from unrestrained economic competition. Progressive reforms did not eliminate these, but by the end of World War I the state had

---

[26] See also Barton, *Lincoln at Gettysburg*, 113–23.

[27] *The Outlook*, February 13, 1918, 243–44.

[28] *Congressional Record*, February 13, 1920, 8785.

[29] *Congressional Record*, February 23, 1925, 4448. Commemorating the men who died to preserve this mighty reality, the Gettysburg Address became an established part of Memorial Day observances.

[30] The consequence of the Civil War, according to Nathaniel Stephenson, was not to restore Union but to create a nation that until then had not existed; *Abraham Lincoln and the Union: A Chronicle of the Embattled North* (New Haven, Conn.: Yale University Press, 1920), esp. 1–18. See also Carl N. Degler, "One among Many: The United States and National Unification," in Gabor S. Boritt, ed., *Lincoln: The War President* (New York: Oxford University Press, 1992), for a comparison of Lincoln and Bismarck.

begun to recalibrate the relation between individual rights and cor-
porate power.[31] A "people's government" based on universal suffrage
and progressive taxation was not what Lincoln had in mind in his
reference to government "of the people, for the people, by the people"; but as this government emerged at the turn of the twentieth
century it established its own legitimating past tense by making Lincoln its founder and symbol. This founder, this symbol, became more
inwardly compelling than ever throughout the Progressive Era's second stage—the New Deal.

During the Second World War the original meanings of the Gettysburg Address—consolation and renewal of militancy—reemerged.
"A new birth of freedom" meant military victory.[32] That democratic
government "shall not perish from the earth" now meant that it
would prevail over fascism.[33] The most frequently quoted line during
World War II, as during the Civil War, was "It is for us the living,
rather, to be dedicated here to the unfinished work which they who
fought here have thus far so nobly advanced."[34] The *New York Times'*
editor thus marked the eightieth anniversary of the Gettysburg Address: "In this tremendous war, whose every day adds to the number
of our dead, Mr. Lincoln's words of eighty years ago are as strong,
inspiring, and immediate as if they were heard today for the first
time."[35] F. Lauriston Bullard concluded his short book on the same
note: "It was his devotion to democracy that justified Abraham Lincoln's appeal at Gettysburg for the completion of 'the unfinished
work' for which the 'honored dead' of that battlefield had given 'the
last full measure of devotion.' It is for that same cause that the United
States is at war today."[36]

War bond advertisements made this point tangible. The back of
the *Philadelphia Inquirer's* February 12, 1943, Sunday supplement,
to take one example, shows a soldier in full battle gear lying face up,
dead. He appears in the picture's foreground, directly in front of the
viewer. In the background, elevated above the fallen soldier, is Dan-

---

[31] Jürgen Habermas, *Legitimation Crisis* (Boston: Beacon Press, 1975).

[32] *New York Times*, March 19, 1943: 22.

[33] *Congressional Record,* House, November, 1941, A819.

[34] See, for example, *Congressional Record,* House, February 1, 1945, A409; April
17, 1945, A1767.

[35] *New York Times*, November 20, 1943.

[36] F. Lauriston Bullard, *"A Few Appropriate Remarks": Lincoln's Gettysburg Address* (Harrogate, Tenn.: Lincoln Memorial University, 1944), 71.

iel Chester French's Lincoln Memorial statue. Lincoln looks down upon the soldier, and both are illuminated by the same mysterious light. On the viewer's left, between Lincoln's statue and the soldier's body, is an extract from the Gettysburg Address: "That We Here Highly Resolve That These Dead Shall Not Have Died in Vain." In a related announcement titled "Remember Dec. 7th!" (date of the attack on Pearl Harbor), the same line appears above a battle-torn flag flying half-mast[37] to consecrate the dead.

The era's political imagery conformed to its biographical statements. James G. Randall, writing during wartime peril, defined the Gettysburg Address as the ornament of democratic Americanism:

> Sensing the greater opportunity of the hour, Lincoln used the Gettysburg occasion for two purposes: in unforgettable phrases he paid tribute to those who had fallen; not failing in that, he coupled the deepest and most dominant sentiments of his people with the political idea that was central in his own mind: the wider world significance of democracy's testing, the enduring importance of success in the American democratic experiment as proving that government by the people is no failure.[38]

Seven years later, Representative Heller of New York marked the invasion of South Korea by observing that "[t]he cause for which the men who fell at Gettysburg gave the last full measure of devotion has not . . . won its final victory." In the face of the communist menace, "anxious humanity still yearns for a new birth of freedom."[39] Commentator M. L. Duttus, too, located the Gettysburg Address in terms of its relationship to America's wars, specifically "at the half-way point of the Republic's progress from the Declaration to the dedication of our own and other nations to stand against aggression in Korea."[40] Forty years of Cold War tension followed World War II, and from the very beginning of this era "Lincoln was a secret weapon against dictatorship." If "government of the people, by the people, for the people is not to perish from the earth, then neighborly relations of people to people must be promoted to spread on this earth.

---

[37] Still Pictures Division, National Archives, Washington, D.C., Office of War Information.

[38] James G. Randall, *Lincoln the President: Springfield to Gettysburg*, 2 vols. (New York: Dodd, Mead, 1945), 2:320.

[39] *Congressional Record*, November 20, 1950, A7375.

[40] *New York Times Magazine*, November 19, 1950: 31.

When that is achieved, Gettysburg will be less a memorial of the past and more a preview of man's destiny in a world of peace."[41] By midcentury two cycles of understanding had emerged. Just as World War II recapitulated the interpretation of Lincoln's wartime genera- tion—consolation and encouragement to finish the fight—the Cold War recapitulated the Progressive Era and New Deal vision of the Address as a symbol of democracy. But something more appeared at midcentury, something impertinently grandiose: Abraham Lincoln's assertion of dedication at a Pennsylvania battlefield had become a preview of human destiny itself. Benjamin Thomas believed as much: "pleading for steadfastness to democratic principles as the best hope of peace, prosperity, and happiness among mankind, his appeal comes as a strong, clear call to every generation of Americans."[42] For Reinhard Luthin (writing in 1960), also a Cold War biographer, the Gettysburg Address "presents to the whole family of man the ques- tion whether a constitutional republic, or democracy . . . can or can not maintain its territorial integrity against its own domestic foes."[43]

"The whole family of man" is a big family, and a big audience. As the United States emerged from World War II, leader of the demo- cratic world—the Free World, as it was then called—the Gettysburg Address became infused by something causing it to outgrow itself. Before the 1945 victory, the Gettysburg Address was read by a nation under siege; after the war, the Address no longer seemed appropriate for America alone; it seemed to have been meant for the world. In 1959 the Abraham Lincoln Sesquicentennial Committee sent Lin- coln scholars on extended lecture tours abroad and distributed to every country microfilmed copies of the *Collected Works of Abraham Lincoln* "so that his philosophy and ideas might be better understood and remembered." The United States Information Agency, Voice of America, and Radio Free Europe made sure everyone got the word. In the committee's last act, Chairman John Sherman Cooper dedi- cated a final report to Congress, writing, "Lincoln is truly the 'Symbol of the Free Man' and as you read these pages, I am sure, you will be

[41] Herman Blum, *The Enduring Impact of Lincoln's Gettysburg Address* (Phila- delphia: n.p., 1963), 9.

[42] Benjamin P. Thomas, *Abraham Lincoln: A Biography* (New York: Alfred Knopf, 1952), 403.

[43] Reinhard H. Luthin, *The Real Abraham Lincoln: A Complete One Volume His- tory of His Life and Times* (Englewood Cliffs, N.J.: Prentice-Hall, 1960), 401.

aware of his world-wide influence on freedom loving peoples everywhere."[44]

As Lincoln's renown spread, the meaning of his words became more encompassing. By 1964, his eulogy for fallen soldiers was becoming, in poet Robert Lowell's words, a symbolic and sacramental act whose meaning "goes beyond sect or religion and beyond peace and war, and is now part of our lives as a challenge, obstacle, and hope."[45] Bruce Catton had come to the same conclusion: Lincoln's eulogy at Gettysburg was not just a test of the country's cohesion, to end slavery, or even to extend human freedom—"It was the final acid test of democracy itself; in a way that went far beyond anything which either government had stated as its war aims, the conflict was somehow a definitive assaying of the values on which American society had been built."[46] The Address, in other words, expressed the Civil War's ultimate meaning, transcending what any one might later say about it.

Transcendence is an attribute of objects that exist outside, above, and independent of the world.[47] Every society depends on some higher jurisdiction to justify itself, and this is why Lincoln's speech still rang true to Robert Lowell in 1964 "when our country struggles with four almost insoluable spiritual problems: how to join equality to excellence, how to join liberty to justice, how to avoid destroying or being destroyed by nuclear power, and how to complete the emancipation of the slaves."[48] Was not the Gettysburg Address silent on these four issues? Or were the historians not listening closely enough?

By the early 1960s, Americans began to read the Gettysburg Address through the lens of racial rather than international conflict. When William Baringer, Executive Director of the Lincoln Sesquicentennial Commission, glanced through the September 20, 1958, *Washington News*, for example, he was struck by Peter Edson's col-

---

[44] *U.S. Abraham Lincoln Sesquicentennial 1959–1960.* Final Report, Washington, D.C., 1960, x, 101.

[45] Robert Lowell, "On the Gettysburg Address," in Allan Nevins, ed., *Lincoln and the Gettysburg Address: Commemorative Papers* (Urbana: University of Illinois Press, 1964), 89.

[46] Bruce Catton, *The Civil War* (1960; reprinted, New York: Fairfax Press, 1980), 169–70.

[47] Robert Bellah, "Transcendence," in *Beyond Belief,* 168–92, 196.

[48] Robert Lowell, "On the Gettysburg Address," 89.

umn: "The words of Lincoln's Gettysburg Address have become something of a mockery: 'Fourscore and seven years ago our fathers brought forth on this continent a new nation, conceived in liberty and dedicated to this proposition that all men are created equal. . . .' If the Civil War Centennial and the Lincoln Sesquicentennial are to mean anything, there are five years in which to make good on Mr. Lincoln's pledge at Gettysburg." Baringer apparently agreed with Edson's interpretation, for in his letter to the Civil War Centennial's first commissioner, Edmund Gass, he explained that his short-lived Sesquicentennial body "will not be able to do that little job of settling the school integration crisis. The Civil War Commission, however, will long endure, and you seem to me just the people for that."[49]

What the Gettysburg Address had to do with a school integration crisis was a matter of interpretation. Since "Lincoln's reaffirmation of the American commitment to the 'proposition that all men are created equal' had been preceded by the Emancipation Proclamation," Lincoln meant emancipation to be a first step toward racial equality. Thus spoke Secretary of State Dean Rusk at the Gettysburg Address Centennial celebration.[50] Poet Archibald MacLeish was present at the Centennial, too, and he echoed Rusk's thought: "[T]here is only one cause to which we can take increased devotion"—the cause of race relations. "Lincoln would be disappointed at the slow pace of their improvement."[51] Like-mindedness reverberated upon itself as William Scranton, Republican governor of Pennsylvania, amplified Rusk's and MacLeish's comments by including the civil rights issue in his official centennial address: "Today, a century later, our nation is still engaged in a test to determine if the United States, conceived in liberty and dedicated to the proposition that all men are created equal, can long endure. Blood has been shed in the dispute over the equality of men even in 1963."[52] According to E. Washington Rhodes, African American editor of the *Philadelphia Tribune*, these events proved that the "hopes of Abraham Lincoln for

[49] Baringer to Gass, October 2, 1958, U.S. Civil War Centennial Commission, U.S. National Archives, Box 79.

[50] *Gettysburg Times*, November 19, 1863, 4. For similar arguments, see Louis A. Warren, *Lincoln's Gettysburg Declaration* (Fort Wayne, Ind.: Lincoln National Life Foundation, 1964); Kenneth M. Stampp, "One Alone? The United States and National Self-determination," in *Lincoln: The War President*, 141.

[51] *Gettysburg Times*, November 19, 1963: 1.

[52] Governor William Scranton to *Gettysburg Times*, November 19, 1963.

a united nation remain unrealized, unfulfilled in American life."[53] Clearly, Rhodes, Scranton, MacLeish, Rusk, and Epson saw Lincoln at Gettysburg affirming his vision of a racially integrated society.

By the last decade of the twentieth century, the Gettysburg Address's interpreters moved farther away than ever from its immediate content. Prior to the 1990s, Lincoln's opening phrase, "Four score and seven years ago," was meaningful as an orienting phrase linking the suffering of the Civil War to America's founding; during the 1990s that phrase came to define the significance of the entire Address. The memory of thousands of young bodies lying in fresh graves had faded—at least for the new generation of historians. "Though seldom recognized as such," explains Webb Garrison, "the Gettysburg Address is a fervent eulogy to the Declaration of Independence. In it the birth of the nation is linked, not to the year the Constitution was ratified, but to 1776, the year of the Declaration."[54] The effluences of abstraction fed on one another. For Allen Guelzo, the Gettysburg Address "was yet another opportunity for Lincoln to establish the Declaration of Independence as the moral spirit animating the Constitution, and to see the war as a struggle for that moral spirit, rather than merely an overgrown dispute about certain procedural niceties of the Constitution."[55]

Among the procedural niceties to which Guelzo refers is the right of states to secede from the Union. To no one attending the Gettysburg Cemetery's November 19, 1863, dedication would Garrison or Guelzo have made sense. Their exegesis seems clever enough today, but after Edward Everett's straightforward account of the battles and the purpose of the war, their version of Lincoln's words would have seemed bookishly irrelevant.

The second series of works not only emphasized the Declaration of Independence but also defined it as Lincoln's instrument for denigrating an elitist or, at best, nonegalitarian Constitution. Garry Wills's *Lincoln at Gettysburg: The Words That Changed America* is the pioneering statement. Asserting that the Gettysburg speech transformed America into an egalitarian society, Wills presents a great

---

[53] *New York Times,* November 20, 1963: 1.

[54] Webb Garrison, *The Lincoln No One Knows: The Mysterious Man Who Ran the Civil War* (Nashville: Rutledge Hill Press, 1993), 240.

[55] Allen C. Guelzo, *Abraham Lincoln: Redeemer President* (Grand Rapids, Mich.: William B. Eerdmans, 1999), 370.

man theory of history and places Lincoln at its center. Reviewers' headlines reflect Wills's conception: "Lincoln's Master Work Transformed America";[56] "Honest Abe's Sleight of Hand Redeemed a Nation";[57] "How We Were Created Equal";[58] "At Gettysburg Lincoln Rewrote History";[59] "How Lincoln's Gettysburg Address Changed the Way a Nation Saw Itself."[60]

No longer was Abraham Lincoln the great symbol of equality, but its maker; no longer the personification of America, but the ultimate source of its virtue. No longer was the Gettysburg Address a mere commemorative text, it was a formative event in its own right, shaping social and political developments: "Because of it, we live in a different America."[61] Lincoln's Address was as authoritative as the Declaration of Independence, Wills asserts, "and perhaps even more influential, since it determines how we read the Declaration."[62] Distinguishing between a Declaration affirming the equality of all men and a Constitution legitimating slavery, Wills asserts that Lincoln invoked the former to cleanse the latter. In this "open-air sleight-of-hand," he subverted the Constitution by convincing his generation that it was designed to institute and preserve equality. Such was Lincoln's achievement. He gave America its own Code Napoleon, or, rather, Code Lincolnian. Lincoln came to Gettysburg not to dedicate a cemetery but, in Wills's view, "to change the world, to effect an intellectual revolution," and he succeeded: "The crowd departed with a new thing in its ideological luggage, that new Constitution Lincoln had substituted for the one they brought there with them. They walked off, from those curving graves on the hillside, under a changed sky, into a different America."[63] Lincoln, godlike, changed that sky, made those people different.[64]

---

[56] *Detroit News,* December 9, 1992: 15A.

[57] *Newsweek,* June 15, 1992: 54.

[58] *New York Times,* June 7, 1992, sec. 7: 1.

[59] *Detroit Free Press,* June 8, 1992: 5A.

[60] *Detroit News,* July 8, 1992: 3D.

[61] Garry Wills, *Lincoln at Gettysburg: The Words That Remade America* (New York: Simon and Schuster, 1992), 147.

[62] Ibid.

[63] Ibid., 38.

[64] Garry Wills's argument resonates with the perspective of the political left. That Lincoln used the Declaration of Independence as a tool to revise the Constitution also convinced conservative scholars. For example, Wilmoore Kendall's belief that Lincoln demeaned the Constitution and confounded the American people's self-

Garry Wills was not the only scholar who thought he discerned in Lincoln's speech a previously unrecognized disdain for the Constitution. Before Wills's book appeared, Andrew Delbanco asserted that Lincoln found the "sheet anchors of the republic in the Declaration of Independence, not the Constitution," and at Gettysburg appealed to "the equality principle of the Declaration" to give force to his speech.[65] "The Gettysburg Address cannot be explained," declared Merrill Peterson, "nor can it be fully understood, except as the culmination of Lincoln's 'grand pertinacity'" (dedication to the Declaration of Independence's concepts of liberty and equality). Lincoln at Gettysburg spoke as a revolutionary, "subtly changed Jefferson's declaration"—for nine years he had been changing it—"by turning an enlightened appeal to reason and nature in behalf of individual liberty into a national sacrament." Lincoln at Gettysburg, Peterson concluded, was a preview of Gunnar Myrdal's (1944) classic, *An American Delimma: The Negro Problem and Modern Democracy.*[66]

Lincoln's reference to "Four score and seven years ago" expressed his belief that the Declaration of Independence's equality proposition transcended the Constitution's legitimation of slavery and that continued union would be unjustifiable without emancipation. According to Neely, Lincoln's "new birth of freedom," reincarnated in his Second Inaugural Address, with its dramatic excoriation of slavery sixteen months after Gettysburg and on the eve of the Confederacy's surrender, defined the war's "ultimate meaning and purpose."[67] According to Donald, Lincoln believed the Constitution had to be bent to conform to the egalitarian Declaration of Independence. Donald, like many new historians, takes the *Chicago Times*'s allegation of Lincoln's belief in racial equality as the actual basis of what he meant to say at Gettysburg.[68]

Thus, as American society confronted its own racism in the 1990s,

understanding conforms perfectly with the claims of his left colleagues; see "Equality: Commitment or Ideal?" *The Intercollegiate Review* (Spring 1989): 25–33.

[65] Andrew Delbanco, "To the Gettysburg Station," *New Republic* 201 (November 20, 1989): 38.

[66] Merrill D. Peterson, "'This Grand Pertinacity': Abraham Lincoln and the Declaration of Independence," *Fourteenth Annual R. Gerald McMurtry Lecture* (Fort Wayne, Ind.: Lincoln National Life Foundation, Inc., May 16, 1991), 2, 18–20.

[67] Mark E. Neely, Jr., *The Last Best Hope of Earth: Abraham Lincoln and the Promise of America* (Cambridge, Mass.: Harvard University Press, 1993), 156.

[68] Donald, *Lincoln,* 562–66.

scholars transformed its founding charter, the Declaration of Independence, into an antiracist document, attributing to Lincoln an abolitionist perception of the Constitution, one that reduced its significance to its sections authorizing slavery.[69] Howard Jones conceived the Civil War itself as Lincoln's instrument "for reshaping the Union of the Constitution into the more perfect Union envisioned by signers of the Declaration of Independence"[70]—the same generation of men who inserted the slavery article in order to ensure the Constitution's ratification. Jeffrey Meyer, too, sees Lincoln at Gettysburg framing the Constitution with the Declaration of Independence: "From that time on, most Americans have accepted Lincoln's interpretation of the meaning of the war and for the terrible bloodshed have sought absolution in the thought that the disaster was necessary to end slavery."[71]

Multiple discoveries by scientists working independently of one another, as we have long known, reveal common cultural concerns and preoccupations. When many scholars starting from different premises and working on different topics reach the same unprecedented conclusion about the meaning of the Gettysburg Address, we know that something is in the air, something we can infer only by examining the content of their consensus. To Neely, Donald, Jones, and Meyer, therefore, we add Harry Jaffa, Phillip Paludan, and George Fletcher. As their efforts to enlarge on Garry Wills accumulate, their argumentation becomes more abstract and ambitious. Jaffa asserts that Lincoln's Address "was more than an exercise in ceremonial propriety: It was a political speech intended to gain support for the Thirteenth Amendment."[72] Phillip Paludan believed that Lincoln transformed the old idea of liberty resting on limited government into the new reality of liberty resting on strong central government.

---

[69] For detail on Lincoln's reverence for the Constitution, see Allen C. Guelzo, "Apple of Gold in a Picture of Silver: The Constitution and Liberty," in Gabor Boritt, ed., *The Lincoln Enigma: The Changing Face of an American Icon* (New York: Oxford University Press, 2000), 86–107.

[70] Howard Jones, *Abraham Lincoln and a New Birth of Freedom: The Union and Slavery in the Diplomacy of the Civil War* (Lincoln: University of Nebraska Press, 1999), 15.

[71] Jeffrey Meyer, *Myths in Stone: Religious Dimensions of Washington, D.C.* (Berkeley: University of California Press, 2001), 204.

[72] Harry V. Jaffa, *A New Birth of Freedom: Abraham Lincoln and the Coming of the Civil War* (Lanham, Md.: Rowman and Littlefield Publishers, 2000), 79.

Six of the seven constitutional amendments passed between 1865 and 1920 strengthened the government, and these "had been charted and defined at Gettysburg in a two-minute speech."[73] Fletcher, extending Paludan's point, explains that Lincoln so managed the Civil War as to make Emancipation the primary goal and to create the need for a new Constitution requiring a Thirteenth, Fourteenth, and Fifteenth Amendment. This new Constitution, to which the Gettysburg Address was a "preamble," pushed the original to the political left by subordinating Union to racial justice.[74] Saving the Union, Meyer adds, was not good enough. The Union had to be kept "forever worthy of saving," which would be possible only if it were free of slavery.[75] To this end, Lincoln took the country to war. "Only in the killing, and yet more killing if necessary," David Blight declares, "would come the rebirth—a *new* birth—of the freedoms that a republic makes possible."[76] Such was Lincoln's chilling message to the grieving masses at Gettysburg Cemetery. Such is the theme of contemporary children's books, textbooks, and television documentaries. Newly understood, the Gettysburg Address becomes a declaration that could have been written by John Brown.

In some contexts, new interpretation refreshes by correcting and enlarging old understandings. In other cases, new interpretation stifles understanding by dulling our sensibilities and reducing our capacity to understand and feel the event as it originally unfolded. What are we to make of the new historians' interpretations of Lincoln at Gettysburg? I believe they distort more than they clarify. President Abraham Lincoln went out of his way to emphasize that emancipation was instrumental to the protection of the Union, and he made this point repeatedly between the time he announced it in September 1862 and the autumn of 1863. For most whites living at the time, the passages "Four score and seven years ago," "the proposition that all men are created equal," and "new birth of freedom" were rarely

---

[73] Phillip Shaw Paludan, *The Presidency of Abraham Lincoln* (Lawrence: University Press of Kansas, 1994), 229, 231. Lincoln's policies, as Paludan represents them, prefigured the amendments to end slavery, afford full citizenship and the right to vote to blacks, allow the collection of federal income tax, prohibit the manufacture and distribution of alcohol, and allow universal suffrage.

[74] George P. Fletcher, *Our Secret Constitution: How Lincoln Redefined American Democracy* (New York: Oxford University Press, 2001), 26–28.

[75] Meyer, *Myths in Stone,* 203.

[76] Blight, *Race and Reunion,* 13.

associated with slavery and emancipation. How, then, to explain the Declaration of Independence's priority in Lincoln's Address? For Fletcher, as for the other new historians, Lincoln considered the Declaration as a prelude to the Emancipation Proclamation. The proclamation, after all, is dated "the year of our Lord one thousand eight hundred and sixty three, and of the Independence of the United States of America the eighty-seventh."[77] But this wording is not Lincoln's; it is a formal phrase used on many official documents, including naturalization certificates, and tells us nothing about Lincoln's motives.

The timing of recent military events is a more plausible, if not entirely satisfactory, explanation of Lincoln's first topic sentence. July 4, 1863, was the turning point of the Civil War: the simultaneous withdrawal of the Confederate army from Gettysburg and the surrender of Vicksburg, which gave the Union control of the Mississippi River and cut the Confederacy in half. Lincoln recognized this correspondence in his July 7 speech following the twin victories: "Gentlemen, this is a glorious theme, and the occasion for a speech, but I am not prepared to make one worthy of the occasion."[78] Among a people that took for granted divine intervention in political affairs, the day was a sign from God.[79] What opening sentence would be more appropriate? On July 4, 1776, America was born; on July 4, 1826, two of "our fathers" who brought forth the nation, Thomas Jefferson and John Adams, died together; on July 4, 1831, James Monroe, a third founding father, died; on July 4, 1863, four score and seven years after the year of "the independence of the United States," the embattled nation turned the tide of war. What was on Lincoln's mind when he wrote the Address can never be known, but the significance of July 4 was so well known that it must have been part of the context in which he pondered his words.

If the United States in 1863 was "conceived in liberty and dedicated to the proposition that all men are created equal," we need to know that in 1863 liberty and equality were paired in the minds of most people with the necessity of order. The Civil War itself, in Michael Kammen's words, "prompted large numbers of Americans to

---

[77] Fletcher, *Our Secret Constitution*, 37.

[78] *Collected Works of Lincoln*, 6:320.

[79] Robert P. Hay, "Providence and the American Past," *Indiana Magazine of History* 65, no. 2 (June 1969): 79–101.

reconsider the ideal of achieving a *balance* between liberty and order in favor of *subordinating* the former to the latter." The code of "liberty and justice for all" first appeared in the 1895 Pledge of Allegiance, but it was not put into practice until the late twentieth century. Not until then did the idea of "ordered liberty" give way to the belief that without justice neither order nor liberty would be possible.[80] Thus, the Gettysburg Address, as conceived today by the new historians, expresses dual priorities—liberty before order, justice before liberty—that would have been incomprehensible to most Americans in 1863.

How did the Civil War generation think about equality? The victory of the Northern fighters, as Lincoln saw it, was a historic victory that renewed hope for the survival of democracy, but this democracy expressed nineteenth-, not twentieth-century values. For Lincoln, as for other former Whigs, "the proposition that all men are created equal" meant that all citizens, although stratified in terms of talent, virtue, and endowment, are equal in terms of legal rights and economic opportunity. Lincoln made this clear when he explained the purpose of the war in 1864 to a regiment of Ohio soldiers. So soon after Andrew Jackson's struggle against gentility and privilege, they understood what Lincoln meant when he said, "It is in order that each one of you may have through this free government which we have enjoyed, an open field and a fair chance for your industry, enterprise and intelligence; that you may all have equal privileges in the race of life, with all its desirable human aspirations. It is for this the struggle should be maintained, that we may not lose our birthright— . . . The nation is worth fighting for, to secure such an inestimable jewel."[81] Plainly, the "inestimable jewel" worth fighting for is the free market, the right of every man to improve himself.[82] Lincoln at Gettysburg referred to capitalism—a fair chance in the race of life— when he recognized the equality of man.[83]

---

[80] Michael Kammen, *Spheres of Liberty: Changing Perceptions of Liberty in American Culture* (Madison: University of Wisconsin Press, 1986), 100.

[81] *Collected Works of Lincoln,* 7:512.

[82] Nevins, ed., *Lincoln and the Gettysburg Address.*

[83] For more on the mid-nineteenth-century meaning of equality, see Barrington Moore, Jr., *Authority and Inequality under Capitalism and Socialism* (Oxford: Clarendon Press, 1987), 28; David M. Potter, "The Quest for National Character," in John Higham, ed., *The Reconstruction of American History* (New York: Harper and Row, 1962), 197–220; David Walker Howe, *The Political Culture of the American Whigs*

Might the achievement of economic equality have something to do with Lincoln's vision of a new birth of freedom? "Freedom" is the Germanic form of the Latin "liberty"; but both words eclipse the concrete state to which they refer—autonomy—because they are both symbols, often allegorical, of America itself. "What [Lincoln] meant by 'a new birth of freedom' for the nation," Carl Sandburg observed, "could have a thousand interpretations."[84] Some interpretations, however, might be more reasonable than others. The new birth, it is said, was a "near escape from destruction of the Union and its anticipated renaissance as a nation after having been purged of the terrible sin of slavery."[85] Svend Petersen made sense when he wrote these words in 1963, and he makes perfect sense today, but in 1863 Northern farmers knew that slavery's extension into the territories and, eventually, formerly free states would place them in impossible competition with slave labor. Nothing, perhaps, feels more like a new birth of freedom than a snatching from the jaws of slavery an open field for industry, enterprise, and intelligence.[86] The weakness of my interpretation of the Gettysburg Address adds no strength to the new historians'. To demonstrate that Lincoln's two-minute speech was a stalking horse for the Thirteenth Amendment and contributed to the centralization of the American state and the racial integration of American society, as they claim, is insurmountably difficult.[87] Speeches that change nations are declarations of new economic, political, or military policies, not funeral eulogies. If the Gettysburg Address was such a policy speech—not the commemora-

---

(Chicago: University of Chicago Press, 1979); John P. Diggins, *On Hallowed Ground: Abraham Lincoln and the Foundations of American History* (New Haven, Conn.: Yale University Press, 2000).

[84] Carl Sandburg, *Abraham Lincoln: The War Years*, 4 vols. (1939; reprinted, New York: Dell, 1965), 2:413.

[85] Svend Petersen, *The Gettysburg Addresses: The Story of Two Orations* (New York: Frederick Ungar, 1963), 63.

[86] That Northerners and Southerners alike felt the new birth of freedom to be their destiny is evident in the extraordinary popularity of "Battle Cry of Freedom," a song equally popular among Federal and Confederate soldiers. Among the latter, of course, freedom referred to local rights, including the right to secede from the Union.

[87] If Donald is right, then overestimation of the power of words must have been characteristic of the mid–nineteenth century. During debates with Lincoln, "[Stephen] Douglas's attempts to prove that the Declaration of Independence did not include African-Americans had already changed the way most whites viewed blacks"; Donald, *Lincoln*, 233.

tion of a historical event but a historical event in its own right—then we must specify what would have happened to American society if Lincoln had decided not to speak at Gettysburg, or if he had made a different speech. If Lincoln at Gettysburg determined how Americans interpret the Declaration of Independence, the Constitution, and the Civil War itself,[88] how would they interpret these if he had not spoken? What alternate interpretations and, above all, what political possibilities (Fascism? Authoritarianism? Permanent Apartheid?) did Lincoln's words negate? What alternative explanations of American democracy (Alexis de Tocqueville's? Louis Hartz's? Barrington Moore's?)[89] must we reject in order to affirm this Lincoln-centered theory?

Matters of fact do not always apply to the Gettysburg Address. A touching speech that affirms the equality of all men makes sense to a society that seeks to abolish invidious distinctions of race, ethnicity, and religion, but did it make sense to Lincoln's society, wherein such distinctions were pivotal objects of commitment and identity? Did it make sense in the situation in which Lincoln found himself—the commemoration of a great battle and dedication of a cemetery for thousands of dead young men for whom these distinctions were valid? Did it make sense to the political officials sharing the platform with Lincoln—particularly state governors representing strong Democratic constituencies: Governor Horatio Seymour of New York, Governor Joel Parker of New Jersey, Governor William Denison and former Governor David Tod of Ohio, Governor Augustus Bradford of Maryland, and Governor Oliver Morton of Indiana? The last was a staunch Republican, but his presence, no less than the Democratic governors', was not lost on Lincoln. He knew that in Indiana, as in Illinois, the 1862 elections created legislatures that favored immediate armistice and repudiation of the Emancipation Proclamation. He knew that his remarks had to conform not only to Everett's statement but also to Reverend Stockton's invocation, Benjamin French's ode, prepared especially for the occasion, James Percival's dirge, and Rev-

---

[88] Garry Wills, "Foreword," in Michael McCurdy, illustrator, *The Gettysburg Address by Abraham Lincoln* (Boston: Houghton Mifflin, 1995).

[89] Alexis de Tocqueville, *Democracy in America*, 2 vols. (New York: Knopf, 1945); Louis Hartz, *The Liberal Tradition in America* (New York: Harcourt, 1955); Barrington Moore, Jr., *The Social Origins of Dictatorship and Democracy* (Boston: Beacon Press, 1966).

erend Baugher's benediction,[90] none of which implied let alone mentioned emancipation.

Lincoln surely hated slavery and wanted to abolish it once and for all. Like many progressive Northerners, he believed personally that the phrase "all men are created equal" referred to the equal right of every man, black or white, to the fruit of his own labor. However, Lincoln knew that most Americans did not feel strongly enough about slavery to sacrifice their own or their children's lives. He used the phrase "all men are created equal" when writing to friends, like Joshua Speed,[91] and when speaking to public audiences, but he knew each would interpret it differently. Lincoln knew that the people of Gettysburg would hear in his words a repudiation of class-based privilege, and he had no reason to torment them by expressing a conviction they did not share. He was not about to tell them, in the midst of thousands of fresh graves, that they had been tricked, that the purpose of the war was different from what they believed it to be. Since most people believed they were fighting to save the Union, the last thing Lincoln was to do, especially in south-central Pennsylvania,[92] was to give the impression he had manipulated them into risking their lives on behalf of emancipation.

The Gettysburg Address assumed the character of a sacred text as it was assimilated into Progressive Era political reform, regional reconciliation, the challenge of World War I, the economic emergencies of the 1930s, and the military crises of the 1940s. Legitimating

---

[90] *Address of Hon. Edward Everett*, 26–28, 83, 85, 88.

[91] See, for example, Lincoln's 1854 letter to Joshua Speed in Basler et al., eds., *Collected Works of Abraham Lincoln*, vol. 2, p. 323. Whether or not Lincoln correctly interpreted Jefferson's use of the phrase "all men are created equal" cannot be discussed within the confines of this paper. Stephen Douglas, while debating Lincoln, asserted that that phrase, an introduction to a long list of grievances against the Crown, referred to colonial injustices that no man living on the soil of England would be asked to endure. Lincoln's response to Douglas was clever and morally persuasive, but it may or may not have captured Jefferson's intent. If read as a statement about internal matters, specifically, racial equality, then the remainder of the Declaration of Independence from Great Britain becomes a non sequitur. And if Southern delegates believed the Declaration of Independence to be an assertion of racial equality, they would have never signed it.

[92] As the official procession returned from the cemetery, an Indianapolis journalist noted contemptuously how "the windows were lined with ladies, and the doorways with men, shouting and waving handkerchiefs as heartily as if the county were not a stronghold of rebel sympathizers"; *Indianapolis Daily Journal*, November 23, 1863: 2.

the costs of global responsibility within a framework of a rapidly expanding electoral democracy, the Gettysburg Address retained much of its original meaning. Radically different interpretations appeared during the early years of the civil rights movement and, thereafter, amid the increasing persuasiveness of African American claims.

That a correspondence exists between the state of the society and the meaning of the Gettysburg Address raises important questions. If each generation sees in the Address what another does not, are the two perceptions equally valid? Does one generation's experience give it insight unavailable to predecessor or successor generations? Or does one generation's experience cause it to distort history in unprecedented ways? The latter possibility cannot be casually rejected. The conditions that produced the Civil War and the beliefs and attitudes of the generation fighting it have been replaced by so many layers of experience that it is difficult to imagine the conditions in which the Gettysburg Address was originally conceived. There is too much to unknow. Yet, the difference between the old and new interpretations is so substantial that the passage of time alone cannot explain it.

Arnaldo Momigliano observed twenty years ago that the present age is an "Age of Ideology," a time of unprecedented skepticism about history, as of every other aspect of national life: "One of the consequences of this attitude is that an increasing proportion of historical research is made in the form of rhetorical and ideological analysis . . . while the interpretation of old facts is more frequent than the discovery of new facts."[93] In this context, the historian is more inclined to issue messages justifying certain moral viewpoints and political policies and less inclined to convey objective information about the past.

The moral concerns of our day center on race. The same perspective that creates the need to know more about slavery's qualities and consequences also promotes a view of history that is sympathetic to African American aspirations and reflects dissatisfaction with American society, a dissatisfaction, often bordering on alienation, with the unequal distribution of resources (evident until recently in the popularity of neo-Marxist critiques) and disdain for those facets of the past in which the political and moral shortcomings of the present

---

[93] Arnaldo Momigliano, "History in an Age of Ideologies," *American Scholar* (1984): 495–96, 506.

are supposedly rooted. Consequently, many historians project upon Lincoln their own disdain for that Constitution, the very Constitution that abolitionists deemed "A Covenant with Death and an Agreement with Hell."[94] Edward Ayers, summarizing the new intellectual mood, concludes: "We are disappointed with those many white men who died for the Union who would not willingly have risked their lives for the end of slavery." White Northerners, once believed to have been content to live with slavery confined to the Southeast, gradually recognized that "the war had to be a war to end slavery, and not merely one to save the Union."[95] The war had to be different because the society was different. And so the war changed—in monographs, textbooks, films, television specials, magazines, high school textbooks, juvenile readers, and the classroom. The Gettysburg Address changed, too. As the new historians make it relevant to the present under the guise of disclosing its true meaning, the text doesn't seem to change at all. Unacceptable as a funeral eulogy for fallen soldiers yet too precious to ignore or discard, the text is conserved by alteration. Gettysburg, like other Civil War battlefields, was an arena for slaughter. To assume that Lincoln came to Gettysburg while the grounds were still strewn with rotting horse carcasses to speak to grieving families about civil rights is an illusion. Between illusion and error, Sigmund Freud taught us, is a great difference. To say that Lincoln wrote his Gettysburg Address on the back of a paper bag on the train ride from Washington is an error; to say that he wrote the Gettysburg Address with a view to reinterpreting the Constitution is an illusion. The first statement is easily refuted by the drafts Lincoln prepared in the White House before he left for Gettysburg. The second statement, that Lincoln wished to give a new, egalitarian spin to the Constitution, is resistant to disproof—illusory—because it reflects the believer's moral preference. "It is characteristic of the illusion," explained Freud, "that it is derived from men's wishes."[96] If only Lincoln had really meant to tell his

---

[94] John L. Thomas, *The Liberator: William Lloyd Garrison* (Boston: Little, Brown, 1963), 384.

[95] Edward L. Ayers, "Worrying about the Civil War," in Karen Halttunen and Lewis Perry, eds., *Moral Problems in American Life: New Perspectives on Cultural History* (Ithaca, N.Y.: Cornell University Press), 156, 157–58.

[96] Sigmund Freud, *The Future of an Illusion* (1927; reprinted, Garden City, N.Y.: Doubleday, 1957), 53.

Gettysburg audience that the purpose of the war was more worthy after the Emancipation Proclamation than before! If only his main goal had been to cleanse the nation by rooting out slavery! If only his secret goal had been to eliminate all racial injustice! Then everything presently linked to emancipation—multiculturalism, diversity, affirmative action, recognition—would be legitimated as part of America's heritage. Slavery itself would be an anomaly rather than an intrinsic part of American history. "Thus we call a belief an illusion when a wish-fulfillment is a prominent factor in its motivation, while disregarding its relations to reality, just as the illusion itself does."[97] An illusion is a belief in which we have a psychological stake, diminishing us if shown to be false, enlarging us if shown to be true. Accordingly, many good people have a stake in the Gettysburg Address and are morally inspired and elevated by what the new historians say about it. What of the new historians themselves? Can they embrace the ideal of racial equality without revising the past? Or is the worthiness of this ideal dependent on Lincoln's having articulated it at Gettysburg?

---

[97] Ibid., 54.

12

Abraham Lincoln's Reputation during His Administration

Hans L. Trefousse

IN 1994 Merrill Peterson published his revealing book *Lincoln in American Memory*. Most appropriately, he entitled his first chapter "Apotheosis," and what followed was the tracing of the deification of the Great Emancipator after his martyr's death.[1] Whether Abraham Lincoln's reputation was in any way comparable while he was still alive is a question that remains to be answered.

Some fifty years earlier J. G. Randall, the famous Lincoln biographer, in an article entitled "The Unpopular Mr. Lincoln" came to the conclusion that his hero was largely unappreciated during his lifetime. "For in the eyes of contemporaries," he wrote,

> Lincoln was a President who offended conservatives without satisfying radicals, who issued a tardy and incomplete emancipation proclamation after showing a willingness to conserve slavery, who had little if any success with Congress, who suppressed civil rights, headed a government marred by corruption, bungled the war, and then lost the peace, his postwar policy being blocked by congressional regional leaders in his lifetime before being wrecked in the reconstruction period.

He concluded that if Lincoln, like Woodrow Wilson, were to be remembered by what his enemies said, his reputation would be very different.[2]

It is, of course, true that Lincoln had many enemies who denigrated him throughout his career. In the South, this feeling was very widespread, as was to be expected; in the North, Democrats attacked

---

[1] Merrill D. Peterson, *Lincoln in American Memory* (New York: Oxford University Press, 1994), esp. 3–35.

[2] J. G. Randall, "The Unpopular Mr. Lincoln," *Abraham Lincoln Quarterly* II, no. 6 (June 1943): 256.

him incessantly for being too radical and too antislavery, while radical Republicans faulted him for being too slow in freeing the slaves. He was viewed as hesitant, wavering, and indecisive. The hostile press characterized him as a baboon and a gorilla, and no terms seemed too demeaning to downgrade the Civil War president.[3]

Yet there was another side to the picture. Surprisingly enough, any number of observers became aware of Lincoln's greatness at an early time. Comparing him to George Washington, they predicted that in the annals of history he would be considered second only to the Father of His Country. It was a comparison that would be repeated many times, a juxtaposition that proved more than justified.

In fact, there was general agreement, even among most of Lincoln's opponents, that the president was honest. "Honest Abe" was no mere election slogan, and in December 1862, shortly after the disastrous defeat at Fredericksburg and in the midst of the cabinet crisis, the confidence of diverse Republicans in his patriotism and integrity remained unshaken.[4] This trust enabled him to weather many a storm and to secure his renomination for the presidency in 1864. Randall's judgment, therefore, would seem to be mistaken.

Interestingly enough, many of the attributes that later contributed to Lincoln's fame, and that were cited throughout his administration, were pointed out even when he was first nominated. The general consensus about his honesty has already been mentioned; it was constantly reiterated. "'Honest old Abe' Nominated," headlined the *New Haven Palladium* on May 19, 1860, and other newspapers used the same expression. Joshua Giddings, the famous abolitionist, wrote the candidate on May 17 that his selection was made on two grounds: "1 That you are an *honest* man," and "2nd That you are not in the hands of Corrupt or dishonest men."[5] As the *New York Tribune*

---

[3] Michael Davis, *The Image of Lincoln in the South* (Knoxville: University of Tennessee Press, 1971), passim; David Herbert Donald, *Lincoln* (New York: Simon & Schuster, 1995), 331–33, 342, 423–24; Stephen B. Oates, *With Malice toward None: The Life of Abraham Lincoln* (New York: Harper & Row Publishers, 1977), 278.

[4] Resolution, Connecticut Assembly, December 31, 1862, in J. H. Trumbull to Lincoln, December 31, 1862, Abraham Lincoln Papers, Library of Congress; Howard K. Beale, ed., *The Diary of Edward Bates 1859–1866* (Washington, D.C.: Government Printing Office, 1933), 269; *New York Herald*, December 31, 1862.

[5] *New Haven Palladium*, May 19, 1860; also in Abraham Lincoln Papers, Library of Congress; *Chicago Tribune*, May 19, 1860; *New York Times*, May 19, 1860; Joshua R. Giddings to Lincoln, May 19, 1860, Abraham Lincoln Papers, Library of Congress.

stated on May 15, 1860, "'HONEST OLD ABE'. With this homely but most expressive phrase the people of the Northwest are wont to designate the man whom the Republican Convention at Chicago yesterday . . . selected as our standard bearer."[6]

Charles Sumner, much more radical than Lincoln, agreed. Although worried that the nominee had very little acquaintance with government and was uninformed on foreign affairs, Sumner characterized him as a "good honest Anti-Slavery man" and wrote to the Duchess of Argyll that those who knew Lincoln spoke of him as a person of "real goodness." By one of these, he was referred to as "the peer of the first men of the nation," while an Illinois correspondent remarked to Senator Lyman Trumbull, "He is a man whose firmness and sincere integrity can never be doubted by those who are not prejudiced and who fully understand his principles . . . well calculated to hold the reigns of this government and administer it wisely."[7] It was therefore not surprising that after the Republican victory in November, the *Chicago Tribune* exalted that "honest old Abe" was elected, while Senator James W. Grimes of Iowa wrote to Trumbull, "Our triumph was achieved more because of Lincolns reported honesty & the known corruptions of the democrats, than because of the negro question."[8]

Visitors who saw him during the interregnum were equally impressed. Salmon P. Chase, later often critical of the president, wrote on January 9, 1861, to George Opdyke that when he visited Lincoln in Springfield a week earlier, he was taken with his "absolute integrity of character." Trumbull learned that religiously inclined citizens "turned out to vote for an *Honest Man*," while the secular German-American leader Carl Schurz was also greatly encouraged by the hope that the foes of freedom would "break down under the honest will-power of a simple man." James Garfield, the later president, meeting the candidate in Columbus, Ohio, while finding him "distressingly homely," nevertheless found that through "all his awkward

---

[6] *New York Tribune*, May 15, 1860.

[7] Charles Sumner to the Duchess of Argyll, May 22, 1860, in Beverly Wilson Palmer, ed., *The Selected Letters of Charles Sumner*, 2 vols. (Boston: Northeastern University Press, 1990), 2:24; A. B. Eaton to Lyman Trumbull, June 25, 1860; Francis Longwith to Trumbull, May 24, 1860, Trumbull Papers, Library of Congress.

[8] *Chicago Tribune*, November 7, 1860; James W. Grimes to Trumbull, November 13, 1860, Trumbull Papers.

homeliness, there is a look of transparent, genuine goodness which at once reaches your heart and makes you trust and love him."[9]

The trust in Lincoln's honesty was not transitory. "We voted for you in the expectation that you were an honest man. We still have confidence in you," a Boston correspondent wrote him on April 2. Sumner on June 4 again informed the Duchess of Argyll that Lincoln was "honest & well-disposed," and Postmaster General Montgomery Blair on August 20 characterized his chief as "one of the most honest men I ever knew." In October Rutherford B. Hayes, now an officer in the army, commented on Lincoln's honesty, as did the Kentuckian Thomas Batman the following month.[10]

Confidence in the president did not diminish in 1862, in spite of the difficulties of that year. Various public bodies voted their appreciation of his honesty; the congregation of the Mikve Israel synagogue in Philadelphia thanked God for it, and various correspondents assured him of their continued trust. Questioning the common saying that no politician was honest, a Baltimore acquaintance wrote to Blair, "I will take the case of our worthy President, the world accords him an honest heart—his political friends know that his judgement is correct, and in addition to that, know him to be a 'true man.'" The Madison, Connecticut, soldier Samuel Shepard, though expressing his doubts about various subordinate officials, still emphasized his continued trust in Lincoln, as did Commodore John P. Sloat, who confessed that he did not want to cast any censure on the president,

[9] Chase to George Opdyke, January 9, 1861, in John Niven et al., eds., *The Salmon P. Chase Papers,* 5 vols. (Kent, Ohio: Kent State University Press, 1993–98), 3:44–45; E. Wright to Trumbull, December 31, 1860, Trumbull Papers; Schurz to Mrs. Schurz, January 29, 1861, in Joseph Schafer, ed., *Intimate Letters of Carl Schurz* (Madison: State Historical Society of Wisconsin, 1928), 240; Garfield to Mrs. Garfield, February 17, 1861, in Theodore Clarke Smith, *The Life and Letters of James Abram Garfield,* 2 vols. (New Haven, Conn.: Yale University Press, 1925), 1:155.

[10] Henry B. Small to Lincoln, April 2, 1861, Abraham Lincoln Papers, Library of Congress; Sumner to Duchess of Argyll, June 4, 1861, in *Selected Letters of Sumner,* 2:69; Montgomery Blair to Benjamin F. Butler, August 20, 1861, in Jessie Ames Marshall, comp., *Private and Official Correspondence of General Benjamin F. Butler during the Period of the Civil War,* 5 vols. (Norwood, Mass.: Plimpton Press, 1917), 1:221; Rutherford B. Hayes to Mrs. Hayes, October 19, 1861, in Charles Richard Williams, ed., *Diaries and Letters of Rutherford B. Hayes,* 5 vols. (Columbus: Ohio State Archeological & Historical Society, 1922–26), 2:120; Thomas Batman to Lincoln, November 18, 1861, Abraham Lincoln Papers, Library of Congress.

as he had every reason to believe that Lincoln's "established character for integrity and a desire to do justice to all" prompted his actions.[11] The *New York Herald* commented on the public confidence in the Executive, and Secretary of the Treasury Chase, politically drifting farther and farther apart from his chief, conceded that he had "the most honest intentions in the world." Even the caustic New Yorker George Templeton Strong, critical as he was of the administration, still expressed his faith in the president. It was therefore only to be expected that the radical abolitionist Congressman Owen Lovejoy, in a speech at Chicago, would avow his "great confidence in the honesty and patriotism of Abraham Lincoln" as well as in the "honesty of his anti-slavery principles."[12]

During the next two years, Lincoln's reputation for honesty did not wane. In February 1863 Andrew Johnson, in a speech at Indianapolis, explained that he supported Lincoln because he had administered the Constitution like an honest man. The Virginia loyalist David Hunter Strother, usually critical of the Executive, listened to one of Lincoln's speeches in Washington in July. Although he thought the speaker's manner was somewhat that of a buffoon and his appearance ungainly, "Yet," he concluded, "his manner impressed you with his honesty and sincerity." And the often critical *New York Herald* took credit in September for always having appreciated his honesty. Even Secretary of the Treasury Chase, a rival for the next year's presidential nomination, again commented on his chief's integrity. Frederick Douglass in a speech at Philadelphia in December said that the president impressed him as an honest man, William M. Chambers of the government's medical department thought of him as a man of more integrity than any man in any country, and the *Chicago Tribune* was

---

[11] Iowa, March 29, Wisconsin, April 5, Minnesota, September 29, Connecticut, December 21, 1862; Abraham Hart to Lincoln, April 23, 1862, Francis Cochran to M. Blair, May 20, 1862, John D. Sloat to Lincoln, July 31, 1862, Abraham Lincoln Papers, Library of Congress; Samuel Shepard to Dr. Tom Thomas, July 30, 1862, in Nina Silver and Mary Beth Sievers, eds., *Yankee Correspondence: Civil War Letters between New England Soldiers and the Home Front* (Charlottesville: University Press of Virginia, 1996), 67.

[12] *New York Herald*, August 2, 1862; Chase, Journal, September 12, 1862, in *Chase Papers*, 1:382; Allan Nevins and Milton Halsey Thomas, eds., *The Diary of George Templeton Strong*, 4 vols. (New York: Octagon, 1974), 3:259; *Chicago Tribune*, August 2, 1862.

convinced that he used the annual message of 1863 "as a vehicle for his plain, earnest, and honest convictions of duty and views of public policy."[13]

It was only natural that these expressions of trust would increase in 1864, an election year. Again and again observers insisted that Lincoln deserved renomination because of, among other factors, his honesty, and his integrity endeared him to the army. As one correspondent remarked, all agreed that "'President Lincoln is an *honest man!*' which Pope said is '*the noblest work of* God.'" A resident of Staten Island, in admiration of his honesty, named his son after the president, and the *Missouri Republican,* conservative as it was, commented on Lincoln's integrity. The Boston financier John Murray Forbes, quite dubious about Lincoln, nevertheless preferred him to other candidates because of his honesty, and Secretary of the Navy Gideon Welles, though uneasy about some of the president's advisers, wrote that he was "honest, sincere, and confiding," unlike some of his associates. And after the president's reelection, William Lloyd Garrison expressed his full faith in Lincoln's "integrity of purpose."[14]

Equally with his honesty, Lincoln's patriotism was recognized very early. "The Administration of Abraham Lincoln will be all that can be asked or desired by all good citizens, north and south," wrote one of Johnson's correspondents on January 2, 1861. Declaring that the president-elect was no abolitionist, he continued, "he loves his country too well to peril anything tending its destruction." In February the *New York Times* expressed its confidence in his "ability and patri-

---

[13] Speech at Indianapolis, February 26, 1863, in LeRoy P. Graf et al., eds., *The Papers of Andrew Johnson,* 16 vols. (Knoxville: University of Tennessee Press, 1967–), 6:152; Cecil B. Eby, ed., *A Virginia Yankee in the Civil War: The Diaries of David Hunter Strother* (Chapel Hill: University of North Carolina Press, 1961), 191; *New York Herald,* September 3, 1863; Gideon Welles, *Diary of Gideon Welles,* 3 vols. (New York: W. W. Norton & Company, 1960), 1:413; John W. Blassingame, ed., *The Frederick Douglass Papers,* 5 vols. (New Haven, Conn.: Yale University Press, 1979–92), 3:608; William M. Chambers to William P. Dole, December 10, 1863, Abraham Lincoln Papers, Library of Congress; *Chicago Tribune,* December 10, 1863.

[14] James H. Hackett to Lincoln, July 1, 1864, James Morris to Lincoln, October 5, 1864, Abraham Lincoln Papers, Library of Congress; *Missouri Republican,* April 9, 1864, also in Abraham Lincoln Papers, Library of Congress; John Murray Forbes to George W. Curtis, April 28, 1864, in Sarah Forbes Hughes, ed., *Letters and Recollections of John Murray Forbes,* 2 vols. (Boston: Houghton, Mifflin, 1899), 2:89; *Diary of Welles,* 2:131; Garrison to Lincoln, January 21, 1865, in Walter H. Merrill and Louis Ruchames, eds., *The Letters of William Lloyd Garrison,* 6 vols. (Cambridge, Mass.: Belknap Press, 1971–81), 5:256.

otism," the legislature of Wisconsin called his inaugural the "words of a true Patriot," Neal Dow commented on Lincoln's wisdom and patriotism on March 15, and one month later the *New York Courier and Enquirer* emphasized that no one doubted his honesty and patriotism.[15]

Not even Union reverses changed this assessment. Following the defeat at Bull Run, Thurlow Weed, the increasingly conservative New York politician, wrote, "I know how faithfully you serve, and how devotedly you love the Union." Hayes, who would later serve as president, confided to his wife in October, "Lincoln is, perhaps, not all that we could wish, but he is honest, patriotic, cool-headed, and safe. I don't know any man that the Nation could say is under all the circumstances to be preferred in his place." In July 1862 the *New York Herald,* though often censorious, conceded that the policies of the president in reference to the management of the war had been "conservative and patriotic," and in June 1863 Benjamin B. French, the Commissioner of Public Buildings, mused that "the more I see of him the more I am convinced of his superlative goodness, truth, kindness & and Patriotism." It was hardly surprising that the president's patriotism was mentioned again and again in the election year of 1864 and that the same sentiments should be voiced at the time of his assassination. Lincoln's patriotism was not only recognized, it was often pointed out as one of his outstanding characteristics.[16]

Despite many complaints about Lincoln's alleged weaknesses, already during his lifetime, many of the president's contemporaries were fully aware of his firmness, ability, and wisdom. Shortly after the election of 1860, P. H. Sylvester, one of the nativist Daniel Ullman's correspondents, wrote, "It needs a man of indomitable iron will at

---

[15] J. Warren Bell to Johnson, January 2, 1861, in *Papers of Andrew Johnson,* 4:116; *New York Times,* February 11, 1861; Resolution, March 12, 1861, Abraham Lincoln Papers, Library of Congress; Neal Dow to George Worthington, March 15, 1861, George Worthington Papers, New York Historical Society; *New York Courier and Enquirer,* April 15, 1861, also in Abraham Lincoln Papers, Library of Congress.

[16] Weed to Lincoln, August 18, 1861, Abraham Lincoln Papers, Library of Congress; Hayes to Mrs. Hayes, October 19, 1861, in *Diaries and Letters of Hayes,* 2:120; *New York Herald,* July 5, 1862; Benjamin B. French, *Witness to the Young Republic: A Yankee's Journal, 1828–1879* (Hanover, N.H.: University Press of New England, 1989), 424; Resolution of Citizens of Kansas in Washington, February 19, 1864, H. C. Page et al. to Lincoln, June 3, 1864, John W. Forney to Lincoln, October 24, 1864, Abraham Lincoln Papers, Library of Congress; *Chicago Tribune,* April 17, 1865.

the head of the administration, a man who will act prudently, promptly, and with decision. Such a man, I think Mr. Lincoln to be." In Indiana Senator-designate Henry S. Lane heard that although on the day of the inauguration the new president would find the national affairs in a state more unsettled and perilous than they had ever been before, according to the leading traits of his character he would adopt a pacific policy, but this inclination would not prevent him from using force to suppress treason.[17]

Many radicals shared these views. Sumner characterized Lincoln as "calm & decided," and Schurz too was impressed with the tenacity of the president-elect. "Lincoln himself stands firm as an oak," he wrote to his wife on the day before Christmas, "and his determination is imparted to the timorous members of the party." A few days later Merritt Ransom of Lewiston, Illinois, commented on the great Republican victory "in Electing honest Old Abe to the Presidency" because he thought Lincoln was "decidedly the man for the times and the best man that could have been selected to fill that important station at the present cricis, for it needs a man of firmness and decision at the helm of government under the present aspect of affairs to steer the ship of state into a safe and commodious harbour." Chase commented on Lincoln's ability as well as his entire reliability for the defense of "our principles," and Schurz became more and more convinced of his steadfastness.[18]

More conservative observers expressed similar opinions. The *New York Times* was certain that although Lincoln was not afraid of concessions, he was firm on principles. The *New York Commercial Advertiser* thought that firmness and vigor were his distinguishing qualities, while the *Manchester Guardian* commented on his outward manifestation of energy and resolution. No wonder his friend Orville H. Browning wrote from Quincy, Illinois, that everybody was delighted with the measures adopted and the vigor with which the president was pushing them. As a St. Louis correspondent asked Blair on

[17] P. H. Sylvester to Daniel Ullman, November 26, 1860, Ullman Papers, New York Historical Society; John B. Dillon to Lane, December 10, 1860, Henry S. Lane Papers, Indiana Historical Society, Indianapolis.
[18] Sumner to Duchess of Argyll, December 18, 1860, in *Selected Letters of Sumner,* 2:39; Schurz to Mrs. Schurz, December 24, 1860, January 21, 1861, in *Intimate Letters,* 236, 240; Merritt Ransom to Trumbull, December 29, 1860, Trumbull Papers; Chase to James S. Pike, January 10, 1861, in *Chase Papers,* 3:46–47.

May 23, 1862, to "Give my compliments to the President and thank him for me for his late proclamation [the revocation of Hunter's orders freeing rebels' slaves in his department]. . . . [H]e has all the backbone required to maintain the constitution their fears to the contrary not withstanding." The appointment of General George B. McClellan after the Second Battle of Bull Run caused the *New York Herald* to hail the great "firmness of the President," and not even the general's dismissal in November and the Emancipation Proclamation changed its mind. Then, on December 20, 1862, Governor Israel Washburn of Maine confessed to Vice President Hannibal Hamlin that he was not doubting the president, for he thought he had "faith and sense enough to know that any backing down is death." The following April Welles praised the president's "intuitive sagacity" and unswerving right intentions, and in July even the Democrat S. S. Cox had good words for the Executive's sagacity. By September his private secretary, John Hay, thought that "[t]he old man sits here and wields like a backwoods Jupiter the bolts of war and the machinery of government with a hand equally steady & equally firm." The French Masons congratulated him on his moderation, prudence, and firmness, while Douglass, in a speech at Philadelphia in December 1863, emphasized the fact that Lincoln said once he made up his mind, he stuck to it.[19]

These expressions of confidence and trust facilitated Lincoln's renomination and reelection. In March 1864 the Annual Conference of the Methodist Episcopal Church expressed its undiminished confidence in the wisdom and ability of the administration, and shortly before the election of 1864 the Vermont soldier Wilbur Fisk analyzed the situation by writing that the rebels were hoping McClellan would make concessions to them but that they knew Lincoln's "straightfor-

---

[19] *New York Times,* February 11, 1861; *New York Commercial Advertiser,* March 4, 1861, also in Abraham Lincoln Papers, Library of Congress; *Manchester Guardian,* April 20, 1861; Orville H. Browning to Lincoln, April 22, 1861, William M. McPherson to M. Blair, May 23, 1862, Abraham Lincoln Papers, Library of Congress; *New York Herald,* September 5, October 3, 17, 19, November 10, 1862; Washburn to Hamlin, December 20, 1862, Israel Washburn Papers, Library of Congress; *Diary of Welles,* 1:265; Samuel S. Cox to Lincoln, July 15, 1863, Abraham Lincoln Papers, Library of Congress; Tyler Dennett, ed., *Lincoln and the Civil War in the Diaries and Letters of John Hay* (New York: Da Capo Press, 1988), 91; E. Benoit to Lincoln, November 18, 1863, Abraham Lincoln Papers, Library of Congress; *Douglass Papers,* 3:606–8.

ward iron determination to punish treason everywhere" and that he would not "surrender one iota of the principles that he has avowed." So it was not surprising that at his second inauguration, *Harper's Weekly* pointed out that no man in office had been so tried as he and that no man had shown himself "more faithful to a great duty."[20]

Many observers also recognized at an early time that Lincoln represented the common man so popular in American tradition. "Honest Abe, as he is called by the people of the West—by whom he is admired and loved as few men ever have been," wrote the *New Hampshire Palladium* after his nomination, "is emphatically a Representative Man of the great party of Free Labor. Having risen by his own genius from an humble position, he now stands in the foremost rank of American statesmen and illustrates in his own history the noble career that lies open in these free States to every citizen." Other papers emphasized his typification of the American dream— the rise from rags to riches by his own efforts, and men who knew him stressed his folksiness and informality with all comers. As the Virginia loyalist David Hunter Strother, upon seeing Lincoln in 1862, stated,

> The President is a representative in all points of the tastes, manners, ideas, and capacities of the American people. He is American internally and externally, mind and person. He is neither great nor small, but a fair, average man of the race. He is the result of our system and that system is entirely responsible for the manner in which he fulfills the duties of his office. If he fails, the system has failed conclusively, and there will be an end to it.[21]

In October 1863 he impressed the inmates of the Five Points House of Industry as a model of a man who rose from the humblest circumstances, and in January 1864 he had the same effect on a young lawyer in Poughkeepsie. Schurz, in a letter about Lincoln to a friend in Germany, put it most succinctly: "He is the people personified; that

---

[20] J. C. Pershing to Lincoln, March 16, 1864, Abraham Lincoln Papers, Library of Congress; Wilbur Fisk to *Green Mountain Freeman,* October 9, 1864, in Emil and Ruth Rosenblatt, eds., *Hard Marching Every Day: The Civil War Letters of Wilbur Fisk, 1861–1865* (Lawrence: University Press of Kansas, 1992), 262; *Harper's Weekly,* March 11, 1865.

[21] *New Hampshire Palladium,* May 19, 1860, also in Abraham Lincoln Papers, Library of Congress; *Chicago Tribune,* May 19, 1860; *New York Times,* May 21, 1860; Strother, *Virginia Yankee,* 121–22.

is the secret of his popularity. His government is the most representative that has ever existed in world history." And historian John Lothrop Motley, writing from Vienna after the election of 1864, fully agreed:

> I do not intend any insipid compliment but merely the renewed expression of a thought which I have a hundred times expressed before, that the American people felt to the core of its heart that it had found in you a most fitting & fortunate impersonation. The great mass of loyal & patriotic citizens have seen their own simple & unsophisticated sentiments embodied in the honest, dispassionate but sagacious & resolute policy of your government.[22]

Lincoln's contemporaries even commented on his excellent sense of timing and his ability to balance both wings of his party to his advantage. As early as 1860, the papers stressed his political moderation, standing as he did halfway between the radicals and the conservatives, and none other than Karl Marx observed in March 1862, "President Lincoln never ventures a step forward before the tide of circumstances and the call of general public opinion forbids further delay. But once 'old Abe' has convinced himself that such a turning point has been reached, he then surprises friend and foe alike by a sudden operation executed as noiselessly as possible."[23] *Harper's Weekly*, commenting on the question of arming the blacks, stated that "it is impossible to act in a matter of this kind faster than the great public opinion approves, and in that perception is the profound wisdom of Mr. Lincoln." Calling for his renomination in January 1864, the *Buffalo Commercial Advertiser* commented on his remaining on the right path while at the same time strengthening his party by conciliating both wings of it. The *Baltimore American* thought Lincoln, while leading the people, nevertheless allowed himself to be guided by the current of the popular will, and the *Chicago Tribune* was impressed by the fact that "all his policy and measures have been framed so precisely according to his own individual opinion and inau-

---

[22] Patrick McCarty et al. to Lincoln, October 16, 1863, Walter C. Allen to Lincoln, January 28, 1864, Abraham Lincoln Papers, Library of Congress; Schurz to Theodore Petrasch, October 12, 1864, in *Intimate Letters*, 309; Motley to Lincoln, November 28, 1864, Abraham Lincoln Papers, Library of Congress.

[23] *New York Tribune*, May 19, 1860; *Chicago Tribune*, May 19, 1860; Karl Marx and Friedrich Engels, *The Civil War in the United States* (New York: International Publishers, 1970), 155.

gurated so exactly at the time and in the manner which best suited
Mr. Lincoln, that they may truly be called entirely his own."[24]

Similarly, Lincoln's basic kindness and decency were frequently
acknowledged. Garfield's recognition of his genuine goodness has already been mentioned. By October 1861 Elizabeth Blair Lee thought
that Lincoln, though slow, was "a good true man," and even Lincoln's
opponents conceded that although some said pirates ought to be
hanged, "the idea of the good natured Old Abe pursuing such a
fiendish policy is laughable." The independent *New York Herald* in
July 1862 spoke of his "characteristic magnanimity," an assessment
with which the secretary of the navy, commenting on his "wonderful
kindness of heart," concurred. The journalist Charles Graham Hal-
pine, though calling the president irresolute and without a large mind
necessary to grasp great questions, nevertheless conceded that he
was a man of kind intentions and kind in spirit.[25] In fact, soldiers
believed that the Chief Executive pardoned too many culprits. Jewish
organizations praised his kindness when he revoked General U. S.
Grant's notorious "Jew Order," newspapermen trusted that "that
kindness of heart for which you are so distinguished" would move
him to seek justice for colleagues being mistreated in Richmond, and
French was more and more "convinced of his superlative goodness,
truth, kindness & Patriotism." London Quakers appealed to him in
view of his kind feelings, while General Meade, of whose conduct
after the Battle of Gettysburg the president had been very critical,
saw him in October and found him, as always, "very considerate and
kind." The army was convinced of his many kindnesses to soldiers,
and several of his neighbors considered him too kind and indulgent
to traitors. It is no wonder that petitioners often relied upon this
characteristic in their appeals.[26]

---

[24] *Harper's Weekly,* June 14, 1862; *Buffalo Commercial Advertiser,* January 11,
1864, *Baltimore American,* March 14, 1864, also in Abraham Lincoln Papers, Library
of Congress; *Chicago Tribune,* July 1, 1864.

[25] Elizabeth Blair Lee to Philip Lee, October 7, 1861, in Virginia Jeans Laas, ed.,
Wartime Washington: The Civil War Letters of Elizabeth Blair Lee (Urbana: Univer-
sity of Illinois Press, 1991), 84; H. L. Abbott to Mother, November 30, 1861, in
Robert G. Scott, ed., *Fallen Leaves: The Civil War Letters of Henry Livermore
Abbott* (Kent, Ohio: Kent State University Press, 1991), 87; *New York Herald,* July
8, 1862; *Diary of Welles,* 1:135; *Chase Papers,* 1:420.

[26] Robert Gould Shaw to Father, November 21, 1862, in Russell Duncan, ed.,
Blue-Eyed Child of Fortune: The Civil War Letters of Colonel Robert Gould Shaw
(Athens: University of Georgia Press, 1992), 258; Isidor Bush to Edward Bates, Janu-

Even the Emancipator's writing and speaking abilities was commented upon well before he assumed office and many times afterward. His famous Farewell Address at the Springfield railroad station is a case in point. As one Illinoisan opined to Trumbull, "What patriot can read his few remarks at the Springfield depot—with the snow & rain pelting him in the face & not have the tear of sympathy start in his eye—& what Christian can refuse the request."[27] The First Inaugural Address was also well received by many observers. "I cannot let one day pass without expressing to you the satisfaction I have felt in reading and in considering the Inaugural address," wrote Edwin D. Morgan, the governor of New York. "None can say, truthfully, they don't understand its meaning. Kind in spirit, firm in purpose, National in the highest degree, the points are all well made, and the case is fairly stated and most honorably met." Republican newspapers agreed, and George A. Nourse in St. Paul felt that the "inaugural does us good like a medicine." One of Lincoln's correspondents thought that it "was the ablest state paper ever laid before the American people."[28]

The July 4, 1861, message to Congress also met with praise. To be sure, any number of newspapers criticized it, but as the Kentucky antislavery activist Cassius M. Clay wrote enthusiastically, it is "a very able paper, and one which will add to your reputation very much. It comes forcibly to the point, in that simplicity of words and structure of sentences, which is the true style of all great effort." Johnson applauded it, the *Chicago Tribune* thought it was "clearly up to the demands of the great occasion that has called Congress together in

---

ary 6, 1863, Sydney Howard Gay to Lincoln, May 26, 1863, Abraham Lincoln Papers, Library of Congress; French, *Witness*, 424; William Wood to Society of Friends, London, September 2, 1863, Abraham Lincoln Papers, Library of Congress; George G. Meade to Mrs. Meade, October 23, 1863, in George Gordon Meade, ed., *The Life and Letters of George Gordon Meade*, 2 vols. (New York: Scribner's, 1913), 2:154; James C. Rice to John P. Usher, April 4, 1864, K. H. Fell to Lincoln, November 18, 1864, Richard J. Oglesby to Lincoln, November 20, 1864, Mrs. S. E. Walworth to Lincoln, December 6, 1864, Mrs. Hiram Barney to Lincoln, February 5, 1864, John C. Dayton to Lincoln, June 20, 1864, Abraham Lincoln Papers, Library of Congress.

[27] G. W. Lands to Trumbull, February 18, 1861, Trumbull Papers.

[28] Edwin D. Morgan to Lincoln, March 5, 1861, Abraham Lincoln Papers, Library of Congress; *New York Times*, March 5, 1861; *Chicago Tribune*, March 5, 1861; George A. Nourse to Trumbull, March 6, 1861, Trumbull Papers; Joseph Blanchard to Lincoln, March 28, 1861, Abraham Lincoln Papers, Library of Congress.

extraordinary session," and *Frank Leslie's Illustrated Newspaper* called it a document "remarkable for its directness and simplicity."[29]

What was true of the Inaugural and the July 4 message also applied to the message to Congress in December 1861. Johnson heard from Perry County, Illinois, how pleased the inhabitants were with this message, James Hamilton praised it, and *Harper's Weekly* commented that public confidence was confirmed by it. And the 1862 message was also received favorably, even by the secretary of the treasury who often criticized his chief, as were its successors, especially the one of 1864, which the *Chicago Tribune* specifically called "in point of style, . . . a well written document."[30]

The year 1862 was marked by two expressions of the president's policy that were of the utmost importance. The first was his answer to Horace Greeley's "The Prayer of Twenty Millions," in which he emphasized his primary aim of saving the Union rather than the extirpation of slavery, and the second was the preliminary Emancipation Proclamation. Speaking of the former, the often critical *New York Times* editorialized, "The letter, like all of Mr. Lincoln's literary attempts, exhibits the peculiarities of his mind and style; but the logical sequence and precision, and the grammatical accuracy of this, is greatly in advance of any previous efforts." The latter met with the approbation of many antislavery elements because of its contents.[31]

In 1863 Lincoln's reply to Erastus Corning in defense of his actions so pleased Welles that he wrote in his diary, "It has vigor and ability and with some corrections will be a strong paper," and the later letter to James C. Conkling, setting forth Lincoln's policies, was generally considered an excellent example of his literary skills. "I expected a good letter—a very good one," commented the Bostonian John Z. Goodrich, "but it suits me even better than expected." Sumner, call-

[29] Clay to Lincoln, July 25, 1861, Abraham Lincoln Papers, Library of Congress; Johnson to Lincoln, July 27, 1861, in *Papers of Andrew Johnson,* 4:609; *Chicago Tribune,* July 6, 1861; *Frank Leslie's Illustrated Newspaper,* July 13, 1861.

[30] A. A. Steele to Johnson, December 14, 1861, in *Papers of Andrew Johnson,* 5:58; James A. Hamilton to Lincoln, December 17, 1861, Abraham Lincoln Papers, Library of Congress; *Harper's Weekly,* December 21, 1861; *New York Herald,* December 2, 1862; Chase to Lincoln, November 28, 1862, in *Chase Papers,* 3:320; *Chicago Tribune,* December 7, 1864.

[31] *New York Times,* August 24, 1862; John Allison to Lincoln, September 23, 1862, Theodore Tilton to Lincoln, September 24, 1862, David Paul Brown to Lincoln, September 25, 1862, George F. Train to Lincoln, September 25, 1862, Abraham Lincoln Papers, Library of Congress.

ing it characteristic, thought it stated the case very well, and letters of congratulation came from all over the country. "His last letter is a great thing," wrote Hay, characterizing it as "a great utterance of a great man."[32]

A few weeks later Lincoln delivered his Gettysburg Address, usually considered one of the greatest public speeches ever delivered in the English language. Edward Everett's reaction is well known, as he confessed to Lincoln, "I should be glad, if I could flatter myself that I came as near to the central idea of the occasion, in two hours, as you did in two minutes." He was not alone. Lincoln's opponents may have totally underestimated the address, but French, among others, spoke of the president's "most appropriate words"; James Scovel, the New Jersey Republican, sent Lincoln an editorial in the *Philadelphia Evening Bulletin* about "your excellent speech at Gettysburg"; and *Harper's Weekly*, characterizing Everett's words as "smooth and cold," highlighted the contrast between them and Lincoln's. "The few words of the President were from the heart to the heart," it stated. "They cannot be read, even, without kindling emotion. . . . It was as simple and felicitous and earnest a word as was ever spoken." Soon requests for copies arrived from all manner of correspondents.[33]

In the spring of 1864 Lincoln sent his famous letter to Albert G. Hodges of the Frankfort, Kentucky, *Commonwealth*, in which he said if slavery was not wrong, nothing was wrong. Even the acerbic Horace Greeley had to admit that while "President Lincoln is not generally esteemed a man of signal ability; yet he has no adviser and (since Jefferson) has had no predecessor, who surpassed him in that rare quality, the ability to make a statement which appeals at once, and

---

[32] *Diary of Welles*, 1:323; John Z. Goodrich to Lincoln, September 3, 1863, Abraham Lincoln Papers, Library of Congress; Sumner to Richard Cobden, September 4, 1863, in *Selected Letters of Sumner*, 2:189–90; I. N. Morris to Lincoln, August 26, 1863, Henry Wilson to Lincoln, September 3, 1863, Abraham Lincoln Papers, Library of Congress; Hay to John G. Nicolay, September 11, 1863, in *Diaries and Letters of Hay*, 91.

[33] Everett to Lincoln, November 20, 1863, in Roy P. Basler et al., eds., *The Collected Works of Abraham Lincoln*, 9 vols. (New Brunswick, N.J.: Rutgers University Press, 1953–55), 7:25; French, *Witness*, 435–36; James M. Scovel to Lincoln, November 23, 1863, Abraham Lincoln Papers, Library of Congress; *Harper's Weekly*, December 5, 1863; David Wills to Lincoln, November 23, 1863, Edward Everett to Lincoln, January 30, 1864, Abraham Lincoln Papers, Library of Congress; Edward Morgan to Mrs. Julian K. Fish, February 8, 1864, Morgan Papers, New York Historical Society.

irresistibly, to the popular apprehension—what we may call the shrewdly homely way of 'putting things.'" Captain John McKenzie of Paducah wrote that "no act of your life, or letter from your pen, has afforded me more satisfaction, than your letter of the 4th April to A G Hodges."[34]

The Second Inaugural Address is generally considered Lincoln's second great contribution to English oratory. It too was appreciated at the time. "What do you think of the inaugural?" Charles Francis Adams wrote to his father, the American minister to Great Britain.

> That rail-splitting lawyer is one of the wonders of the day. Once at Gettysburg and now again on a greater occasion he has shown a capacity for rising to the demands of the hour which we should not expect from orators or men of the schools. This inaugural strikes me in its grand simplicity and directness as being for all time the historical keynote of this war; in it a people seemed to speak in the sublimely simple utterance of ruder times. . . . Not a prince or minister in all Europe could have risen to such an equality with the occasion.

Others agreed, and even Benjamin Moran, at the American legation in London, otherwise no great admirer of the president, called the inaugural address "brief and sensible."[35]

The president's most controversial policies were those concerning slavery. Pushed by the radicals to inaugurate emancipation as speedily as possible, constrained by the conservatives to do the exact opposite, Lincoln carefully balanced these pressures in such a way that he was able to move toward the complete abolition of slavery by gradual steps, striking when he deemed the time ripe.[36] For this gradual approach, he was constantly criticized by the radicals, and when he did move, the conservatives were unhappy. But even in connection with this difficult issue, there were a considerable number of observers who appreciated his accomplishments and were delighted with them.

---

[34] Greeley "Lincoln to Hodges," *New York Tribune*, April 29, 1864, John M. Mackenzie to Lincoln, April 28, 1864, Abraham Lincoln Papers, Library of Congress.

[35] C. F. Adams, Jr., to C. F. Adams, March 7, 1865, in Wortington Ford, ed., *A Cycle of Adams Letters, 1861–1865*, 2 vols. (Boston: Houghton, Mifflin, 1920), 2:257–58; French, *Witness*, 466; Sarah Agnes Wallace and Frances Elma Gillespie, eds., *The Journal of Benjamin Moran*, 2 vols. (Chicago: University of Chicago Press, 1948–49), 2:1395.

[36] Hans L. Trefousse, *Lincoln's Decision for Emancipation* (Philadelphia: Lippincott, 1975), 17.

On March 13, 1862, after Lincoln's publication of the appeal to the border states for compensated emancipation, the Massachusetts businessman Steven Minot Weld at Fairfax Court House, Virginia, commented favorably. "The President's Proclamation," he wrote to his father, "is liked very much by all officers I have seen." Douglass, showing a thorough understanding of Lincoln's problems, in an address at Rochester said that he should live to see the president of the United States deliberately advocating emancipation was more than he had ever ventured to hope. To be sure, there were "spots on the line," but a blind man could see where the president's heart was.[37] After the abolition of slavery in the District of Columbia, the European revolutionaries Alexandre A. Ledru-Rollin, Joseph Mazzini, and Karl Blind expressed their satisfaction by stating, "Since we have seen the cause of Unity and Emancipation represented by a republican as sincere as energetic, we have never, . . . doubted your ultimate success."[38]

The preliminary Emancipation Proclamation, though regretted by conservatives, brought forth similar expressions of approval. "God bless you for the word you have spoken! All good men upon the earth will glorify you, and all the angels in Heaven will hold jubilee," wrote three Erie, Pennsylvania, residents. Missouri radical B. Gratz Brown considered it "the noblest act of the age," and expressed the hope that "a great free nation . . . may in the Hereafter give you all honor as the first President of the Republic who dared to plant himself and his nation upon the principle of Freedom." Garfield was equally affected, and any number of religious institutions passed resolutions of appreciation.[39] Lincoln's refusal to withdraw the document received similar encomiums; as the *Chicago Tribune* editorialized, "the President stands firm, and History will vindicate his courage and no-

---

[37] Weld to Father, March 13, 1862, in Stephen Minot Weld, *War Diaries and Letters of Stephen Minot Weld* (Boston: Riverside Press, 1912), 72; *Douglass Papers*, 3:518.

[38] Ledru-Rollin et al. to Lincoln, April 24, 1862, Abraham Lincoln Papers, Library of Congress.

[39] W. B. Lowry et al. to Lincoln, September 23, 1862, B. Gratz Brown to Lincoln, September 27, 1862, Presbyterian Synod of Genessee, September 18, 1862, General Association of the Congregational Church, New York State, September 25, 1862, Reformed Presbyterian Church, Pittsburgh Presbytery, October 1, 1862, Abraham Lincoln Papers, Library of Congress; Garfield to Mrs. Garfield, September 27, 1862, in Smith, *Garfield*, 1:245.

bleness"; and when the great day came, admirers sent laudatory poems. General Julius Stahel wished that he might "long be spared to enjoy the anniversary of this day when [Lincoln's] wisdom & patriotism shall have restored peace & plenty to our united country," and correspondent after correspondent sent him parallel congratulations. Douglass considered the promulgation of the proclamation a great noble act belonging to the whole human family, and the abolitionist Gerrit Smith thought that the president was right to delay its publication as he did, because he had power only as commander in chief. "Stand by the government!" he concluded in his letter to the president.[40] Giuseppe Garibaldi was equally taken by the document. "Heir of the thought of Christ and of Brown," he wrote, "you will pass down to posterity under the name of *the Emancipator*, more enviable than any crown and any human treasure!"

By the fall of 1864 his adherents were still so pleased with Lincoln that a Nevada doctor informed him that, delighted as he was that the president had the nerve and good sense to strike the everlasting death blow to the blighting curse of slavery, he would hang the Emancipator's miniature in his parlor. And when Lincoln used his powers to facilitate the passage of the Thirteenth Amendment in the House, Garrison once more expressed his full faith in the president's integrity of purpose to stand by every word of the proclamation and hoped that God would grant him success. Then, after the amendment passed, a delighted Henry Ward Beecher, the famous Brooklyn minister, wrote to the Emancipator, "Every step which you have, one by one taken, toward emancipation & national liberty, is now confirmed beyond all change. . . . You have brought the most dangerous and extraordinary rebellion in history, not only to a successful end, but, have done it without sacrificing *republican government* even in its form. . . . Your position is eminent & impregnable."[41]

Lincoln's popularity in the army was a well-known fact. General McClellan confirmed it in a letter of May 14, 1862 to the commander

---

[40] *Chicago Tribune*, December 18, 1862; Barry Gray to Lincoln, January, 1863, Julius Stahel to Lincoln, January 1, 1863, and numerous other letters, January 1863, Abraham Lincoln Papers, Library of Congress; *Douglass Papers*, 3:549; Gerrit Smith to Lincoln, February 27, 1863, Abraham Lincoln Papers, Library of Congress.

[41] Garibaldi et al. to Lincoln, August 6, 1862, C. W. Shang to Lincoln, October 23, 1864, Abraham Lincoln Papers, Library of Congress; Garrison to Lincoln, January 21, 1865, in *Letters of Garrison*, 5:256; Beecher to Lincoln, February 4, 1865, Abraham Lincoln Papers, Library of Congress.

in chief; in April 1864 Secretary of the Interior Usher heard that four-fifths of the army desired Lincoln's renomination; and by the fall of 1864 reports from unit after unit testified to the overwhelming majority he would and did obtain in the November election. As a member of William T. Sherman's forces in Atlanta wrote to his sister on September 27, "I hope Old Abe will be elected. I know he would be if they would give the soldiers a vote."[42] And the still controversial military skill of the commander in chief was frequently acknowledged. Hay, as early as September 1862, was sure that it was due to "his indomitable will, that Army movements have been characterized by such energy and celerity for the last few days"; Secretary Chase gave him credit for the capture of Norfolk; and the *Washington Daily Chronicle* highlighted his great sagacity in retaining General Grant, who had just captured Vicksburg. Apparently, contrary to some modern historians, a number of the president's contemporaries appreciated his military abilities.[43]

All these praises of Lincoln's honesty, firmness, timeliness, patriotism, and goodness led to a general recognition that he was an extraordinarily great man. As early as January 14, 1861, one of Washburn's correspondents exulted that friends had been scared the previous week when "our candidate" was about to speak. "But," he continued, "they are now content. Yet what a man he is! He has yielded nothing in fact although he says he would vote for some propositions which I could not . . . ; yet what he has said is so guarded that while it tends to conciliate, it makes no sacrifice of principle." In February a Lewiston, Illinois, resident already expressed the hope

---

[42] McClellan to Lincoln, May 14, 1862, in Stephen W. Sears, ed., *The Civil War Papers of George B. McClellan: Selected Correspondence, 1860–1865* (New York: Ticknor & Fields, 1989), 264–65; James C. Rice to John P. Usher, April 4, 1864, Robert E. Fisk to John Hay, September 22, 1864, Abraham Lincoln Papers, Library of Congress; Alfred L. Hough to Mary (Hough), September 23, 1864, in Robert G. Athearn, ed., *Soldier in the West: The Civil War Letters of Alfred Lacey Hough* (Philadelphia: University of Pennsylvania Press, 1957), 218; Wilbur Fisk to *Green Mountain Freeman*, in *Hard Marching*, 264–65; Jenkin Lloyd Jones, *An Artillery Man's Diary* (Madison: Wisconsin Historical Commission, 1914), 265, 267; Charles LaForest Dunham to Miss Hersey Dunham, September 27, 1864, in Arthur H. De Rosier, *Through the South with a Union Soldier* (Johnson City: Publications of East Tennessee State University Research Advisory Council, 1969), 152.

[43] *Diaries and Letters of Hay*, 46; Chase to Janet Chase, May 11, 1862, in *Chase Papers*, 3:197; *Washington Daily Chronicle*, May 25, 1863, also in Abraham Lincoln Papers, Library of Congress.

that God had raised Lincoln up "to be the chosen instrument to restore peace and harmony to the nation," and the inaugural did nothing to dispel this notion. In July 1861 *Harper's Weekly,* confessing that the president had not been its first choice, nevertheless pointed out that "thus far Mr. Lincoln seems to us to have been fully equal to the stupendous task which Fate has set before him."[44] Nor did reverses destroy trust in the president. The cabinet, not he, was blamed for disasters. Even in slave-holding Kentucky citizens appreciated his honesty of purpose, his strong vein of integrity and his common sense. Commenting on the enthusiasm of the crowd in front of the Capitol on August 6, 1862, French mused that it showed how the president was beloved. "He is one of the best men God ever created," the commissioner confided to his diary.[45]

As time went on, Lincoln's reputation, if anything, increased. The New York War Democrat John K. Porter thought Thurlow Weed was the ablest man in the United States but one, the president, for whom he was gladly willing to lay down his life. From Rome, an Italian admirer, Ferdinand Beneventano de Bosco, wrote in French, "your manner of governing has inspired the most lively admiration for your performance and for your actions," and by August 1863 Hay, more adulatory than ever, reported to his colleague John G. Nicolay,

> The Tycoon is in fine whack. I have rarely seen him more serene & busy. He is managing this war, the draft, foreign relations, and planning a reconstruction of the Union, all at once. I never knew with what tyrannous authority he rules the Cabinet, till now. The most important things he decides & there is no cavil. I am growing more and more convinced that the good of the country absolutely demands that he should be kept where he is till this thing is over. There is no man in the country so wise, so gentle, and so firm. I believe the hand of God placed him where he is.[46]

[44] D. Dawes Elliot to Washburn, January 14, 1861, Israel Washburn Papers; Myron Phelps to Trumbull, February 27, 1861, Trumbull Papers; *Harper's Weekly,* July 16, 1861.

[45] Bruce Tap, *Over Lincoln's Shoulder: The Committee on the Conduct of the War* (Lawrence: University Press of Kansas, 1998), 15; Thomas Batman to Lincoln, November 18, 1861, Abraham Lincoln Papers, Library of Congress; French, *Witness,* 405.

[46] John K. Porter to Lincoln, October 27, 1862, Ferdinand Beneventano de Bosco to Lincoln, May 20, 1863, Abraham Lincoln Papers, Library of Congress; Hay to Nicolay, August 7, 1863, in *Diary and Letters of Hay,* 75–76.

Even Governor Horatio Seymour of New York, a strong political opponent, after the elections of 1863 that resulted in a loss for the Democrats, admitted to a fellow Democrat that he was not discouraged, because most probably "in the end the interest of the country may be advanced by giving to the Administration undisputed sway." At New Year's Eve 1863 John W. Forney, the Philadelphia journalist, said that Lincoln was the most truly progressive man of the age because he always moved in conjunction with propitious circumstances, not waiting to be dragged by the force of events or wasting strength in premature struggles with them.[47]

The election year 1864 and its aftermath brought forth further proof of Lincoln's popularity. The endorsement in state after state of the president for renomination showed this fact very clearly, and individuals confirmed it. At the beginning of 1864 the Virginia Unionist John Minor Botts favorably described Lincoln's character to a friend. "I doubt," he wrote, "if he is not quite equal, if not superior to any of those by whom he is surrounded." A Republican in southern Illinois was delighted that in Egypt, as the region was called, it was no longer dangerous to support the president. In his letter to Lincoln, he mentioned that "[t]he eyes of the people of this nation, as well as those of every people under heaven who love liberty and free institutions, are turned toward you"; and he insisted that the nation's heart was laboring to give expression to its confidence in and appreciation of his noble services. The Philadelphia attorney Benjamin H. Brewster was convinced that the "Providence of Almighty God placed" Lincoln where he was for the good of the country, and a Lutheran minister in Cumberland, Maryland, concurred. "I am so very glad, that you intend to be our next President again," he wrote, "for you are the only man by the Lords will worthy to be our Chief Magistrate, because I am most sure, that you will carry on the war, untill we have a real free Country."[48] The nomination of General McClellan on a peace platform brought even the radical editor of *Wilkes' Spirit of the Times* to fall in line by endorsing a president "whom the rebels deeply hate, whose honesty and patriotism there has been no one to

---

[47] Seymour to Ledyard Linecklean, November 14, 1863, Helen Fairchild-Horatio Seymour Papers, New York Historical Society; *Diary and Letters of Hay*, 146–47.

[48] Botts to John B. Fry, January 22, 1864, J. Russell Johnson to Lincoln, June 20, 1864; Benjamin H. Brewster to Lincoln, August 29, 1864, G. Henry Vosseler to Lincoln, September 3, 1864, Abraham Lincoln Papers, Library of Congress.

dispute, and who represents a 'platform' which insists on the integrity of the whole national domain." And after Lincoln's successful reelection, George E. Wiss, the American consul in Rotterdam, contrasted that moment in history when the new president was standing alone at the inaugural, surrounded by a few friends and many enemies, without an army, navy, or treasury, with his current position, in possession of the greatest army and navy of the world, having regained so vast a ground of the rebellion and changed the mind of the nation into acknowledging freedom of a suppressed race. "Should any one have forgotten, how you have commenced, and what you have achieved?"[49] he asked rhetorically. It was clear by end of 1864 that Lincoln had the trust of the majority of the nation.

By far the most astonishing and to some degree the most impressive proof of a great number of public figures' recognition of Lincoln's achievement was his frequent comparison with Washington and the previously cited recurrent prediction of his future stature among presidents, often ranking him as next only to the Father of His Country. As early as August 16, 1861, the *Philadelphia Press* remarked that like Lincoln, Washington had also been attacked, charged with imbecility, ignorance, and indifference. Three days later his friend Browning chided him for having been despondent at their last meeting and not hopeful of his future. "In this you are wrong, most decidedly, and do yourself great injustice," Browning insisted. "You have your future in your own hands, and the power to make your name one of the most justly revered, and illustrious in the annals of the human race."[50] The *New York Herald,* not yet unfriendly, on September 7 maintained that there was no man in the North who did not believe that the president was as "earnestly loyal to the Government as Washington was," and in March 1862 it boasted that "[i]n this crisis, for the first time since the days of George Washington the administration of the federal government has been lifted to Washington's platform of nationality." During the fall the *Chicago Tribune* declared that not since the days of Washington had there been so

---

[49] *Wilkes' Spirit of the Times,* October 1, 1864, also in Abraham Lincoln Papers, Library of Congress; George E. Wiss to Lincoln, November 21, 1864, Abraham Lincoln Papers, Library of Congress.

[50] *Philadelphia Press,* August 16, 1861, also in Abraham Lincoln Papers, Library of Congress; Browning to Lincoln, August 19, 1861, Abraham Lincoln Papers, Library of Congress.

good a president. A Quincy, Illinois, correspondent expressed the opinion that if Lincoln only would rid himself of bad advisers and turn things around, people would say that Washington liberated his country but Lincoln saved it.[51]

The period of the publication of the Emancipation Proclamation—often the source of vicious attacks at home and abroad—brought forth a spate of comparisons with the first president. John Bittmann, an advocate of colonization, thought that the pen of History was "recording incidents . . . under your Excellency's Administration as glorious in manliness,—as profound in patriotism,—and as earnest in the social and intellectual advancement of your countrymen, as that of your immortal predecessor, The Father of his Country." In February 1863 John C. Hamilton, a particularly observant Republican, remarked that "there is a *remarkable* analogy in the inner view of Washingtons official civil career with that of President Lincoln"; and he surmised that the results of his career would be "equally glorious and beneficial with that of the Father of his country."[52] Motley agreed. Delighted at the victories at Gettysburg and Vicksburg, he wrote that never since Washington had any American president taken office under such great responsibility or in so dark an hour, and that the wise and the good in every land had followed with appreciation Lincoln's steady march along "the steep & rugged path of Duty." Charles W. Goddard, an American in Constantinople, predicted that the Emancipation Proclamation was destined to "an immortality as luminous as the Declaration of Independence & the Farewell Address of Washington," and Brigadier General James C. Rice thought that Lincoln, like Washington, would ever live in the hearts of his countrymen. Others were certain that posterity North and South would bless the president forever.[53]

As in the case of other laudatory remarks, the election year of 1864 naturally caused these comparisons and forecasts of future fame to multiply. On January 2, 1864, *Harper's Weekly,* commenting on Lincoln's popularity, predicted that if he were to be renominated, he

[51] *New York Herald,* September 7, 1861, March 21, 1862; *Chicago Tribune,* October 15, 1862; Isaac N. Morris to Lincoln, November 20, 1862, Abraham Lincoln Papers, Library of Congress.

[52] John Bittmann to Lincoln, January, 1863, John C. Hamilton to Lincoln, February 2, 1863, Abraham Lincoln Papers, Library of Congress.

[53] Motley to Lincoln, July 25, 1863, Charles W. Goddard to Lincoln, October 19, 1863, James C. Rice to Henry Wilson, November 11, 1863, William H. Underwood to Lincoln, December 6, 1863, Abraham Lincoln Papers, Library of Congress.

would be reelected with a greater majority than that given to Washington and, after the renomination, confirmed this opinion. "No public man in our history since Washington has inspired a deeper popular confidence," it insisted. In June the U.S. Sanitary Commission sent him a cane made from the arch erected for Washington in 1789 because he approached so near the character of his illustrious predecessor and gave similar gratification to the ladies of Trenton. Word came from Kentucky that if Washington, an instrument of Divinity, made good in revolution and delivered the American people from tyranny, Lincoln, equally an instrument of Providence, had sanctified that revolution and saved the American people from a worse despotism.[54] And on October 12 Schurz put the matter most succinctly. "In fifty years, perhaps much sooner," he wrote, "Lincoln's name will stand written upon the honor roll of the American Republic next to that of Washington, and there it will remain for all time." Alfred L. Hough agreed. If everything went well after the election, he thought, "future history will place Mr. Lincoln's name next to Washington; The first the founder the second the preserver of our country." William Kellogg, an old Peoria acquaintance, expressed similar sentiments.[55] No wonder the old Garrisonian abolitionist Oliver Johnson was able to comment, "A redeemed, disenthralled and regenerated nation will forever speak your name with gratitude and reverence, as worthy to stand side by side with that of the 'Father of his Country.'" The American consul in Hamburg was of the same opinion.[56]

It is therefore obvious that Lincoln, far from being underestimated during his lifetime, was in fact appreciated by any number of observers. Notwithstanding the incessant attacks upon him by enemies both left and right, he succeeded in impressing enough of his countrymen with his abilities not only to win renomination and reelection, but also to be likened to the Father of His Country, whose fame, it was predicted, he would share in the future. The predictions certainly came true.

---

[54] *Harper's Weekly*, January 2, June 25, 1864; New Jersey Dept., Great Central Fair, U.S. Sanitary Commission to Lincoln, June 10, 1864, Rufus K. Williams to Lincoln, October 3, 1864, Abraham Lincoln Papers, Library of Congress.

[55] Schurz to Theodore Petrasch, October 12, 1864, in *Intimate Letters,* 309; Alfred L. Hough to Mary (Hough), November 20, 1864, in *Soldier in the West,* 230–31; William Kellogg to Lincoln, December 10, 1864, Abraham Lincoln Papers, Library of Congress.

[56] Oliver Johnson to Lincoln, December 7, 1864, J. H. Anderson to Lincoln, December 2, 1864, Abraham Lincoln Papers, Library of Congress.

13

The Lincoln Grail: The Great Collectors and Their Great Collections

Harold Holzer

THE NEW YEAR 1849 found Abraham Lincoln approaching something of a personal and professional crisis. In a month he would be forty years old. But his steady march up the political ladder was grinding to a halt. He was now a lame-duck congressman with only a few weeks left in Washington. It is no wonder that, on January 5, he wrote a rather maudlin letter to an admirer who probably seemed to him one of the last of his supporters willing to admit his admiration. Wrote Lincoln, "Your note, requesting my 'signature with a sentiment' was received. . . . I am not a very sentimental man; and the best sentiment I can think of is, that if you collect the signatures of all persons who are no less distinguished than I, you will have a very undistinguishing mass of names."[1] Barely a decade later, of course, Lincoln was elected president. And after preserving the Union, he would emerge as the most "distinguished" name in American history, notwithstanding his own grim prediction of 1849.

There is much irony in the fact that Lincoln, a man capable of writing such discouraging and self-deprecating words to the first collector ever known to have expressed interest in his signature—a man, by the way, who totally lacked the collecting impulse himself (Lincoln was a voracious reader who never owned a library)—eventually came

---

[1] Lincoln to C. U. Schlater, in Roy P. Basler et al., eds., *The Collected Works of Abraham Lincoln*, 9 vols. (New Brunswick, N.J.: Rutgers University Press, 1953–55), 2:19. The irony of this request from Schlater was first pointed out in Frank J. Williams and Mark E. Neely, Jr., "Lincoln Collecting: What's Left to Collect," *Manuscripts* 38 (winter 1986): 17, 19.

to inspire such passionate acquisitiveness among generations of Americans.

Without knowing it, C. U. Schlater, the correspondent who wrote to Lincoln to request his autograph in 1849, presaged a fiercely competitive national obsession. Schlater was the earliest "collector" ever to seek out a relic associated with Lincoln.

The efforts of the hundreds of collectors who followed in his footsteps might be said to reflect reverence for the man who, in historian David Herbert Donald's words, "embodies what ordinary, inarticulate Americans have cherished as ideals." Their lifelong pursuit of Lincoln speaks too of the uniquely American impulse to pursue the cherished touchstones that testify to the endurance of the nation. As Donald put it, the "Lincoln cult is almost an American religion."[2]

It is not an exaggeration to say that Lincoln collectors have changed history—certainly our *understanding* of history. As the great Lincoln scholar J. G. Randall acknowledged in 1936, "The hand of the amateur has rested heavily upon Lincoln studies. And not only of the amateur historian, but of the collector, the manuscript dealer, the propagandist." Yet many years later, when historian Don E. Fehrenbacher was asked, shortly before he died, what new contributions might yet be made to the seemingly endless list of books about Lincoln, he replied, "I think it would be interesting and useful to present a concise, comprehensible, and well-researched history of the major Lincoln collectors and what happened to their collections."[3]

Until now, their history has seldom been told. Most professional historians prefer not to acknowledge amateurs. The commercial impulse that inevitably informs collecting at many levels makes most scholars uncomfortable: theirs, the critics argue, is a quest for profit, not knowledge. But such doubts ignore the genuine passion that animates great collectors, not to mention their triumphs of discovery and preservation. What is more, exploring the growth of the country's most sustained collecting passion can open a window on the evolution of patriotic spirit and collective memory. As the cultural historian Michael Kammen has pointed out, collecting Lincoln relics, from

---

[2] David Herbert Donald, *Lincoln Reconsidered: Essays on the Civil War Era* (New York: Alfred A. Knopf, 1956), 144, 146, 164–165.

[3] J. G. Randall, "Has the Lincoln Theme Been Exhausted?" *American Historical Review* 41 (January 1936): 270; Don E. Fehrenbacher to Harold Holzer, July 23, 1997.

the first, was a manifestation of patriotism and "elaborate religious mythology."[4]

Lincoln collecting has not only helped to save irreplaceable historical material, it also inspired the first known domestic reverence for the American past, which otherwise found no outlet in the culture until the Colonial revival of the centennial year of 1876.[5] The lure of Lincolniana gripped politicians, men of religion, businessmen, and bibliophiles—people in all walks of life, from the son of a landscape gardener to J. P. Morgan himself and, more recently, his modern equivalents, Malcolm Forbes, Richard Gilder, and Lewis Lehrman. The collecting began virtually from the moment that Lincoln was transformed from mortal to martyr in 1865.

In a very real sense, the first successful and influential Abraham Lincoln collector was Lincoln's own son Robert. So possessive was he about his father's presidential papers that he summoned Supreme Court Justice David Davis back to Washington immediately after his father's assassination to take charge of the material. Robert worked with the late president's private secretaries to sort and store the material.[6] Just four months later, he journeyed to Springfield, Illinois, to take possession of the records and papers that remained at the old Lincoln-Herndon law office. Although he believed that their "pecuniary" value was small, he wanted to get them away from his father's longtime law partner, William H. Herndon. Robert proceeded faithfully and stubbornly—some might say obsessively—to preserve, protect, and cloak them from all public view and most scholarly scrutiny for the next sixty years. A frustrated Albert Beveridge, laboring on a major biography of Lincoln, once admitted that he was prepared to use "dynamite, or chloroform, soothing syrup, or quinine, cocaine, or T. N. T." to get access to the well-guarded archive. He never did.[7]

---

[4] Michael Kammen, *Mystic Chords of Memory: The Transformation of Tradition in American Culture* (New York: Knopf, 1991), 157, 204. Kammen noted that Lincolniana once even absorbed one of the twentieth century's greatest art collectors, J. P. Morgan.

[5] See Karal Ann Marling, *George Washington Slept Here: Colonial Revivals and American Culture, 1876–1986* (Cambridge, Mass.: Harvard University Press, 1988), 25–51.

[6] John S. Goff, *Robert Todd Lincoln: A Man in His Own Right* (Norman: University of Oklahoma Press, 1969), 80–81.

[7] David C. Mearns, *The Lincoln Papers: The Story of the Collection*, 2 vols. (Garden City, N.Y.: Doubleday, 1948), 1:vii, 18. The papers were finally opened to the public, and scholars, on July 26, 1947; see 93, 133–34.

During all that time Robert kept the papers as close to him as possible whenever, and wherever, he traveled, even if it meant hiring a special railroad car just to transport the dozens of trunks in which he had stored the priceless archives. (As president of the Pullman Company he had unlimited access to such perks.)[8]

When Robert died, the treasure was sitting only a few yards from his bedside, stored in a special office he built to house them. Even then, under the terms of a maddening stipulation in his will, another quarter of a century would have to pass before the records of his father's correspondence were at last opened to the public. And not for twenty-five years more would historical detectives probing hidden closets in his Vermont mansion stumble across unimagined, additional material, which Robert had somehow managed both to amass and to shield from the light of history. Here was a hitherto unknown collection of family photographs, as well as an "insanity file" he had assembled to vindicate his stern, long-ago decision to have his mother committed to an institution for the mentally ill. It is instructive to recall that those treasures were ultimately unearthed not by a historian, but by a curator-collector.[9]

Robert Lincoln might be called the first Lincoln collector. But he was by no means the last. Perhaps his unyielding insistence on family privacy perversely inspired others to defy him, thus unleashing the Lincolniana virus among his contemporaries. Few who caught it ever found a cure, or sought one.

The zeal to own what Lincoln owned, to touch what Lincoln touched, and in so doing to keep his memory alive inspired many, consumed a few, and enlightened generations, for many of the greatest collections ended up in public archives. The story of these great private collectors has yet to be told in full. This essay represents a modest beginning.

Practically from the moment Lincoln took his last breath, private collectors moved in to enshrine him, and to surround themselves

---

[8] Ralph Geoffrey Newman, *Preserving Lincoln for the Ages: Collectors, Collections, and Our Sixteenth President* (Fort Wayne, Ind.: Louis A. Warren Lincoln Library and Museum, 1989), 4–7.

[9] Mark E. Neely, Jr., and R. Gerald McMurtry, *The Insanity File: The Case of Mary Todd Lincoln* (Carbondale: Southern Illinois University Press, 1986), x–xi, 132–33.

with relics that testified to his life and legend. Though they lacked Robert Lincoln's inherited access, they seized every opportunity to capture the relics and artifacts floating around in the public domain: letters Lincoln had sent, photographs he had signed, beds in which he had slept, paintings for which he posed, books he had read. Rumors circulated for years that some overzealous, unscrupulous collectors seized *more* than opportunity: they apparently rifled through government offices in Illinois and seized documents as well. Indeed, when the Lincoln Legal Papers project launched its comprehensive search of Illinois court records in the 1990s, researchers found a number of important handwritten documents, unnoticed for years precisely because relic hunters had years earlier clipped from them the one valuable asset they recognized: their Lincoln signatures.

Some early collectors had been Civil War soldiers, developing their reverence for their commander in chief, as historian William C. Davis has put it, as "common men" in an "uncommon crisis." One, remarkably, fought not for Lincoln's Union, but for the enemy armies of the Confederacy. Another took up residence in the house where Lincoln lived and, later, in the house where Lincoln died.[10]

Yet another collector was at first so enraptured by the idea of collecting—any kind of collecting—that he once purchased and proudly defended the authenticity of a tiny fragment of snakeskin he claimed came from the serpent that originally tempted Eve in the Garden of Eden. Only later did he shun such indiscriminate buying and concentrate on more credible material: Lincolniana.

And still another collector was a busy manufacturer who happened to love old photographs. Chancing one day upon a janitor sweeping a pile of glass negatives into the street for disposal, he asked if he might instead take them home. Holding one negative to the light, a shock of recognition swept over him as he made out the features of Lincoln. Here was an original glass negative from the old Brady galleries. In another instant, they might have been tossed into the trash bin of history. These were the early collectors, mad for Lincoln because they had seen him, served under him, or heard tales about him from the men of their father's generation.

---

[10] William C. Davis, *Lincoln's Men: How President Lincoln Became Father to an Army and a Nation* (New York: Simon & Schuster, 1999), 7.

They would be followed, after the Lincoln birthday centennial in 1909, and well into the new century, by a new breed, distanced from Lincoln by time but as determined to rescue, restore, and retain his relics as their predecessors. Now came a Chicago lawyer, an Illinois governor, and more recently, among the post–World War II collectors still working to unearth new material at the dawn of a new millennium, a professional curator who cultivated Lincoln descendants, an ambitious professional illustrator who built the largest holding of Lincoln photographs ever collected, a former candidate for governor of New York, and a Rhode Island judge they call "maximum Frank."

They all have something in common: they have quested after what might be called "the Lincoln Grail" during thirteen consecutive decades of uninterrupted private collecting, exerting significant impact on collective memory.

The first generation—those who pursued the symbolic pieces of a secular American cross—lived in Lincoln's shadow and attempted to freeze his image in time. The very first, of course, was Robert Todd Lincoln (1843–1926), son of the president, self-appointed guardian of his reputation, and legally empowered custodian of his father's papers.

Then there was Osborn Hamilton Oldroyd (1842–1930), truly in a class by himself. At age eighteen, Oldroyd first read about Lincoln in an 1860 campaign biography that he was selling at his modest newsstand in Mount Vernon, Ohio. After serving in the Union army during the Civil War, he married a woman from Lincoln's hometown of Springfield and began amassing a collection that would soon boast Lincoln's gray shawl, an inscribed family bible, and furniture from his law office and his White House bedroom. Later, Oldroyd and his collection moved into Lincoln's own former Springfield residence, where he remained as custodian even after Robert Lincoln donated the home to the state in 1887. Six years later, Oldroyd moved on to Washington and this time took up residence in the house where Lincoln died. Oldroyd dwelled in the Petersen House for more than thirty years, still surrounded by his Lincoln treasures, enthusiastically guiding visitors through the collection, and producing books and pamphlets about the sixteenth president. His collection was eventually purchased for $50,000 by the federal government for its Ford's Theatre Museum, but only after Henry Ford attempted to buy it for himself. Oldroyd stayed on as curator emeritus until the end of his long, single-minded life.[11]

Oldroyd outdid the competition for the highest-echelon materials, but he did have contemporary colleagues in the Lincoln field during what the great Lincolniana dealer Ralph G. Newman called "the era of the contemporaries": William Vaughan Spencer, Irish-born Andrew Boyd, and Charles Henry Hart, whose book collections spurred efforts to catalog all the material that had been published to date about the sixteenth president, a task that would benefit historians—as well as future collectors—for generations.[12]

Right behind these pioneers came "the Big Five," the name given the first leaders of the field who dominated Lincoln collecting at the turn of the century. Jay Monaghan, who published the first compilation of the Lincoln Papers in 1948, acknowledged that "the Big Five possessed a 'corner' in the field. Their word was law."[13]

The scholar of the group was Daniel Fish (1848–1924) of Minneapolis, a Civil War veteran who became a lawyer and journalist, and eventually a jurist and, not unimportantly, adjutant general of the Grand Army of the Republic. Fish was "bitten by the bug of Lincoln bibliomania," as he put it, after doing research for a Lincoln speech. By the time the self-described "boy soldier of the Union" died, he owned important memorabilia, manuscripts, and a thousand books. Fish also wrote the first truly comprehensive bibliography of Lincoln publications, a major contribution to the field.[14] Ultimately, his collection was sold to the Lincoln National Life Insurance Company

---

[11] Wayne C. Temple, *By Square and Compasses: The Building of Lincoln's Home and Its Saga* (Bloomington: Illinois Lodge of Research and the Masonic Book Club, 1984), esp. ch. 11; Louis A. Warren, "Moving a National Museum," *Lincoln Lore,* no. 146 (January 25, 1932); William Burton Benham, *Life of Osborn H. Oldroyd: Founder and Collector of Lincoln Mementos* (Washington, D.C.: [Beresford], 1927). Oldroyd's books included a study of the assassination and a collection of tributes by other writers. Louis A. Warren dryly noted of Oldroyd the author: "[He] was primarily a collector." See Warren, "Oldroyd's Publications," *Lincoln Lore,* no. 868 (November 26, 1945).

[12] Newman, *Preserving Lincoln for the Ages,* 8–9; Louis A. Warren, "Lincoln Bibliographers," *Lincoln Lore,* no. 61 (June 9, 1930).

[13] Jay Monaghan, ed., *Lincoln Bibliography 1839–1939,* 2 vols., Collections of the Illinois State Historical Library 31, Bibliographic Series 4 (Springfield: Illinois State Historical Library, 1945), 1:xix.

[14] See Daniel Fish, *Lincoln Literature: A Bibliographical Account of Books and Pamphlets Relating to Abraham Lincoln* (Minneapolis: Minneapolis Public Library Board, 1900).

and became the core of the holdings at what is now the Lincoln
Museum in Fort Wayne, Indiana. Fish is credited, in Monaghan's
words, with having "defined the limits of [printed] Lincolniana," ex-
cluding kitsch and embracing "exclusively . . . books and pamphlets,
including in the latter class everything that approaches to the dignity
of the brochure."[15]

William Harrison Lambert (1842–1912), a much-honored Civil
War veteran who built his own successful insurance company in Philadelphia, began a forty-year career as a Lincoln collector after his
father inspired him with his first Lincoln book. He specialized in
books that Lincoln had once read himself, along with a fabulous archive of autograph material, most notably Lincoln's letter to General
John C. Frémont revoking the latter's order of emancipation in Missouri. A 1906 fire destroyed the original legal books Lambert had
assembled from Lincoln's Springfield law office, along with furniture
from the Lincoln White House, but his manuscripts had just been
moved to a bank vault and were saved. The Lambert collection was
sold at auction two years after the death of the man even his rivals in
the field acknowledged had owned the best Lincoln collection of anyone outside the Lincoln family.[16]

Lambert's rival Charles Woodbury McLellan (1836–1918) of
Springfield claimed that he was in the same room as Lincoln when
the news arrived that he had won the Republican presidential nomination in 1860. True or not, McLellan went on to become a cotton
broker, of all things, and eventually served as a commissary in the
Confederate armed forces. Somehow he evolved into an important
New York–based banker. Reading Herndon's biography of Lincoln
aroused McLellan's interest in the field, and he collected passionately
after he retired from business in 1906. Within thirty years he owned
more than six thousand items, including Lincoln's famous, handwritten "Mediation on Divine Will," such early examples of Lincoln's
handwriting as the muster roll from Captain Abraham Lincoln's
Black Hawk War regiment, and five great contemporaneous paintings. In 1923 John D. Rockefeller arranged for the purchase of the
collection, for $42,500, for his alma mater, Brown University. Today

---

[15] Ralph Newman attested to Fish's scholarship; see *Preserving Lincoln for the
Ages*, 9; see also Monaghan, *Lincoln Bibliography*, 1:xix.

[16] *In Memoriam: William Harrison Lambert* (New York: Lincoln Fellowship,
1912); original in the Lincoln Museum, Fort Wayne, Indiana.

it is the nucleus of its John Hay Library's 23,000-item Lincoln holdings. (The Brown collection is one of the best in the nation, but Lincoln students often mistakenly attribute its status solely to its John Hay collection; McLellan surely deserves equal credit.)[17]

Joseph Benjamin Oakleaf (1858–1930), a lawyer and public official from Moline, Illinois, born in the year of the Lincoln-Douglas debates, was inspired to collect Lincolniana after reading the serialized version of Nicolay and Hay's great multivolume biography. He began his efforts by attempting to purchase every book they had read, and largely succeeded. Later he purchased a number of letters written by Lincoln's wife, Mary, and the luminous husband-and-wife companion portraits painted in the White House by Francis B. Carpenter in 1864. Oakleaf lectured widely, on both Lincoln collecting and Lincoln's legal career, and eventually wrote a useful supplement to Fish's Lincoln bibliography, updating it with 1,576 new titles. He was probably the first Lincoln collector to rent a separate apartment—and a four-room one at that—to house his collection. Indiana University purchased the collection in 1942, but it has never been fully cataloged.[18]

Judd Stewart (1867–1919), the only one of the Big Five born after Lincoln's death, was probably the most indiscriminate of these leading early collectors. A conservative Republican offended by Theodore Roosevelt's split with the party in 1912, he wrote several tracts

[17] Mark E. Neely, Jr., *The Abraham Lincoln Encyclopedia* (New York: McGraw-Hill, 1982), 204–5; Edith R. Blanchard, "The McLellan Lincoln Collection," *Books at Brown* 4 (January 1947). A copy of the original letter from the Comptroller of Brown University acknowledging receipt of the collection and disclosing the price paid was published in *The Rail Splitter: A Journal for the Lincoln Collector* 6 (summer 2000): 23.

[18] Louis A. Warren, "Oakleaf Lincolniana to Indiana University," *Lincoln Lore*, no. 676 (March 23, 1942); J. L. McCorison, Jr., "The Great Lincoln Collectors and What Became of Them," *Lincoln Herald*, 50–51 (December 1948–February 1949): 2–16; Monaghan, *Lincoln Bibliography*, 1:xxiii–xxiv. See also Joseph B. Oakleaf, *Lincoln Bibliography* (Cedar Rapids, Iowa: Torch Press, 1925). Examples of Oakleaf's lectures include "Abraham Lincoln as a Criminal Lawyer," at the Illinois State's Attorneys' Association, December 7, 1912 (published in 1923), and "An Address on the Collection of Lincoln Literature" before the Illinois Bar Association on February 12, 1913 (also published in 1923), and both in Monaghan, *Lincoln Bibliography*, 2:156–57. A recent effort to present highlights from the collection is Cecil K. Byrd and Ward W. Moore, eds., *Abraham Lincoln in Print and Photograph: A Picture History from the Lilly Library* (Mineola, N.Y.: Dover Publications, 1997), which acknowledges the Oakleaf acquisition as the "nucleus" of the Lilly Library collection; see v.

arguing that Lincoln and Roosevelt would have differed politically had they been contemporaries. His collecting career was more distinguished, although Stewart did purchase memorabilia and curios with the same zeal with which he bought books and manuscripts. And one of his greatest so-called "finds," letters that Lincoln allegedly sent to Southern leaders on the eve of the Civil War, was ultimately proven a forgery.[19]

But his collection also boasted three thousand unassailable books, broadsides, and pamphlets, including the proof copy of Lincoln's First Inaugural Address, which he published, with his own foreword, in 1920. He also owned Lincoln's magnificent handwritten note to the parents of Ephraim Elmer Ellsworth, one of the great condolence letters in American literature. And Stewart published one of the first illustrated studies of Lincoln portraits, a lavish catalog of the pictorial treasures within his own vast collection. After his death, Stewart's heirs sold the collection to railroad tycoon Henry E. Huntington, and it became the core of the huge Lincoln archive at the Huntington Library in San Marino, California.[20]

That was the Big Five. Their competition—and their successors—were in turn known as the "New Seven." And they were nearly as successful as the five who first dominated the field.

Charles F. Gunther (1837–1920), for example, did not quite make the "Big Five," but his collection did eventually grow to include the bed on which Lincoln died, furniture from the Lincolns' Springfield home, and the president's famous 1865 letter to General Ulysses S. Grant urging that the war be "pressed" to a speedy conclusion. A wealthy, free-spending candy manufacturer—he was the collector who believed he owned the skin of the snake from the Garden of Eden—Gunther's Lincoln collection eventually went to the Chicago Historical Society.[21]

Henry Horner (1879–1940) became the law partner of the son of

---

[19] Neely, *The Abraham Lincoln Encyclopedia*, 291; Judd Stewart, *Abraham Lincoln on Present-Day Problems. And Abraham Lincoln as Represented by Theodore Roosevelt* (Columbus, Ohio: n.p., 1912).

[20] [Judd Stewart], *Lincoln's First Inaugural[:] Original Draft and its Final Form* (n.p.: n.p., 1920); *Catalogue of the Portraits of Lincoln in the Lincoln Collection of Judd Stewart* (Plainfield, N.J.: n.p., n.d.). The book included 629 prints, including cartoons.

[21] Neely, *The Abraham Lincoln Encyclopedia*, 56; Clement M. Silvestro, "The Candy Man's Mixed Bag," *Chicago History* 2, no. 2 (1972): 86–89.

Lincoln's onetime law associate, Henry Clay Whitney, sparking his interest in Lincolniana. Later a judge and two-term governor of Illinois, Horner's collection of six thousand books included a jokester from which Lincoln read aloud during cabinet meetings. A frequent lecturer, his topics included the "universality" of Lincoln for citizens of the world, and Lincoln's role as commander in chief. Horner donated the collection, which he lovingly referred to as "a bachelor's children," to the Illinois State Historical Library the year of his death, 1940. Sixty years later, plans were announced to build a Lincoln "Presidential Library" in Springfield dedicated, in part, to displaying the Henry Horner collection in Lincoln's hometown.[22]

John Edgar Burton (1847–1930) of Lake Geneva, Wisconsin, son of a shoemaker, was one of the wealthiest men ever to pursue Lincoln collecting. He made his fortune in mining investments and spent it on Lincolniana. Beginning his Lincoln pursuits in the 1860s, he eventually bought so much material that the "Big Five" grew jealous, exchanging letters criticizing him. "He pays enormous prices," J. B. Oakleaf complained at one point to Fish, noting disdainfully that Burton lived in a three-story house that was crammed from top to bottom with what he dismissed as "curios." Burton also horrified his competitors by openly advertising to purchase "Books, Pamphlets, or documents regarding Abraham Lincoln, at a reasonable cash price."[23]

But among the so-called curios for which Burton paid those "cash" prices was an autographed presentation copy of the Lincoln-Douglas debates and pages from the boy Lincoln's sum book. Still, the "Big Five" ultimately enjoyed the last laugh on their competitor. Burton was ruined in 1915 and was forced to sell his treasures at New York auctions in 1915 and 1916. His entire collection—boasting nearly twenty-five hundred Lincoln books along with significant one-of-a-kind items—fetched the grand total of only $11,126. But before his fall, Burton, Monaghan said, "added rules of his own to the game and set his colleagues to arguing happily over each other's definitions of

[22] Monaghan, *Lincoln Bibliography,* 1:xxv, xxvii; 2:220; Henry Horner, *The Universality of Lincoln* (Springfield, Ill.: Abraham Lincoln Association, 1932); Neely, *The Abraham Lincoln Encyclopedia,* 156; Newman, *Preserving Lincoln for the Ages,* 23.

[23] John Edgar Burton, *Burton's Want List Regarding Abraham Lincoln and Lincolniana* (Milwaukee: n.p., 1905); Neely, *The Abraham Lincoln Encyclopedia,* 41–42; R. Gerald McMurtry, "John E. Burton: Lincoln Collector," *Lincoln Lore,* no. 1605 (November 1971): 1–3.

the field. Some five hundred collectors followed suit, rummaging attics and bookstores, exulting over an early imprint, complaining when the discovery did not qualify as "Lincolniana." Burton had re-energized the field.[24]

Another of its luminaries was William E. Barton (1891–1930) of Sublette, Illinois. Best known as a Lincoln biographer, he was a Congregational minister by vocation who served parishes in Ohio, Illinois, Tennessee, and Massachusetts. Collecting—and writing about—Lincoln became his avocation. His holdings eventually grew to four thousand Lincoln titles, augmented by pieces he purchased at auction at the Burton sale, and all of which he proudly displayed at a Massachusetts summer home that he named "The Wigwam" in honor of the Chicago convention hall where Lincoln was nominated for president in 1860. Barton's heirs donated the holdings to the University of Chicago.[25]

Henry Horner's childhood friend Alfred Whital Stern (1882–1961) was a prominent Chicago lawyer known to an entire generation of colleagues as "Abraham Lincoln's best (posthumous) friend." His huge collection, built over thirty-five years, included such treasures as an original 1860 Lincoln life mask and the handwritten recollections of the artist who sculpted it. Its greatest single treasure was arguably the large scrapbook that Lincoln personally assembled of the newspaper reprints of his 1858 campaign debates with Stephen A. Douglas, a scrapbook that served as the basis for the first printed version of the Lincoln-Douglas debates. Stern donated all of his holdings— seven thousand pieces in all, including books, broadsides, sheet music, manuscripts, and ephemera—to the Library of Congress on the eighty-seventh anniversary of the Gettysburg Address in 1953, providing with it an endowment to fund its "perpetual enlargement." Stern, the Library of Congress declared in accepting the gift, had "spared neither pains, nor expense, to make his collection at once worthy of the spirit who called it into being and his fellow-citizens who, in successive generations, may return to it for example and inspiration."[26]

---

[24] McMurtry, "John E. Burton: Lincoln Collector"; Monaghan, *Lincoln Bibliography,* 1:xix; Anderson Auction Company, *The Large and Important Library of John E. Burton* (auction catalog) (New York: n.p., 1915).

[25] Neely, *The Abraham Lincoln Encyclopedia,* 20.

[26] *A Catalog of the Alfred Whital Stern Collection of Lincolniana in the Library of Congress* (Washington, D.C.: n.p., 1960), esp. v.

Illinois-born Oliver Rogers Barrett (1873–1950), arguably the greatest of all mid-twentieth-century Lincoln collectors, traced his interest in the field to a childhood trauma: as a grade-schooler, he had been punished for bad behavior by being forced to sit next to his only African American schoolmate. When he complained to his mother about this "humiliation," she refused to sympathize; instead she proudly told him Lincoln's life story and took him to visit Springfield. Barrett became a Lincoln collector while still a boy and continued for the rest of his life. His fabled collection inspired a book by Carl Sandburg (the only volume ever devoted to a Lincoln collector and collection). The poet maintained that the Barrett collection reflected the "toil" and "pursuit" of "more than half a century." To a grateful Sandburg, "the collector's flair leading Barrett since he was a boy has resulted in a mass of source materials wherein are many items that would have probably been lost for historical purposes but for the sagacity and method by which they were sought out."[27]

Two years after Barrett's death, his collection was sold at the Parke-Bernet Galleries in New York, after Illinois declined to purchase it for the State Historical Library for $220,000. The dispersed treasures included Lincoln's letters to his only intimate friend, Joshua Fry Speed, and the rhyming doggerel from Lincoln's childhood sum book: "Abraham Lincoln / his hand and pen / he will be good but / god knows When." As for the prized debates scrapbook, rival collector Alfred Stern bought it at the Barrett sale for $24,000. Lincoln's ivory-handled seal sold for just $650 and a chair from his White House bedroom for $110, the intimate Lincoln-Speed letters for only $35,000. In all, the sale sent 842 items back into the private hands, and to such public institutions as the Library of Congress, the Illinois State Historical Society, Lincoln Memorial University, and the Chicago Historical Society.[28]

Then there was Frederick Hill Meserve (1865–1962). In an incredibly long life, this intrepid detective-scholar did more to identify and preserve the pictorial record of Lincoln's life and times than any other contemporary. A New York textile executive who loved pictures, he bought the remains of Mathew Brady's original archive of

[27] Carl Sandburg, *Lincoln Collector: The Story of Oliver R. Barrett's Great Private Collection* (New York: Harcourt Brace, 1949), 3–4.

[28] *The Oliver R. Barrett Lincoln Collection* (auction catalog) (New York: Parke-Bernet Galleries, 1952); Newman, *Preserving Lincoln for the Ages,* 16–17.

photographic negatives in 1902 (Brady had earlier sold them to meet his debts). Of his ten thousand pieces, seven were priceless, original Lincoln glass negatives. Their discovery, Sandburg said, transformed Meserve from "a patient and devoted collector" into "a tireless zealot."[29]

Meserve studied and published as he acquired, and one of his book projects became an instant classic. Featuring prints that he developed by hand from his own plates and negatives, Meserve issued a plush chronology of all one hundred known Lincoln photographs. The printing of one hundred limited-edition copies at $35, each boasting photos hand-pasted to rag-paper pages, itself went on to become one of the most desirable of all Lincoln collectibles. Meserve issued supplements in 1928, 1952, and a final volume in 1955, at the age of ninety. At his death, his collection passed to his daughter Dorothy Kunhardt (a celebrated author of children's books like *Pat the Bunny*), and at her passing, to her son Philip, a journalist and historian, who eventually sold the holdings to the National Portrait Gallery. The Kunhardt grandsons and great-grandsons still consult the collection to create books and television documentaries, including a documentary mini-series on Lincoln. The elder Meserve's death at age ninety-seven signaled the end of the third great era of Lincoln collecting. "Quiet, modest, and unassuming," Sandburg recalled, Meserve had been "a born natural' in his particular field."[30]

There have, of course, been others: F. Lauriston Bullard, who gave his collection to Boston University; Elwin Page of New Hampshire; Massachusetts State Senator Edward C. Stone; Claude E. Simmonds of New Paltz, N.Y.; Michael McCarthy of Brockton, Mass.; William Kaland of New York; and Roy Crocker of the Lincoln Savings and Loan Association in California, whose collection included the "signature" of Lincoln's stepmother: "Her Mark."[31]

[29] Frederick Hill Meserve and Carl Sandburg, *The Photographs of Abraham Lincoln* (New York: Harcourt, Brace, 1944), 17.

[30] Ibid., 24; Frederick Hill Meserve, *Lincolniana: Historical Portraits and Views Printed Directly from Original Negatives . . . in the Collection of Americana of Frederick Hill Meserve* (New York: privately printed, 1915).

[31] The Kaland Collection of documents, books, and prints, was sold by the Swann Galleries in New York on May 23, 1985; see *Abraham Lincoln and His Contemporaries* (auction catalog) (New York: Swann Galleries, 1985). The Crocker Collection was offered by Sotheby Parke-Bernet on November 28, 1979; see *Important Lincolniana . . . The Roy P. Crocker Historical Document Collection of the Lincoln Savings and Loan Association* (auction catalog) (New York: Sotheby Parke-Bernet, 1979).

Ralph Newman, who had purchased 80 percent of the manuscripts at the Barrett auction, added to the list James W. Bollinger, Albert H. Griffith, Frederick R. Risdon, John W. Starr, and Carl Haverlin. And he noted that the richly varied collection of Philip David Sang (1902–75), which included much Lincolniana, was so enormous that it required five separate auctions to dispose of it—1,342 items in all, including Lincoln's famous letter advising "wanting to work is so rare a merit, that it should be encouraged."[32]

Well-publicized auctions such as the Sang sale have the effect of recycling much important material, invariably attracting new generations of collectors. Accordingly, a robust modern era has succeeded the age of Haverlin and Sang. Is there a new "Big Five" or "Little Seven?" There certainly remains a high-end echelon, and no end of aspirants to the exclusive pantheon.

Lloyd Ostendorf (b. 1925), for example, has amassed not one but two great collections of Lincoln photographs, the first of which he sold to the Lincoln Museum in Fort Wayne, the second of which he began successfully to build as soon as he sold the first. A professional illustrator who began his career as an apprentice to *Terry and the Pirates* cartoonist Milton Caniff, he discovered many new Lincoln camera poses and published three editions of a definitive book on the photographs of Lincoln, updating and replacing the work of Meserve. Some have challenged the authenticity of his latest finds, which include a purported second page of the reading copy of Lincoln's Gettysburg Address, and a photograph that he argues depicts Lincoln after death. Whatever one feels about his more recent discoveries, however, few doubt the importance of his contributions to the field over nearly half a century of collecting.[33]

Dr. John K. Lattimer (b. 1916), a widely respected New York urologist, developed a passionate, some say macabre, interest in relics of the Lincoln assassination, becoming the nation's greatest private collector of murder-and-deathbed artifacts. He owns the blood-

---

[32] John Y. Simon, "Ralph G. Newman, 1911–1998," *Civil War History* 45 (March 1999): 61; Newman, *Preserving Lincoln for the Ages,* 18–21, 29; Abraham Lincoln to George D. Ramsay, October 17, 1861, in *Collected Works of Lincoln,* 4:556; *Highly Important American Historical Documents, Autograph Letters, and Manuscripts[,] the property of the Elsie O. and Philip D. Sang Foundation* (auction catalogs), 5 vols. (New York: Sotheby Parke-Bernet, 1978–80).

[33] See *Lincoln's Photographs: A Complete Album,* rev. ed. (Dayton, Ohio: Rockywood Press, 1998). Some of his controversial new finds are illustrated on 416–17.

stained collar torn from Lincoln's shirt after he was shot, the knife used by one of Booth's co-conspirators to stab the secretary of state, and the nooses used to hang the assassins. He possesses other prizes, too, like Mary Lincoln's traveling commode. True, he also bought, and believes in, a shriveled little artifact auctioned off as what was left of Napoleon's private parts, allegedly severed from his corpse by his vengeful attending physician. In a historical twist that eerily echoes his passion for the assassination, Lattimer himself was shot from behind a few years ago, but unlike Lincoln, he was saved by modern medicine. Not long thereafter, he appeared before the Lincoln Group of New York to energetically debate an author who claimed that Lincoln's own physicians had botched the job of saving his life after he was shot by Booth.[34]

James T. Hickey (1921–96), the longtime curator of the Lincoln Collection at the Illinois State Historical Library, simultaneously built a great private collection of Lincolniana—his own—arousing admiration, envy, and some raised eyebrows as well over this unique dual role.[35] His personal holdings included the long-lost album of Lincoln family photographs, along with one-of-a-kind ambrotypes of the Lincoln children, all of which he eventually sold to the Lincoln Museum in Fort Wayne, rather than to the archive that employed him for most of his adult life. Illinois did get the leather photo album itself, but only after it was emptied of its contents. And the final disposition of the remainder of his rich collection remains a matter of speculation. Hickey amassed his extraordinary range of family relics through his close personal friendship with Lincoln's last living descendant, Robert Todd Lincoln Beckwith. Most of that collection still remains intact, its final fate unknown.[36]

[34] Dr. Lattimer described his collection briefly in Lattimer, *Kennedy and Lincoln: Medical and Ballistic Comparisons of Their Assassinations* (New York: Harcourt Brace Jovanovich, 1980), xx–xxi; see also Harold Holzer, "Collecting Relics of an Assassination," *Americana Magazine* (May–June 1981): 70–73.

[35] Louis A. Warren, founder of the Lincoln National Life Historic Research Foundation, now the Lincoln Museum in Fort Wayne, also had a personal collection of research material. See Louis A. Warren, "Lincoln Lore Source Material," *Lincoln Lore*, no. 261 (April 9, 1934); see also Mark E. Neely, Jr., "James T. Hickey, Lincoln Curator," in *The Collected Writings of James T. Hickey from Publications of the Illinois State Historical Society, 1953–1984* (Springfield: Illinois State Historical Society, 1990), vii–viii.

[36] Mark E. Neely, Jr., and Harold Holzer, *The Lincoln Family Album: Photographs from the Personal Collection of a Historic American Family* (New York: Doubleday, 1990), vii–ix.

Malcolm Forbes (1919–90) was the billionaire collector on a grand scale of presidential autographs, vintage toy soldiers, antique toy boats, and the glorious Fabergé Easter eggs of the Russian imperial family (at one time he owned more of those than the Kremlin). Forbes began pursuing Lincoln with a vengeance in the 1970s, paying mind-boggling prices at auction sales to the delight of headline writers and the dismay of poorer collectors. Forbes set a record when he paid $231,000 for a Lincoln document in 1984, telling the *New York Times:* "I think it's a bargain." A few months later, he broke his own record by outbidding millionaire and later presidential candidate Ross Perot at $297,000 for a printed, souvenir copy of the Emancipation Proclamation, signed by Lincoln, but hardly unique: forty-eight copies were known to exist. Lincoln scholars Frank J. Williams and Mark E. Neely, Jr., called it "a titanic struggle over an inconsequential document." Forbes would go on to shatter his own price records again and again, amassing the most distinguished collection of the roaring 1980s.[37] Today his treasures are showcased at the small but extraordinary Greenwich Village museum that bears his name. There is nowhere else that one can see the text of Lincoln's over-sentimental attempt at poetry, "My childhood home I see again," displayed near a handwritten copy of Julia Ward Howe's rather more successful verse, "The Battle Hymn of the Republic."[38]

Of this modern collecting group, only Ostendorf and Lattimer lived to enter the twenty-first century alive and well and continuing their Lincoln pursuits with strong appetites and open checkbooks. Their enduring strength has been their willingness to specialize. But a younger generation of mega-generalists charged into the new millennium with limitless resources, insatiable commitment, wide-ranging interests, and something new as well: a public-spirited willingness to use their treasures to educate others.

The California-based collector Louise Taper, for one, converted an early and casual interest in Mary Lincoln, and early employment on the set of the *Sandburg's Lincoln* miniseries, into one of the great private collections of the 1980s and 1990s, focusing on artifacts, doc-

[37] Frank J. Williams and Mark E. Neely, Jr., "The Crisis in Lincoln Collecting," *Books at Brown*, 31–32, Harold Holzer, ed., *Lincoln and Lincolniana* (Providence, R.I.: Friends of the Library of Brown University, 1985), 84–85.

[38] See Harold Holzer, "Collecting's First Family," *Americana Magazine* (March–April 1983): 41–47.

uments, and relics (including the First Lady's mourning jewelry). The most important woman Lincoln collector of all time, she also owns a Lincoln stovepipe hat, White House china, pages from Lincoln's sum books, and countless documents. But she not only buys, she shares. Through her efforts, her funding, and her loans, the Huntington Museum mounted the 1995 traveling exhibition *The Last Best Hope of Earth*, one of the most popular shows of Lincoln manuscripts in history. The Lincoln field will likely feel her influence for decades to come.[39]

Likewise will be felt the influence of Richard Gilder and Lewis Lehrman, the unique collecting partners who have beaten Forbes's old auction records for historical documents, creating a collection so large it reposes at the Morgan Library in New York, and so vast and broad that scholars now consult it as routinely as they do the Library of Congress or the Lincoln Museum. But the Gilder-Lehrman collection does not wait to be reached; it reaches out, mounting traveling exhibitions, sponsoring lectures, inspiring books, financing magnet history schools, supporting scholars, and endowing the most generous annual history award in America, the Lincoln Prize (as well as prizes for the year's best book on slavery, and for the best Lincoln contribution on the Internet). Theirs is perhaps the model twenty-first-century collection: privately owned, and publicly shared.[40]

Finally, there is the chairman of the Lincoln Forum. Frank J. Williams, owner of ten thousand books, pamphlets, sculptures, paintings, and prints, including one of the finest autographed Lincoln photos in private hands, has generously opened the doors of his home to dozens of historians pursuing research projects relating to Lincoln and the Civil War. Somehow he simultaneously pursues not only a judicial career, but also one combining writing and editing, lecturing, and organizational leadership in the Lincoln community. And his passion for the field might never have been stimulated had not his grade-school teacher seated him at the rear of the classroom, away from his friend, but directly beneath an inspiring picture of Lincoln.[41]

---

[39] See, for example, John Rhodehamel and Louise Taper, eds., *"Right or Wrong, God Judge Me": The Writings of John Wilkes Booth* (Urbana: University of Illinois Press, 1997), x; Harold Holzer, "How I Met Lincoln," *American Heritage Magazine* (August 1999): 62.

[40] See Harold Holzer, "Prizing History: An Interview with Richard Gilder and Lewis Lehrman," *American Heritage Magazine* (May–June, 2000): 95–98.

[41] See Harold Holzer, "Profile: Frank J. Williams," *Blue & Gray Magazine* 1, no. 6 (July 1984): 16–19; Harold Holzer, "How I Met Lincoln," 62.

Today the Frank and Virginia Williams collection is more than the sum of its parts. It symbolizes an ethic of public service as well. Frank Williams's story—like those of all the others—exemplifies the best of what increasingly animates collecting and collectors. Lincoln inspired them, and they in turn preserved much of him for us.

The great Lincoln collectors have long been denied the credit they are due. They have too often been misjudged as selfish acquistors with no sense of obligation to the field. In fact, these collectors have performed an enormous public and historical service by preserving and cataloging archives and relics of the Lincoln era that might have vanished without their intervention, whatever its motivation. Many have conducted rigorous study of their own holdings, for the benefit of others. Increasingly, they have shared their treasures with the public through publications and exhibitions. And notwithstanding J. G. Randall's old warning against amateurs and collectors, the fact is that without the great *private* Lincoln collections, the great *public* Lincoln collections—in Chicago, Springfield, Fort Wayne, and San Marino, to name a few—would not only be weaker, they would hardly exist. They would certainly offer less to modern students of Lincoln.

It is fair to say that where private collectors are concerned, their gain has been our gain. They have preserved touchstones to history that otherwise might have been lost to us. They have helped save the past for the benefit of the future.

The tradition continues. The search goes on, the hunger still burns, and the competitive juices flow. In late 1999, the Lincoln community was electrified by rumors that the famous Galloway letter of 1859—in which Lincoln not only warned that Douglas's policies would revive the African slave trade, but also modestly confessed, "I do not think myself fit for the Presidency"—might soon be offered for sale by the family that has owned it for generations. The transaction was never consummated, but it served as a reminder of how many important Lincoln relics remain in private hands. Not long thereafter, yet another private collector unexpectedly sent to unsuspecting, astonished curators at the Illinois Historical Library a trove of unknown personal letters from Mary Lincoln, including her intricate funeral instructions. The library wisely purchased the letters, inspiring national press coverage. Such acquisitions still matter.[42]

---

[42] *Collected Works of Lincoln,* 3:394–95.

Surely anyone who believes that Lincoln collecting in the twenty-first century will not be as vigorous as it was in the nineteenth and twentieth centuries underestimates the lure of the Lincoln grail, and the determination of the men and women who pursue it. The original relics may be scarcer, but the hunt continues.

As this book went to press in 2002, many significant Lincoln (and other historical) treasures from the storied Forbes collection, including the handwritten manuscript of Lincoln's last speech, unexpectedly went on the auction block. The entire Lincoln field was both jolted and invigorated by yet another round of record-setting bids, as the archive fetched $30 million at Christie's New York.[43]

But as Malcolm Forbes himself famously replied when asked why he had just paid an astronomical sum for an historic letter: "What price history?" Besides, Forbes explained shortly before his death in 1990, "The point is, when you're gone, the things you have collected will go back on the block, and many other people will have the fun of collecting a bit of what you did." Twelve years later, other people did.[44]

"Human instinct is such that every person is a collector of some sort or other," Oliver Barrett once told an audience of Lincoln enthusiasts. "Some collect books. Others collect money—and yet others children. In this world you gather what you like best, if you can." For a century and a quarter, Lincoln collectors have liked Lincoln best—and could.[45]

[43] "Bragging Rights," *Wall Street Journal* (March 29, 2002); Rita Reif, "History That's Signed or Delivered," *The New York Times* (March 24, 2002).

[44] *The Forbes Collection of American Historical Documents, Part One* (Catalogue, ed. Chris Coover, New York: Christie's, 2002), 10–11.

[45] Carl Sandburg, *Lincoln Collector*, 14.

CONTRIBUTORS

Jean H. Baker, professor of history at Goucher College, is the author of *Mary Todd Lincoln: A Biography* (1987), a life story of the Civil War first lady that David Herbert Donald called "one of the few books that deserve to be called definitive." She has written extensively about Civil War–era politics and is the author of an acclaimed biography of Adlai E. Stevenson.

Iver Bernstein is professor of history at Washington University in St. Louis. He received his B.A. from Brown University, and his Ph.D. from Yale, where in 1985 he won the George Washington Eggleston Prize for his doctoral thesis, later expanded into the definitive book *The New York City Draft Riots: Their Significance for American Society and Politics in the Age of the Civil War* (1990).

Gary W. Gallagher is John L. Nau III Professor of History at the University of Virginia. His previous books include *The Confederate War* (1997) and *Lee and His Generals in War and Memory* (1998). He has recently published *Lee & His Army in Confederate History* (2001).

Harold Holzer is co-chairman of the United States Lincoln Bicentennial Commission, and the author, co-author, or editor of twenty books on Lincoln and the Civil War. His recent books include *Prang's Civil War Pictures: The Complete Battle Chromos of Louis Prang* (2001) and *State of the Union: New York and the Civil War* (2002). He serves as vice president for communications and marketing at The Metropolitan Museum of Art.

John F. Marszalek is William L. Giles Distinguished Professor of History at Mississippi State University. He is the author of eleven books on subjects ranging from African American history to sex in the Andrew Jackson White House. His two books on William T. Sherman are *Sherman's Other War: The General and the Civil War Press* (1981) and *Sherman: A Soldier's Passion for Order* (1993).

James M. McPherson won the Pulitzer Prize for *Battle Cry of Freedom: The Civil War Era* (1988). His recent books include *Abraham Lincoln and the Second American Revolution* (1991), *Drawn with the Sword* (1996), and *For Cause and Comrades: Why Men Fought in the Civil War* (1997), which won the Lincoln Prize. Professor McPherson has taught history at Princeton University for forty years.

J. Tracy Power won second place in the 1998 Lincoln Prize competition for his book *Lee's Miserables: Life in the Army of the Northern Virginia from the Wilderness to Appomattox* (1998). A former teacher of history at Midlands Technical College and the University of South Carolina, he now works in historic preservation at the South Carolina Department of Archives and History.

Gerald J. Prokopowicz is the longtime resident Lincoln historian at the Lincoln Museum in Fort Wayne, Indiana. His newest book is *All for the Regiment: The Army of the Ohio, 1861–1862* (2001). He is also the author of *America's Sixteenth President: Abraham Lincoln* (1999), part of the "Famous American Series" published for the National Park Service.

Dawn Ruark is the textual editor of *The Papers of Ulysses S. Grant*. She is a Ph.D. candidate in American history at Southern Illinois University Carbondale and intends to write a dissertation on Gustave Koerner.

Barry Schwartz won several awards for his recent book, *Abraham Lincoln and the Forge of National Memory* (2000). A professor of sociology at the University of Georgia who has written for such professional journals as *American Journal of Sociology*, Schwartz is the author of three other books, including *George Washington: The Making of an American Symbol*, a study of hero worship in American history and culture.

John Y. Simon is professor of history at Southern Illinois University Carbondale. He has written or edited, in addition to the published volumes of *The Papers of Ulysses S. Grant*, four books, among which is *The Personal Memoirs of Julia Dent Grant*.

Craig L. Symonds is professor of history at the U.S. Naval Academy at Annapolis, where he has taught for twenty-five years. He is the author of seventeen books, including biographies of Civil War military figures Joseph E. Johnston, Franklin Buchanan, and Patrick Cleburne. His newest work is *The American Heritage History of the Battle of Gettysburg* (2001).

Hans L. Trefousse, Distinguished Professor Emeritus at Brooklyn College and the City University of New York Graduate Center, has written biographies of Benjamin Butler, Benjamin Franklin Wade, Carl Schurz, Thaddeus Stevens, and Andrew Johnson, among other noted books. His chapter in this collection is an excerpt from his forthcoming study of Lincoln's reputation.

Frank J. Williams, founding chairman of the Lincoln Forum, is also a member of the U.S. Lincoln Bicentennial Commission, the president of the Ulysses S. Grant Association, and the former president of both the Abraham Lincoln Association and the Lincoln Group of Boston. He is also the author of several books, a peripatetic speaker on the Lincoln theme, and a major collector of Lincolniana.

THE LINCOLN FORUM

www.thelincolnforum.org

James M. McPherson
Edna Greene Medford
Richard Moe
Michael P. Musick
Mark E. Neely, Jr.
Stephen B. Oates
Phillip Shaw Paludan
Paul L. Pascal
Daniel E. Pearson
William D. Pederson
Dwight Pitcaithley
Gerald J. Prokopowicz
Ronald D. Rietveld
Steven K. Rogstad

Stuart Schneider
Hon. Paul Simon
William Spears
Edward Steers, Jr.
Craig L. Symonds
Louise Taper
Wayne C. Temple
Tim Townsend
Thomas R. Turner
Laurie Verge
Daniel R. Weinberg

Lloyd Ostendorf, 1921–2000
Ralph G. Newman, 1911–1998
Don E. Fehrenbacher, 1920–1997

Lifetime Members

Jack A. P. Albertson, El Centro, Calif.
John S. Allard, New Durham, N.H.
Russell Allen, Clinton, Conn.
Wendy Allen, New Milford, Conn.
Floyd D. Armstrong, Pensacola, Fla.
Carl Barone, West Hempstead, N.Y.
James R. Baum, Providence, R.I.
Richard Bernal, Burlingame, Calif.
Michael R. Beschloss, Washington, D.C.
Nathaniel and Harriet Boone, Manchester Center, Vt.
Gabor S. Boritt, Gettysburg, Pa.
Timothy Branscum, Amherst, Ohio
Paul and Jacqueline Bremer, Grand Rapids, Mich.
Roger D. Bridges, Fremont, Ohio
Peter G. Brown, Dallas, Tex.
George Buss, Freeport, Ill.
Norman Callan, Altoona, Pa.
Martin and Diane Carlino, East Patchogue, N.Y.

Wayne Carmony, Manilla, Ind.
Russell W. Casto III, Nitro, W. Va.
Joan L. Chaconas, Brandywine, Md.
Keith and Carolyn Chamberlin, Ada, Mich.
Andrew J. Clarke, Baldwin, N.Y.
Catherine Clinton, Riverside, Conn.
George M. Craig, Elmhurst, N.Y.
Gary Crawford, Alexandria, Va.
Hon. Mario M. Cuomo, New York, N.Y.
Richard Nelson Current, South Natick, Mass.
Max Daniels, Wheaton, Ill.
Bruce Davis, Camden, S.C.
Gerald J. Desko, Willsboro, N.Y.
Virginia and Bob Douglas, Dayton, Ohio
Jo Dzombak, Latrobe, Pa.
Mark A. Fields, Indianapolis, Ind.
A. Barry Freed, Bellevue, Wash.
Dale G. Frye, Tyrone, Pa.
Malcom Garber, Seattle, Wash.

James Getty, Gettysburg, Pa.
Stephen and Patricia Gilroy, East
    Norwich, N.Y.
Paul and Edith Goldman, Brooklyn,
    N.Y.
Tina Grim, Gettysburg, Pa.
William Hanchett, San Diego, Calif.
Harold Hand, Orwigsburg, Pa.
Stanley L. Harbison, Ypsilanti, Mich.
Tony Harris, Somerset, N.J.
Pamela D. Hawman, Birdsboro, Pa.
Merrill and Jean Hoefer, Freeport,
    Ill.
Terry Holahan, Silver Spring, Md.
Everett J. Hopkins, Wakefield, R.I.
Bill Jacques, Putney, Vt.
Richard A. Jamison, Downers Grove,
    Ill.
Robert and Jean Jenkins, Cambridge,
    Md.
Albert C. Jerman, Arlington, Vt.
Gary D. Joiner, Shreveport, La.
Dr. and Mrs. James A. Jordan,
    Lauderdale-by-the Sea, Fla.
Gerald and Judith Kambestad, Santa
    Ana, Calif.
Donia M. Kirmssé, Pasadena, Calif.
Michael D. Lacey, Valparaiso, Ind.
Everett and Antigoni Ladd,
    Arlington, Va.
Daniel M. Laney, Austin, Tex.
John K. Lattimer, New York, N.Y.
Naomi Lazarus, New York, N.Y.
Lewis L. Lehrman, Greenwich,
    Conn.
Than H. Lenox, Lebanon, Ind.
Allen and Sandra Levinsky, Portland,
    Maine
George P. Lordan, Jr., Salem, Mass.
Deborah Mark, New York, N.Y.
John Marszalek, Mississippi State,
    Miss.

B. F. and Dorothy McClerren,
    Charleston, Ill.
Carolyn and David McMorrow,
    Wareham, Mass.
Jennifer McNamara, Madison, N.J.
Edna Greene Medford, Bowie, Md.
Sin-u Nam, Woodbridge, N.J.
Stephen B. Oates, Amherst, Mass.
Norris and Helen Owen, Bloomfield,
    Ind.
T. Michael Parrish, Austin, Tex.
Brenda and Paul L. Pascal,
    Washington, D.C.
William D. Pederson, Shreveport,
    La.
Donald and Janet Pieper, Shell
    Beach, Calif.
John Plumpton, Toronto, Ontario,
    Canada
Jody Potts, Dallas, Tex.
Fred and Bonnie Priebe, Belleville,
    Mich.
Albert S. Redway, Hamden, Conn.
William Reese, New York, N.Y.
Rose and Don Reever, Addison, Ill.
Dennis Rohatyn, San Diego, Calif.
Greg Romano, Lawrenceville, N.J.
Shirley and Duke Russell,
    Hollywood, Calif.
Joseph and Catherine Schaller,
    Columbus, Ohio
Stuart Schneider, Teaneck, N.J.
Bob Siefken, Bishop, Calif.
Hon. Paul Simon, Carbondale, Ill.
JoAnne Six-Plesko, Madison, Wis.
Jack L. Smith, South Bend, Ind.
Samuel, Laurie, and Rebekah Smith,
    Longwood, Fla.
Dr. Stephen A. Smith, Bridgeport,
    W. Va.
Tefft W. Smith, Washington, D.C.
Rich Sokup, Freeport, Ill.

Richard Somer, Clinton, N.Y.
William Spears, Wichita Falls, Tex.
Paul T. Stazesky, Newark, Del.
Richard Stazesky, Wilmington, Del.
Dr. Michael P. Stevens,
Fredericksburg, Va.
David and Clarisse Stiller, Costa
Mesa, Calif.
Evelyn Strassberg, Cliffside Park,
N.J.
Michael Strassberg, Hamilton
Square, N.J.
James R. Stultz, Moundsville, W. Va.
Craig L. and Marylou Symonds,
Annapolis, Md.
Louise Taper, Beverly Hills, Calif.
Myles Taylor, Rockville, Md.
Dr. and Mrs. Wayne Temple,
Springfield, Ill.
James R. Thomas, Allendale, N.J.
Hans L. Trefousse, Staten Island,
N.Y.

Thomas R. Turner, East
Bridgewater, Mass.
Wouter K. Vanderwal, Alexandria,
Va.
Laurie Verge, Clinton, Md.
Dr. and Mrs. Grant Hulse Wagner,
Wichita Falls, Tex.
Bob and Anne Walters, Newtown
Square, Pa.
Donald Ward, Prospect, Ky.
Jan Warner, Phoenix, Ariz.
Budge Weidman, West Springfield,
Va.
Daniel R. Weinberg, Chicago, Ill.
John Welch, Boston, Mass.
Robert F. Wernle, Crawfordsville,
Ind.
Robert S. Willard, University Park,
Md.
Dr. Irma Zelig, New York, N.Y.
Jay M. Zerin, Pomona, N.Y.
Michael L. Zurcher, Ft. Wayne, Ind.

Members

Norman L. Abrams, San Anselmo,
Calif.
Wes Achauer, Zanesville, Ohio
Donald B. Aitken, Toronto, Ontario,
Canada
Bruce A. Allard, Warren, R.I.
Edwin Allard, New York, N.Y.
Patrick N. Anderson, Alexandria, Va.
Betty Anselmo, Tiverton, R.I.
Lawrence Appel, New York, N.Y.
Rebecca Asbeck, Clifton Park, N.Y.
David Auburn, Williamstown, Mass.
Kathryn Allen and John Baackes,
Menands, N.Y.
Bruce Baggarly, Mattapoisett, Mass.
Heather A. Bailey, Denver, Colo.

Richard Baney, Indian Harbor
Beach, Fla.
Garnet R. Barber, Thornhill,
Ontario, Canada
Paul Barker, Toronto, Ontario,
Canada
Ron and Joan Barnett, Omaha, Nebr.
John and Susan Barr, Kingwood, Tex.
William C. and Jean A. Barr,
Manchester, Vt.
Col. Lawrence A. Barrett, USAF
Ret., Redlands, Calif.
Rick Barry, Warwick, R.I.
Steven Franckhauser and Amy Barry,
Wayne, Pa.
Becky Bayless, Harbor City, Calif.

Margaret Bearden, Cape Coral, Fla.
Jim Begin, Princeton, N.J.
Mike Bell, Cheyenne, Wyo.
Carol S. Bessette, Springfield, Va.
James A. Billings, Copper Harbor,
    Mich.
Marjorie Bingham, Minnetonka,
    Minn.
Robert D. Blais, Seekonk,, Mass.
Ginny Boardman, Phoenix, Ariz.
Dr. Norman F. and Doris W. Boas,
    Mystic, Conn.
Rosamary and George Bogert,
    Osprey, Fla.
Joe Boland, Lititz, Pa.
Bernie Bolcar, Vandergrift, Pa.
Richard K. Books, Oklahoma City,
    Okla.
Harold E. Boyer, Beaver Falls, Pa.
Catherine Boyers, Winchester, Pa.
Charles G. Boyle, Long Island City,
    N.Y.
Charles Brame, Alta Loma, Calif.
Timothy Branscum, Amherst, Ohio
Peggy Brown, King George, Va.
Spence Brown, Manassas, Va.
Carey W. Brush, Richmond, Va.
Larry Bryggman, Stanfordville, N.Y.
Montague Buck, Washington, D.C.
John and Linda Bugash, Red Lion,
    Pa.
Robert S. Burdick, Green Bay, Wis.
Thomas E. Burke, St. Charles, Ill.
Michael Burkhimer, Havertown, Pa.
Alexis Bushnell, Iowa City, Iowa
Stephen P. Bussman, Ft. Payne, Ala.
Sally Butler, Ft. Wayne, Ind.
Thomas Butler, Ft. Wayne, Ind.
Chester S. Byers, Littlestown, Pa.
David Byers, Storrs, Conn.
Fred and Claire Calabretta,
    Westerly, R.I.

John Callahan, Cranston, R.I.
Ken Camerlain, Richardson, Tex.
Nora H. Caplan, Gaithersburg, Md.
Joseph R. Card, Binghamton, N.Y.
Paul J. Carey, Ocala, Fla.
Arnold Carlson, Brooklyn, Conn.
Burrus Carnahan, McLean, Va.
Dr. Robert G. Carroon, West
    Hartford, Conn.
Donald Cascio, Hamden, Conn.
Kenneth P. Cash, Independence,
    Ohio
Steven L. Chaffin, Corona, Calif.
Newell L. Chester, Coon Rapids,
    Minn.
Kenneth L. Childs, Columbia, S.C.
Joel Christman, Cincinnati, Ohio
Donald Cleary, Maplewood, N.J.
Col. Allen E. Cleghorn, APO, AP
Ron Cobb, St. Louis, Mo.
Mr. and Mrs. Sheldon S. Cohen,
    Chevy Chase, Md.
Alice Colonna, Woodbridge, Conn.
Amy Conard, Ballwin, Mo.
John A. Corry, Bronxville, N.Y.
Ed and Candice Cotham, Houston,
    Tex.
Sheila M. Cronin, Chicago, Ill.
Janice E. G. Curry, Fall River, Mass.
Jackie and Joe Cutlip, Bedford, Tex.
Walter R. Dallow, Sacramento, Calif.
Alphonse D'Angelo, Franklin
    Square, N.Y.
Brooks Davis, Chicago, Ill.
David R. Deatrick, Jr., Prospect, Ky.
Dolores DeBenedictis, Penn Valley,
    Calif.
R. Michael Demech, Washington
    Crossing, Pa.
Donald DeRiggi, Glen Cove, N.Y.
Tom DeStefano, Haledon, N.J.
W. I. "Red" and June Dietz,
    Titusville, Fla.

Nicholas DiGiovanni and C. Thierry, Wayland, Mass.

Robert DiMarco, King of Prussia, Pa.

Robert Doerk, Ft. Benton, Mont.

Stan Domosh, Delran, N.J.

John Doolittle, Dexter, N.Y.

Dean A. Dorrell, Washington, Ind.

Charlie Doty, Washington, D.C.

Barbara M. Dragowski, Arlington, Va.

Frederick R. Drews, Boiling Springs, Pa.

Tim and Kevin Duffey, Upper Arlington, Ohio

James T. Dunleavy, Sunnyside, N.Y.

Kay duPont, Atlanta, Ga.

Alexander F. Durvin, Jr., Ft. Washington, Md.

Elaine and Melvin Ecker, Boca Raton, Fla.

Betty Edmonson, Tucson, Ariz.

David J. Eicher, Waukesha, Wis.

Thomas G. Eldred, Union Springs, N.Y.

Paul F. Ellis-Graham, Highland Mills, N.Y.

Francis and Jeanne Elmore, Woodbridge, Va.

Luann Elvey, East Tawas, Mich.

Robert L. Farkas, West Seneca, N.Y.

Lenore Farmer, Pittsburgh, Pa.

Avram Fechter, Washington, D.C.

Dr. Norman B. Ferris, Murfreesboro, Tenn.

Anthony Flynn, Wilmington, Del.

Joseph R. Fornieri, Fairport, N.Y.

Thomas E. Fox, Brockton, Mass.

John Hope Franklin, Durham, N.C.

William K. and Sue A. Frary, Lebanon, Ohio

Charles Frascati, Baltimore, Md.

Sara J. Gabbard, Ft. Wayne, Ind.

Ralph Gary, Grapevine, Tex.

Robert Geise, Selinsgrove, Pa.

Don Gerlinger, Milwaukee, Wis.

Arthur C. Germano, Lynnfield, Mass.

Nancy Gerstad, Chicago, Ill.

Larry Gibbs, Country Club Hills, Ill.

Dennis and Norma Gilpatrick, Magnolia, Tex.

Lora Gisondi, Columbus, Ohio

Don Glickman, Clifton, N.J.

Mo Gootee, Columbus, Ohio

Jeff Gordon, New York, N.Y.

Don Gorman, Elmwood Park, N.J.

Fredrick C. Graff, Medina, Ohio

Jim and Verna Grant, Palmyra, Va.

O. Alfred Granum, Downers Grove, Ill.

Donald and Kathy Gray, Bronxville, N.Y.

Lois Greenbacker, Durham, Conn.

Sally Greer, Kingwood, Tex.

Carlton G. Grode, Neenah, Wis.

Hal Gross, Fresh Meadows, N.Y.

Burnell R. Gulden, Lafayette, Ind.

Shirley Gulvin, Lincoln, R.I.

Lee Gunter, Naperville, Ill.

Deborah Fitts and Clark Hall, Middleburg, Va.

Chuck Hand, Paris, Ill.

Wesley Peter and Loretta Carter Hanes, Washington, D.C.

Kathryn M. Harris, Springfield, Ill.

William C. Harris, Raleigh, N.C.

James Hashman, Mount Vernon, Ohio

Frederick Hatch, Washington, D.C.

Capt. and Mrs. A. Michael Hayes, Jr., Courtland, Va.

Mark S. Heaney, Schererville, Ind.

Dr. C. David Hein, Frederick, Md.

Elaine Henderson, New Milford, Conn.

Homer E. Henschen, Carlisle, Pa.
Robert D. Hesterly, Fairfield, Ill.
James L. Hindle, Cranston, R.I.
Richard N. Hinton, Downers Grove, Ill.
Norbert Hirschhorn, New Haven, Conn.
Tom Holson, Bakersfield, Calif.
Thomas Horrocks, Boston, Mass.
Robert A. Howard, Carlisle, Pa.
Barbara Hughett, Chicago, Ill.
H. Draper Hunt, South Portland, Maine
Syed Husein, Tacoma, Wash.
Patrick Imburgia, Mission Viejo, Calif.
Doris B. Ingman, Richmond Hill, N.Y.
William C. Ives, Chicago, Ill.
James Jackson, Lightfoot, Va.
Laurie W. Jeffrey, New York, N.Y.
Lee Jensen, Hortonville, Wis.
Janice J. Jerabek, Pleasanton, Calif.
Thomas C. Johnsen, Belmont, Mass.
William D. Jones, Norwalk, Ohio
Vickey Kalambakal, Torrance, Calif.
Ronald A. Kanen, Tallahassee, Fla.
Richard Katula, Wakefield, R.I.
Kurt M. Kausler, St. Louis, Mo.
Samual R. Kay, Plymouth Meeting, Pa.
Philip Kayman, Chicago, Ill.
Jane Keel, Bloomington, Ill.
Richard J. Kelly, Malta, N.Y.
Hon. Jack Kemp, Washington, D.C.
Phil Kendall, Grand Junction, Colo.
Nancy and Paul Kennedy, Troy, Mich.
Bob Kermen, Yreka, Calif.
M. Buckley and M. Khosravi, Clifton, Va.
Won S. Kim, Irving, Tex.

Bob and Nancy Kincaid, Columbus, Ohio
Robert A. Kinsley, York, Pa.
Jane Kleindienst, Bakersfield, Calif.
Bernie Kopera, Orland Park, Ill.
Steven R. Koppelman, Randolph, N.J.
Andrew Korinda, Boonton, N.J.
Louis Koser, Seattle, Wash.
John G. and Elsa Kunna, Liberty Corner, N.J.
Sy Kushmar, Canton, Mich.
Diane M. Kushner, Malvern, Pa.
Ray Kuzniar, Wauconda, Ill.
Brian Lamb, Washington, D.C.
Charles E. Lang, Lakeland, Fla.
Robert G. Langford, Morris Township, N.J.
Tom Lapsley, Fairview, Ore.
Rev. Kenneth Craig Larter, Merchantville, N.J.
Tammy Lasater, Santa Clara, Calif.
Gary Lash, Fredonia, N.Y.
James A. Lastovica, Omaha, Nebr.
Bill and Stephanie Latour, Dearborn, Mich.
Gregory Lawrence, Lansing, N.Y.
Jan Leaf, Roseville, Minn.
Gerald R. and Marion C. Leblanc, Sun City Center, Fla.
Dan LeBlond, Plymouth, Mich.
Rob Leete, Holt, Mich.
Frederick A. Lehrer, Stamford, Conn.
Robert E. Leigh, Hotchkiss, Colo.
Bill Lennox, Pickerington, Ohio
Robert J. Lenz, Bloomington, Ill.
Dave Leroy, Boise, Idaho
Lincoln Memorial Shrine, Redlands, Calif.
Frank van der Linden, Bethesda, Md.

Louise Lindinger, Cherry Hill, N.J.

David A. Linehan, Seattle, Wash.

Ron and Susan Littmann, Boulder, Colo.

Mark Lore, Winchester, Va.

Richard Lore, New Bern, N.C.

The Louisiana Lincolnator, Shreveport, La.

Ronald J. Lovett, Niskayuna, N.Y.

Thomas P. Lowry, Woodbridge, Va.

Tony Lynch, Bethesda, Md.

John Lynn, San Francisco, Calif.

Dan Madsen, Aurora, Colo.

Tom Mangrum, Lexington, Va.

J. Kenneth Mangum and Ryan T. Mangum, Phoenix, Ariz.

Bob Marecek, Berwyn, Ill.

Paul R. Martin III, Yorktown Heights, N.Y.

Richard E. Martin, Mount Joy, Pa.

Patrick A. Martinelli, Gettysburg, Pa.

Richard Masloski, New Windsor, N.Y.

Melvin F. Maurer, Westlake, Ohio

John McClary, Decatur, Ill.

Phyllis McClure, Washington, D.C.

Kathleen M. McCollough, Lincoln, Ill.

Stephen and Susan McKenrick, Fayetteville, Pa.

Joseph and Nadine McLachlan, Alexandria, Va.

Rick McLaughlin, Delanson, N.Y.

Joseph E. McMenamin, Springfield, Ill.

Patricia A. McNamee, North Providence, R.I.

Donald E. Meeder, Ft. Lauderdale, Fla.

Michael and Michele Meyrowitz, Okemos, Mich.

John G. Miller, New York, N.Y.

William K. Miller, Duluth, Minn.

Michael R. Morrell, Columbia, Md.

Larry Morris, Evansville, Ind.

Chris and Nan Mosher, Arlington, Va.

Jim Motroni, Jr., Vashon, Wash.

Jim Motroni, Sr., San Mateo, Calif.

Rea and Betty Mowery, San Diego, Calif.

Irving and Julie Moy, Plainville, Conn.

Grant S. Moyer, Moorestown, N.J.

Walter and Peg Mulcahy, Northville, N.Y.

Greg Munson, Chalfont, Pa.

Roselen Murphy, Oak Park, Ill.

Michael Murzyn, Chicago, Ill.

John F. Myers, Brewster, Mass.

Randy and Maureen Myers, Whittier, Calif.

Kim Napolitano, Newport, R.I.

Roger Norton, Ft. Meyers, Fla.

Mark O'Connor, Medfield, Mass.

Bob Odell, Lempster, N.H.

Jane F. O'Donnell, Gainesville, Fla.

Kerry D. Olsen, Rochester, Minn.

Loyette A. Olsen, Winfield, Kans.

Mr. and Mrs. Thomas O'Neill, Ft. Wayne, Ind.

Ernie Ortoli, Monroeville, Pa.

Dr. Patricia Ann Owens, Mount Carmel, Ill.

Mr. and Mrs. H. Ashley Page III, Homewood, Ala.

Robert A. Patnode, Oklahoma City, Okla.

Robert and Marianne Paul, San Diego, Calif.

William C. Perkins, Purchase, N.Y.

Geoffrey and Anne Perret, Beverley, England

Catherine Peterson, Arlington, Va.

Lee Petry, Knoxville, Tenn.
Helen A. Phung, Attleboro, Mass.
Janice Pietrone, Glenshaw, Pa.
Matt Pinsker, Lancaster, Pa.
Grant Murray Platt, Englewood, Colo.
Jerald E. Podair, Appleton, Wis.
Timothy C. Poirier, Indialantic, Fla.
Harold B. Pommier, Batavia, Ill.
Robert A. Price, Edina, Minn.
Daniel W. Pritchett, Dover, Del.
Ed Grosel and Terry Pyles, Pickerington, Ohio
James G. Pyrros, Bloomfield Hills, Mich.
Steven S. Raab, Ardmore, Pa.
Joseph and Lauretta Rayzak, Hicksville, N.Y.
J. Dan Recer, Easton, Md.
Stephen Recker, Pasadena, Calif.
William H. Redd, Falls Church, Va.
Priscilla D. Reetz, Brewster, Mass.
Owen R. Resweber, Jr., Annandale, Va.
Michael Bishop Rieg, Lansdale, Pa.
John Roach, Staten Island, N.Y.
Ron Robinson, Richardson, Tex.
Steven K. Rogstad, Racine, Wis.
Ronald A. Rollins, Oberlin, Ohio
Jeff Rombauer, Maple Valley, Wash.
Alan M. Rosen, Lincoln Park, N.J.
Katharine B. Ross, Wilmington, Del.
Snowden and Marianne Rowe, Cincinnati, Ohio
Douglas S. Russell, Iowa City, Iowa
Donald A. Rydgren, Hockessin, Del.
Gerald and Lillian Safferman, Pittsboro, N.C.
David C. St. John, Arlington, Va.
Keith St. Onge, Edwardsville, Ill.
Tim Saiter, Paris, Ill.
Ross and Lorraine Sargent, Arlington, Va.

Sally Saunders, Freeport, Maine
Sheryl Scarborough, Laurel, Md.
Steve W. Schaefer, Madison, Ga.
Jerry Schanke, Reston, Va.
Philip Schoenberg, Flushing, N.Y.
Glenna Schroeder-Lein, Springfield, Ill.
Karen Schult, Berkley, Mich.
Thomas Seaver, Milford, Mass.
Arthur A. Seif, Berkeley Heights, N.J.
Bill Seitzer, Chestertown, Md.
Milton Seltzer, Wantagh, N.Y.
Joseph Semenza, Phoenix, Ariz.
Linda Serna, Globe, Ariz.
Jonathan C. Shea, Richardson, Tex.
Maurice P. Shea III, Naples, Fla.
Dennis P. Sheehan, Litchfield, N.H.
Glenn V. Sherwood, Longmont, Colo.
Robert Shields, Wilmington, Del.
Robert E. Shipley, Aston, Pa.
Jan Shupert-Arick, Ft. Wayne, Ind.
Donald A. Siller, Chesterfield, Mo.
Ann Simley, Novato, Calif.
Eileen Simon, Irvine, Calif.
Peter Skelly, Janesville, Wis.
Henry and Miriam Slings, Spring Lake, Mich.
Albert M. Smith, Belmont, Mass.
Charles A. Smith, Falls Church, Va.
Donna Fuller Smith, Boynton Beach, Fla.
Dennis Smyth, Moorestown, N.J.
Charles W. Snyder, Savannah, Ga.
Ronald and Darlene Stafford, Annapolis, Md.
Kim L. Stam, Twain Harte, Calif.
Joseph M. Stanichak, Aliquippa, Pa.
Brandt N. Steele, Greencastle, Ind.
Troy M. Stewart, Jr., Huntington, W. Va.

Phil Stichter, Columbus, Ohio

Jim and Laurie Stiles, Prairie Village, Kans.

Eleanor Stoddard, Chevy Chase, Md.

Phillip C. Stone, Bridgewater, Va.

Richard Strong, Yucaipa, Calif.

Howard Strouse, Pickerington, Ohio

James L. Swanson, Chicago, Ill.

Wendy Swanson, Falls Church, Va.

John B. Swearingen, Lumberton, Tex.

James I. and Louise C. Tarman, State College, Pa.

Lawrence and Lynda Taylor, Gettysburg, Pa.

Jean Tedder, Fairfax, Va.

Doug Teske, Columbus, Ohio

Brad and Pat Tillery, Wilmington, N.C.

Donald R. Tracy, Springfield, Ill.

Mrs. Donald Trescott, Rumford, R.I.

Tony Trosley, Champaign, Ill.

William R. Tucker, Rantoul, Ill.

Martin D. Tullai, Lutherville, Md.

Carl Turk, Roselle, Ill.

James and Lois Ullman, Newport News, Va.

Joseph F. Unger, Park Ridge, Ill.

Thomas R. Valaika, Reno, Nev.

Dr. Kim H. and Sylvia Vance, Virginia Beach, Va.

Gordon R. Vincent, Basking Ridge, N.J.

David Walker, Van Wert, Ohio

Robert L. Walter, North Ft. Myers, Fla.

Dean R. Warner, Reston, Va.

David A. Warren, Crystal Lake, Ill.

Jack Waugh, Pantego, Tex.

Dr. Janet Weeks, Dalton, Pa.

Dennis Weiserbs, Roanoke, Va.

S. Jerry Weissman, Elkins Park, Pa.

Richard Wengenroth, New York, N.Y.

Robert Whelan, Wilkes-Barre, Pa.

Charles and Vicki Whitelaw, Annapolis, Md.

Mr. and Mrs. Robert Wilburn, Blairsville, Pa.

James and Susan Wilcox, Sherman Oaks, Calif.

Maggie Wildman, Evanston, Ill.

Arthur R. Williams, Leawood, Kans.

Tom Williams, Victorville, Calif.

Fred Willmer, St. Clair Shores, Mich.

Sharon E. Wilson, Brentwood, N.Y.

Steven M. Wilson, Harrogate, Tenn.

Ernest Winberg, Winthrop, Maine

H. Donald Winkler, Gatlinburg, Tenn.

Michael Wolf, New York, N.Y.

Jacqueline D. Wright, Springfield, Ill.

Carolyn P. Yoder, Lawrenceville, N.J.

Ronald Young, Brownstown, Pa.

INDEX

Abolition, as goal of Civil War, 94

Abraham Lincoln Encyclopedia, The (Neely), 3

Abraham Lincoln Sesquicentennial Committee, 171

Activist government, 49–50

Adams, Charles Francis, 202

Adams, John, 17, 120, 179

"Adjustable buoyant chambers," Lincoln's patented invention of, 51, 58

Admiral, creation of rank of, 51–52

"Age of Ideology," 184

Albert, Prince, 55

Alexandria, Va., 83

Alton, Ill., 136, 149, 150

American Dilemma, An (Myrdal), 176

"American System," of import duties, 154–55

"American Way of War," 61

Anaconda Plan, 5–6, 63, 87

Anderson, Robert, 68–69, 74

Anthony, Susan B., 125

Antietam, Battle of, 10, 11, 58, 89, 80

Appomattox, Va., 33, 95

Arkansas, 34

Arkansas, Battle of, 8

Armies of the Cumberland, Ohio, and Tennessee, Union, 94

Armstrong, Jack, 81

Army, British, 51

Army, C.S., 8–9, 19, 27–28, 34, 36, 69, 88, 179; desertion from, 108–9; interior line advantage of, 8, 12, 13, 27; Lincoln's strategy of destruction of, 10–13; morale in, 93; North invaded by, 9, 10. *See also specific armies*

Army, Union, 8–9, 34, 63, 216; commanding general of, 19–20; desertion from, 99, 106; discipline in, 117–18; draft and, 21, 84, 99; in eighteenth century, 16–17; enlistment in, 6, 9, 117–18; first officer killed in, 83–84; former slaves in, 14, 38, 71, 94, 120, 197; hiring of substitutes to serve in, 84; Lincoln's popularity in, 204–5; morale in, 99, 104; political and ethnic-based appointments in, 23–24; shortage of ranking officers in, 20. *See also specific armies and units*

Army of Northern Virginia, C.S., 94, 101; 1874 election as viewed by, 105–6; Lincoln's desire for destruction of, 9–13, 24, 77–78, 87, 92; morale in, 95–98, 102, 103–10

Army of Tennessee, C.S., 72–73, 92, 94; changes of command of, 101; destruction of, 110

Army of the Potomac, Union, 8, 22, 24, 25, 27–28, 47, 77, 79, 91, 96; changes of command of, 6, 10, 11, 22, 23, 94; conflicts of personalities in, 28; Lincoln as hypothetical

Illinois, 24, 51, 71, 79, 81, 86, 113, 127, 159, 182, 221; 1868 senatorial race in, 65; Lincoln's support in, 207
Illinois State Historical Library, 221, 223, 226, 229
Illusion and error, 185–86
Import duties, 154–55
Indiana, 86, 127, 182
Indiana University, 219
Indian wars, 16, 17
Ingersoll, Robert, 115
Intelligence reports, 38, 43–44, 46
Interior lines, 8, 12, 13, 27, 87
Internet, 228
Iowa, 189
Iowa-class battleships, 62
Ironclad Board, 60–61
Ironclad warships, 60–61, 64

Jackson, Andrew, 1, 17, 27, 80, 85, 80, 116, 180
Jackson, Thomas J. "Stonewall," 9; Shenandoah Valley Campaign of, 34–47
Jaffa, Harry, 177
Japanese Super-battleships, 62
Jefferson, Thomas, 1, 17, 179, 201
"Jew Order," of Grant, 198
John Hay Library, 219
Johnson, Andrew, 33, 191, 199–100
Johnson, Edward "Allegheny," 42
Johnson, John, 110
Johnson, Oliver, 210
Johnston, Joseph E., 13, 19–20, 33, 71, 75, 94, 101
Jones, Howard, 177
July 4, significance of, 179

Kaland, William, 224
Kammen, Michael, 179–80, 212–13

Kansas-Nebraska Act (1864), 83, 136, 147
Kellogg, William, 210
Kelly, William Aiken, 104
Kentucky, 5, 8, 20, 69, 74, 88, 127, 140, 206, 210
Kerrison, Charles, 98
Knox, Henry, 16
Knox, Thomas W., 70–71
Korea, Republic of (South Korea), 170
Kunhardt, Dorothy, 224
Kunhardt, Philip, 224

Lambert, William H., 166, 218
Lamon, Ward Hill, 89
Lane, Henry S., 194
Lang, David, 99
Last Best Hope of Earth, The, 228
Lattimer, John K., 225–26, 227
Ledru-Rollin, Alexandre A., 203
Lee, Elizabeth Blair, 198
Lee, Robert E., 20, 31, 33, 58, 72, 80, 94, 97, 101, 102; army commanded by. See Army of Northern Virginia, C.S.; peace negotiations and, 31, 33; Shenandoah Valley Campaign and, 35; soldiers' regard for, 96; in Virginia campaign, 9–13, 24, 27, 29
"Leg holders," 13, 27, 87
Lehrman, Lewis, 228
Liberty, 179–81
Library of Congress, 4, 86, 222, 223, 228
Lieutenant general, creation of rank of, 24
Lincoln, Abraham: accessibility of, 63, 117; activist governmental philosophy of, 49–50; aggressiveness in officers preferred by, 56–58, 64; appointment-making

Progressive Era: Gettysburg Address as interpreted in, 166–69, 171, 183; Lincoln as symbol of, 169
Psychological warfare, 72

Quakers, 198

Race: current concerns linked to, 186; in later interpretation of Gettysburg Address, 161–62, 167, 172–81, 184–86. *See also* Emancipation Proclamation; Slavery; Slaves
Radio Free Europe, 171
Randall, James G., 170, 187, 212, 229
Ransom, Merritt, 194
Rawlins, John A., 29
Raymond, Henry J., 100
Reagan, Nancy, 122, 123
Reconstruction, 76
Remensnyder, Junius B., 168
Republican National Convention: of 1866, 65; of 1870, 53
Republican Party, 23, 27, 36, 56, 66, 173, 182, 189, 210, 220; Grant and, 24–25; Lincoln's balancing of wings of, 188, 197, 202–3; newspapers of, 164–65, 199; as party of abolition, 93, 100, 147; wartime name of, 93
Rhodes, E. Washington, 173–74
Rice, James C., 209
Richmond, Va., 4, 71, 87, 93, 95, 96, 97, 102, 198; Lincoln in, 80, 84; Pennsylvania Campaign and, 8–11, 13, 22, 27, 29; Shenandoah Valley Campaign and, 34, 35, 36–37, 38, 40, 41, 43, 46, 47
Rifled weaponry, 60, 63
Ripley, James W., 62–63

Risdon, Frederick R., 225
River Queen, 32, 33, 74, 75
Rockefeller, John D., 218
Roosevelt, Eleanor, 125
Roosevelt, Franklin D., 1
Roosevelt, Theodore, 1, 167, 219–20
Rose, Ernestine, 150
Rosencrans, William S., 88
Royal Navy, British, 51, 55
Rusk, Dean, 173–74
Russell, Lord John, 55
Rutledge, Ann, 114, 125

St. Clair, Arthur, 16
St. Louis, Mo., 67
Sale, John F., 97–98
Sandburg, Carl, 181, 223, 224
Sandburg's Lincoln, 227
Sang, Philip David, 225
Sanitary Commission, U.S., 210
San Jacinto, 55
San Marino, Calif., 220
Savannah, Ga., 29, 30, 72, 73–74
Saxton, Rufus, 46
Scarlet Letter, The (Hawthorne), 159
Schlater, C. U., 211–12
School integration, 173
Schurz, Carl, 189, 194, 196–97, 210
Scott, Sir Walter, 128
Scott, Winfield, 18, 20, 21–22, 80; Anaconda Plan of, 5–6, 63, 87; military career of, 19; removed from command, 7, 22
Scovel, James, 201
Scranton, William, 173–74
"Second causes," 155
Second Inaugural Address, 1, 2, 15, 118, 176, 202
Sectionalism, 153
"Seeing the elephant," 62
Seminoles, 17

THE NORTH'S CIVIL WAR SERIES
Paul A. Cimbala, series editor